YOUTH VIOLENCE

Other books in the Current Controversies Series:

The AIDS Crisis
Drug Trafficking
Energy Alternatives
Europe
Gun Control
Iraq
Police Brutality
Sexual Harassment
Women in the Military

YOUTH VIOLENCE

David L. Bender, *Publisher*
Bruno Leone, *Executive Editor*

Bonnie Szumski, *Managing Editor*
Carol Wekesser, *Senior Editor*

Michael D. Biskup, *Book Editor*
Charles P. Cozic, *Book Editor*

CURRENT CONTROVERSIES

Cover photo: Uniphoto

Library of Congress Cataloging-in-Publication Data

Youth violence / Michael D. Biskup, book editor, Charles P. Cozic, book editor.
p. cm. — (Current controversies)
Includes bibliographical references and index.
ISBN 1-56510-017-4 (lib. : acid-free paper) — ISBN 1-56510-016-6 (pbk. : acid-free paper)
1. Juvenile delinquency—United States—Prevention. 2. Juvenile delinquency—United States. 3. Juvenile corrections—United States. 4. Capital punishment—United States. I. Biskup, Michael D., 1956- . II. Cozic, Charles P., 1957- . III. Series.
HV9104.Y6855 1992
364.3'6'0973—dc20 92-23592
CIP

Contents

Chapter 4: How Can Gang Violence Be Reduced?

Chapter 5: Should Violent Youths Receive Harsh Punishment?

Foreword

By definition, controversies are "discussions of questions in which opposing opinions clash" (Webster's Twentieth Century Dictionary Unabridged). Few would deny that controversies are a pervasive part of the human condition and exist on virtually every level of human enterprise. Controversies transpire between individuals and among groups, within nations and between nations. Controversies supply the grist necessary for progress by providing challenges and challengers to the status quo. They also create atmospheres where strife and warfare can flourish. A world without controversies would be a peaceful world; but it also would be, by and large, static and prosaic.

The Series' Purpose

The purpose of the Current Controversies series is to explore many of the social, political, and economic controversies dominating the national and international scenes today. Titles selected for inclusion in the series are highly focused and specific. For example, from the larger category of criminal justice, Current Controversies deals with specific topics such as police brutality, gun control, white collar crime, and others. The debates in Current Controversies also are presented in a useful, timeless fashion. Articles and book excerpts included in each title are selected if they contribute valuable, long-range ideas to the overall debate. And wherever possible, current information is enhanced with historical documents and other relevant materials. Thus, while individual titles are current in focus, every effort is made to ensure that they will not become quickly outdated. Books in the Current Controversies series will remain important resources for librarians, teachers, and students for many years.

In addition to keeping the titles focused and specific, great care is taken in the editorial format of each book in the series. Book introductions and chapter prefaces are offered to provide background material for readers. Chapters are organized around several key questions that are answered with diverse opinions representing all points on the political spectrum. Materials in each chapter include opinions in which authors clearly disagree as well as alternative opinions in which authors may agree on a broader issue but disagree on the possible solutions. In this way, the content of each volume in Current Controversies mirrors the mosaic of opinions encountered in society. Readers will quickly realize that there are many viable answers to these complex issues. By questioning each author's conclusions, students and casual readers can begin to develop the critical thinking skills so important to evaluating opinionated material.

Current Controversies is also ideal for controlled research. Each anthology in the series is composed of primary sources taken from a wide gamut of informational categories including periodicals, newspapers, books, United States and foreign government documents, and the publications of private and public organizations. Readers will find factual support for reports, debates, and research papers covering all areas of important issues. In addition, an annotated table of contents, an index, a book and periodical bibliography, and a list of organizations to contact are included in each book to expedite further research.

Perhaps more than ever before in history, people are confronted with diverse and contradictory information. During the Persian Gulf War, for example, the public was not only treated to minute-to-minute coverage of the war, it was also inundated with critiques of the coverage and countless analyses of the factors motivating U.S. involvement. Being able to sort through the plethora of opinions accompanying today's major issues, and to draw one's own conclusions, can be a complicated and frustrating struggle. It is the editors' hope that Current Controversies will help readers with this struggle.

"As youth violence escalates, concern grows over the safety of neighborhoods, the victims of violence, and the future of violent youths themselves."

Introduction

On February 26, 1992, New York City mayor David Dinkins prepared to address students at Thomas Jefferson High School in Brooklyn. Because of the school's reputation for violence, extra security guards and police officers patrolled the school building. Shortly before Dinkins's speech, gunshots rang out in a hallway. Two teenage boys had been shot. Both died, victims of a younger student's rage.

This anecdote is just one of many that seem to haunt newspaper headlines. Youth violence is becoming more commonplace, involves younger children, and has devastating effects. One Baltimore student told a newspaper, "You've got to be prepared—people shoot you for your coat, your rings, your chains, anything." According to the FBI, the number of juveniles arrested for homicide between 1981 and 1990 increased 60 percent, far more than the 5.2 percent increase among adults. Many experts believe youth violence has reached epidemic proportions and much of their concern focuses on younger violent children. Says Danny Dawson, head of a county juvenile division in Florida, "Ten years ago, it was a shock to see a seven-, eight-, or nine-year-old come into the system. Now it's not, it's a trend."

While a certain amount of violence has always been a trademark of adolescence, the proliferation of guns among youth has made its consequences far more tragic. As George E. Butterfield, deputy director of the National School Safety Center, states, "Some students wouldn't think twice about carrying a gun. Their attitude is: 'I carry a comb, I carry makeup, I carry a piece of candy. Why not carry a gun?'" Indeed, a 1991 U.S. Centers for Disease Control (CDC) survey showed that one in twenty students in grades nine through twelve carries a firearm at least once a month. According to the CDC, in 1986 firearm homicide became the second-leading cause of death among fifteen- through nineteen-year-olds. For many years it has been first among blacks in that age group.

Many of these deaths are the result of an increase in gang violence. As more teenagers swell the ranks of gangs and obtain guns, violence escalates and threatens more neighborhoods. Gang shootings, once endemic to America's big cities, are a growing problem in smaller ones as well. Cities with no previous history of gang warfare, such as Salt Lake City, Utah, and Albuquerque, New Mexico, must now contend with this new phenomenon.

In some neighborhoods, the increase in youth violence has turned schools into war zones. For example, a Long Beach, California, junior high school constructed a ten-foot-high, three-hundred-foot-long concrete wall for protection against random gunfire and drive-by shootings from nearby streets. Teachers and students are now more afraid than ever that an angry student could pull out a gun and threaten them. Such schools are no longer places of education. Says Pat Tornillo, president of a Florida teachers union: "Students can't learn the lessons they need to succeed in life if their attention is on first learning how to survive the day in school."

As youth violence escalates, concern grows over the safety of neighborhoods, the victims of violence, and the future of violent youths themselves. The following chapters of *Youth Violence* examine the root causes of why youths commit violence and the social and legal proposals to reduce the problem. As Barbara Lautman, director of the Center to Prevent Handgun Violence, testified to Congress, "If we don't act now, America's future may be filled with the constant crackle of gunfire and the sounds of frightened students diving for cover. We cannot tolerate our children dying in ever-increasing numbers."

Chapter 1

Is Youth Violence a Serious Problem?

CURRENT CONTROVERSIES

Chapter Preface

In April 1989, a young Wall Street investment banker was jogging in New York City's Central Park when a gang of teenagers between the ages of 14 and 17 attacked her. After knocking her down and beating her with rocks, bricks, and a lead pipe, stabbing her in the head five times, and repeatedly raping her, they left her for dead. She was found hours later, lying in a coma and suffering from multiple skull fractures and loss of blood.

The attackers showed no remorse for their actions. In fact, according to Susan Baker and Tipper Gore in *Newsweek*, one of the attackers told the Manhattan district attorney's office that "it was fun." After being jailed they casually whistled at a policewoman and sang the popular hit song "Wild Thing." Perhaps more than the attack itself, the juveniles lack of sorrow for their wantonly vicious acts horrified the nation.

This crime served to highlight the increasing incidence of youth violence in the United States. Dean Murphy in the *Los Angeles Times* reports, "The skyrocketing juvenile murder rate is all the more alarming, some psychologists say, because it mirrors an overall increase in violent crime by adolescents." The Federal Bureau of Investigation reported that the number of juveniles arrested for homicide between 1981 and 1990 increased by 60 percent nationwide.

Furthermore, a 1992 issue of the *Journal of the American Medical Association* reports that gunshot wounds are the second-leading cause of death among teenagers in the United States.

Despite these statistics, some researchers maintain that youth violence is not widespread. In his book *Last One Over the Wall*, Jerome G. Miller, former head of the Massachusetts juvenile corrections system, states that the public's perception of increased youth violence results from several misleading factors such as the increase in the adolescent population, inaccurate media stories, inflated arrest records (multiple youths are arrested for one crime), and police overcharging suspects (charges are usually reduced in court). Experts such as Miller contend that violent acts by youths are relatively rare and not a serious problem.

Much attention has been focused on youths who assault and kill. In this chapter the authors debate whether these acts indicate that youth violence is a serious problem for society.

Youth Violence Is Increasing

by Paul M. Barrett

About the author: *Paul M. Barrett is a staff reporter for the* Wall Street Journal.

Judonne Cole and Jermaine Daniel face each other in the concrete courtyard of their inner-city housing project. They had argued about a girl. Now, a crowd gathers as Jermaine flicks insults at Judonne.

Suddenly, Judonne pulls out a gun and shoots Jermaine three times in the chest.

The dead boy is 15. The shooter is 14. They had been best friends.

Appalling as this brutal event was, even more appalling is that it only attracted attention in Washington, D.C. because, through a chance encounter several years ago, Jermaine had been befriended by the city's police chief. But the chief soon left office, and the streets reclaimed Jermaine.

Numbed to Killings

His death is part of an ominous new escalation in the wave of black juvenile violence in Washington and other big cities. The victims and assailants are getting younger, the fatal disputes even more trivial. Drugs, though ubiquitous in the backdrop, don't figure directly in much of the bloodshed. "We now see senseless violence for the sake of violence," says Washington's U.S. attorney, Jay Stephens. Killings breed more killings. Death becomes normal, people numb to the waste of life.

Most young victims, absent any local celebrity, go to burial anonymously. On a warm late-winter evening, more than 100 people gather in the Fairlawn neighborhood of southeast Washington to mark the death of Michael Hilliard, 16, who was shot in the back of the head while walking away from an argument at an afternoon basketball game. Michael's two brothers slump on a funeral-home couch weeping miserably. But otherwise the scene is like a church bake sale or a bingo night: people gossiping or nodding to each other blankly, looking bored; little children racing in circles, performing kung-fu kicks.

Standing outside after paying his respects, a police officer who knows the family says, "There's no sense of anything special happening. Another 16-year-old bites the dust."

Fight or Shoot

At Shaed Elementary here, children are being taught "non-violent conflict resolution" in special classes led by a team from the Washington Hospital Center. But it's an uphill struggle: When one class of 10- and 11-year-olds is asked how many know someone who has been killed, 14 of the 18 students raise their hands and volunteer the circumstances. Brian, a chunky extrovert in the front row, tells of the death of Akim, 18: "They shot him." Why? "Over a radio."

In the back of the class, Philip, skinny and shy, nods and whispers, "I saw a boy shot for his sneakers."

"Values have changed," says Daniel Austin, a teacher at the school. "Parents send kids to school and say, 'Hit back.' . . . No one just walks away. They fight it out, shoot it out."

> ***"The victims and assailants are getting younger, the fatal disputes even more trivial."***

Why do kids shoot rather than punch or kick? "Just beating someone doesn't get it any more," says Keisha, a 16-year-old high-school sophomore. "Times change. Kids are not satisfied with doing a beating. They want to end it."

This is far from just a drug problem. Juvenile drug-offense arrests in Washington have declined for two years, while the percentage of all teen-agers arrested who test positive for drug use has also dropped. Yet record numbers of people 17 or younger have been arrested on murder or weapons charges. In the three years from 1986 through 1988, 43 juveniles were arrested for homicide. In just two years, 1989 and 1990, police arrested 129 juveniles for homicide.

The U.S. reported that a black male, age 15 to 19, is almost three times more likely to die from a shooting than from illness. A white teen-ager is 11% more likely to die from a bullet than a disease.

A Window on the Mayhem

Broken homes and easy access to guns have existed for a long time without the current degree of slaughter. "In this town, the weapons have always been out there; it's the behavior of the young people that's changed," says Maurice Turner, the former police chief who tried to help Jermaine Daniel.

A neighborhood such as northeast Washington's Edgewood section, where Jermaine Daniel lived and died, provides a window on the mayhem.

The Edgewood Terrace Apartments, a mixture of public and private housing, sprawl across eight acres at the foot of a gently sloping hill. Less than a mile away, college students, most of them white, stroll to classes on the well-tended campus of Catholic University.

The project, opened in the early 1970s, was to be a model of how to mix working-class tenants with the poor, using strict screening of applicants to keep out malingerers and criminals. The experiment worked briefly. But soon the management, trying to keep apartments occupied and government subsidies flowing, became less choosy about tenants and less scrupulous about maintenance.

"We now see senseless violence for the sake of violence."

In the years since, much of the complex has deteriorated. Plywood boards cover windows in abandoned units that stink of backed-up sewage. Broken glass glitters on empty basketball courts; the bent backboards have no rims. Green-black water fills the bottom few feet of a swimming pool that hasn't been used for 10 years.

The crack of gunfire surprises no one. Roughly three people get killed every two weeks in the square-mile area that includes the project, according to police. Most of the shootings, like most of the other crimes, are committed by people younger than 20, police say, and the average age keeps dropping.

Routine Gunfire

Leaders of the Edgewood Community Coalition, a nascent group struggling to restore order and hope to the area, explain the lethal gunplay as a product of poverty and poor education and lack of jobs and role models. But the sheer number of bullets flying also seems linked to a pervasive devaluation of human life.

"Almost any night you hear the guns," says Virginia Matthews, a coalition member who lives in one of a row of modest single-family houses across Edgewood Street from the project. Hunched nervously on her sofa, the 81-year-old retired school teacher says: "The other night, I heard 13 shots in a row. I sat here and counted them." Neighbors on both sides have had bullets smash through their front doors. Shots shattered the upstairs bedroom window of a house up the street.

Within the Edgewood Terrace compound, teen-agers, mostly boys, lounge in small groups, often attended by younger hangers-on. "Our biggest problem with the youth is absence of supervision," says Clifton Johnson, another coalition member. "Either there's a single parent working, or the parents don't care, or they care but just can't control" their children. The coalition is trying to launch an after-school program, but so far the teen-agers are staying away.

Jermaine Daniel and Judonne Cole were rising through the ranks in this loosely organized army of young people. Jermaine, a gregarious, chubby-cheeked boy nicknamed "Fats," lived with his mother, Diane, an unemployed secretary. Jermaine's father, Henry, is in the Lorton federal prison in Virginia, serving a 10-to-30 year term for manslaughter and drug crimes. One of Jermaine's two older brothers is also serving time in Lorton. For at least a couple of years, Diane Daniel has traveled regularly to and from New York, leaving Jermaine largely on his own, according to people who know the family. Ms. Daniel, who declined to be interviewed for this article, was out of town when her son was killed.

Always Happy-Faced

Judonne, now being held in a juvenile jail, lived in the same seven-story brown brick building with his grandmother and two older brothers. Judonne's mother, a heavy drug user, according to people who know her, surrendered responsibility for the boys a few years ago. The grandmother, though praised by neighbors as principled and well-meaning, by all accounts couldn't control her grandsons.

Judonne's brother, Tony, 17, says the slim, quiet boy "was always happy-faced." Billy, a classmate of Jermaine and Judonne's at Langley Junior High School, says the two were "best friends" who "did their schoolwork; you have to give them that."

> ***"Times change. Kids are not satisfied with doing a beating. They want to end it."***

By the age of 12 or 13, though, Jermaine and Judonne were also involved in selling drugs and even stealing cars, police say. They were arrested on a number of occasions, usually together. "That's how you knew where they were," says a police officer in the area. "When one was locked up, the other one was, too."

A former Edgewood resident and convicted drug dealer who calls himself "Fish" says boys like Jermaine and Judonne learn by imitating their elders. A frequent visitor to his old turf, Fish explains: "Everybody wants to be presentable. White man got your sports jacket and tie. Kid here wants his Guess jeans and his flashy coat." Fish adds: "They can't get no jobs . . . so what else these boys going to do?"

Easy Access to Guns

Getting arrested is an essential element of the outlaw reputation at Edgewood. What's more, "Everyone from Edgewood got to carry a gun to be a man," says Tim Edmonds, 20, who lives in another housing project nearby.

Most young people in the area say their friends acquire guns for protection from drug dealers, from drug customers and from the "stick-up boys" who prey on everyone else. But teen-agers also carry weapons for style. The nine-millimeter semiautomatic pistol, often featured in such TV shows as "Miami

Vice," is the current fashion rage. Jermaine was seen on a couple of occasions with "a nine." He is also said to have carried a .357 magnum, a cousin of the cannon-like .44 magnum made famous in Clint Eastwood's "Dirty Harry" movies.

Movies and television help dissolve inhibitions about guns, says William, an 18-year-old senior at Duke Ellington High School. "There's no reality for these kids; everything is fantasy, killing doesn't mean anything."

"Record numbers of people 17 or younger have been arrested on murder or weapons charges."

Washington has one of the toughest anti-handgun laws in the country; it bans gun sales. But any Edgewood 14-year-old can get one. Thousands of guns are sold legally each year in Maryland, Virginia, and West Virginia; many of them make their way onto the underground market in Washington. Robberies of out-of-state gun shops also help supply the capital, according to James Perry, a crack dealer-turned-youth counselor who uses a wheelchair since getting shot in 1989.

A Deadly Combination

Forty dollars buys a .22 caliber pistol in Edgewood. A nine-millimeter costs as little as $200. For short-term needs, you can rent a .38 caliber revolver from Friday night through Saturday for $40 to $60. Addicts who steal guns will trade them for as little as a $20 vial of crack. Or you can borrow, says Mr. Perry: "'Can I use your gun?' 'Sure, bring it back in an hour.'"

"Kids says they need protection," he says. "But if they're armed, as soon as they get into an argument—boom!—they're going to use it." If someone has the reputation for carrying a gun, he adds, that makes it more likely that antagonists will pull theirs first.

Jermaine had a reputation for carrying a gun. He also had a talent for taunting, or "dis'ing," short for disrespecting. Together, the two are a deadly combination. Among the younger residents of Edgewood Terrace, almost any provocation—the mildest dis'ing—requires retaliation.

The confrontation between Jermaine and Judonne sounds almost inevitable as retold by their friends and family. "They both going out with the same girl," says Billy, the Langley Junior High classmate. "Fats, he don't know. He find out and get mad. That starts something. . . . Judonne, he just wants to end it."

Judonne's Story

The police, based on what they say were Judonne's statements after his arrest, give the following, slightly different account:

Judonne got angry after he learned that Jermaine had threatened to slap the girlfriend. Once a confrontation seemed likely, Judonne went to his apartment and got his .45 caliber Smith & Wesson. He feared that Jermaine would have his .357.

Judonne test-fired his own weapon outside his building. Then he went to meet Jermaine in the courtyard. Jermaine quickly realized that Judonne was armed. As an audience gathered, Jermaine teased Judonne, daring him to shoot. "You better kill me," he said several times.

Judonne fired, and fired twice more. He told police he meant to shoot Jermaine in the legs, not the chest.

Judonne ran, but turned himself in three hours later. "I killed my friend," he said.

Judonne's government-paid lawyer, Gretchen Franklin, says she will introduce "exculpatory" evidence at his trial. At a preliminary juvenile court proceeding she pleaded with the judge, "This is a 14-year-old child we've got here." Next to her sat a forlorn-looking boy dressed in jeans and a blue sweatshirt, staring at his sneakers.

Judonne's brother, Tony, discusses the shooting with a tight, sardonic smile, his eyes hidden behind a pair of wrap-around sunglasses. "This wasn't barbaric," he insists. "It wasn't intentionally loading up to go and shoot someone."

As Tony speaks, a uniformed patrolman sprints past, walkie-talkie squawking. He shouts to his partner: "Let's roll! Let's roll! Kid with a gun!"

Young men standing in a nearby doorway, small boys climbing on a twisted chain-link fence—they all look up, but no one seems scared or dismayed. The spectators go back to their business as the cops turn the corner and disappear.

The Number of Victims of Teenage Violence Is Increasing

by David Freed

About the author: *David Freed is a staff writer for the* Los Angeles Times.

In the Aliso-Pico housing project near downtown Los Angeles, 11-year-old Frankie Mugia and his sister Crystal, 6, have had to sleep on the floor of their second-story bedroom to avoid bullets. Their window has been shot out by gunfire.

How often do you hear gunshots?

"Every day," Frankie says.

How often do you see guns?

"Every day."

If children are the future, then firearms are altering the future of Los Angeles County.

In 1972, the coroner's records show, one in 10 fatal shootings involved children or teen-agers as victims. In 1992 the ratio is more than one in four.

In 1987 the district attorney's office prosecuted 945 youths for carrying firearms: By 1991 the number had more than doubled.

And the *Los Angeles Times* Poll found that one in five households with children in Los Angeles County has been victimized by gun-related crime since 1990.

Indifference to Violence

Triggermen in gang shootings often are not yet old enough to shave. Some schools have had to do away with book lockers because students use them to stash pistols and other contraband. Inner-city children who cannot tell one bird's song from another can often distinguish the caliber and proximity of a gun by the crack of its report.

Doctors believe there may be tens of thousands of children in Los Angeles County whose psychiatric health and emotional growth are being disrupted by constant exposure to violence, especially gunfire.

"Look at the level of meanness and cruelty that these children are experiencing out there—and yet we expect them to grow up and be Jack and Jill," said Dr. Range Hutson, director of emergency admitting at Los Angeles County-USC Medical Center.

"We are creating a generation of people who just don't care about what it is they do to each other."

Conflicting Opinions

Some contend that tightening control of gun and ammunition sales is the answer.

Others argue that more guns in the hands of law-abiding citizens would help deter criminals, thus making the streets safer for both children and adults. According to the *Times* Poll, 9% of firearms owners in Southern California say they have used their guns to thwart burglaries, car thefts or other crimes. Many blame leniency in the courts and a decline in family discipline for the proliferation of gun-related violence. Today's juvenile delinquent with a gun, they say, is tomorrow's armed robber or killer.

Still others contend that the carnage can only increase as long as residents of the county's most upscale and influential areas, where shootings are a relative rarity, remain apathetic.

"Nobody [cares] so long as it stops in the barrio and the ghetto," said Deputy Probation Officer James J. Galipeau. "Until the white middle class sees the real threat is to them and their children, nothing's going to get done."

A Major Urban Problem

The toll among children, meanwhile, continues to mount.

A review of medical records published in 1988 by doctors at Martin Luther King Jr.-Drew Medical Center, which receives a high portion of medical emergencies in central Los Angeles, found that the number of children admitted to the center with gunshot wounds began to grow dramatically in 1980.

"Triggermen in gang shootings often are not yet old enough to shave."

Between 1974 and 1980, no child under the age of 10 was hospitalized there for gunshot wounds, the study found. By 1987, however, doctors at the center had treated and admitted at least 34 children for gunshot wounds, all 9 or younger.

Ten had been shot unintentionally by other children or had accidentally shot themselves; 11 were hit by stray bullets fired by gang members or in retaliation for gang-related activities of their older siblings; 10 were inadvertently shot with guns that were aimed at other relatives during family disputes; two were shot during robberies, and one was hit by sniper fire.

"We are creating a generation of people who just don't care about what it is they do to each other."

Three of the 34 children died of their wounds; three others suffered brain damage requiring them to be institutionalized; one suffers from recurrent bowel obstructions; two underwent colostomies; one lost an eye; two lost parts of a hand, and another suffers from radical nerve damage to the wrist.

"Childhood gunshot wounds," the study concluded, "have become a major urban medical problem."

If anything, the situation in Los Angeles has worsened in recent years.

In the 1970-71 fiscal year, four children 9 or younger were murdered with guns in Los Angeles County, coroner's records show. In 1991 there were 10, plus two who were accidentally shot to death. Since April 1992, gunshots have killed three children, the youngest 18 months old.

No Longer Off-Limits

At Childrens Hospital near Hollywood, 31 children age 14 or younger were treated for gunshot wounds in 1991, compared to 21 the year before.

"Children used to be off-limits to criminals . . . and that's no longer true," said Dr. Nancy Schonfeld, director of emergency services at Childrens Hospital. "It's really sick."

One evening in July 1991, Bianca Duran, 10, her two younger brothers and their seamstress mother, Enriqueta, were caught in a gang cross-fire while playing in San Fernando's Las Palmas Park.

A shotgun blast raked the mother's right arm and back as lead pellets ripped into Bianca's stomach, head and hand. Other pellets hit Bianca's 8- and 9-year-old brothers in their backs.

Bianca, the most seriously injured, underwent surgery and was in the hospital for three days.

"It hurt a little," she said.

Bianca and her brothers have fully recovered from their wounds, at least physically. Sometimes when she sleeps, according to her mother, Bianca whimpers, thrashes violently, then awakes with a start—as if she is reliving the shooting in the park.

"Before this happened," Duran said, "the city was so beautiful. But now. . . ." Her words trailed into tears.

In February 1992, another little girl, Cristal Anguiano, 12, was caught in a gang gunfight as she ran to buy ice cream from a passing truck outside her home in South Los Angeles. She was shot in the heart but managed to carry her 2-year-old brother, Rafael, to safety.

Haunted by Violence

Beyond the number of children killed and wounded, there is an additional toll taken on inner-city youngsters who are regularly exposed to the sound and sight of gunfire.

Many psychiatrists, counselors and others contend there may be tens of thousands of children who are suffering from a form of post-traumatic stress disorder (PTSD), like that experienced by some combat veterans.

In 1987, a study by the National Institute of Mental Health estimated that 1% of American adults had post-traumatic stress as a result of exposure to shootings or other violent episodes. Victims typically complained of nightmares, a feeling of "jumpiness" and trouble sleeping.

Children exposed to shooting incidents, according to a report by Los Angeles psychiatrists Spencer Eth and Robert S. Pynoos, are often haunted by "the sight, sound and smell of gunfire, the screams or sudden silence of the victim, the splash of blood and tissue on the child's clothes, the grasp of a dying parent and the eventual police sirens."

"Children used to be off-limits to criminals . . . and that's no longer true."

Sixth-grader Curly James Jr., who lives in a South-Central Los Angeles housing project, came home from school one day in 1991 and was watching cartoons when he looked out his living room window and witnessed the fatal shooting of a gang member.

The 11-year-old boy can describe in vivid detail how the gunman fired over the heads of several toddlers playing on the lawn, how the victim grimaced in pain as he fell to the ground, clutching the grass with both hands.

A Developing Problem

That night, after he had finally fallen asleep, Curly awoke to screaming from across the courtyard, looked out his bedroom window and saw an apartment engulfed in flames. Gang members had thrown a Molotov cocktail into the apartment in retaliation for the shooting, killing a pregnant woman and her 1-year-old child.

The boy helped police identify the man later convicted of the shooting—and the youngster sometimes has nightmares. "Every time I go to school," he said, "I see his face."

A survey headed by UCLA resident psychiatrist Eugene Jennings found in 1991 that of 40 randomly selected high school students in Compton and South-

Central Los Angeles, seven met the criteria for being diagnosed as suffering post-traumatic stress disorder. None had received counseling.

Several others who had witnessed violent acts and were found not to have the disorder complained of upsetting memories and mental images that sometimes affected their moods and ability to study.

> ***"There may be tens of thousands of children who are suffering from a form of post-traumatic stress disorder."***

"If the sample is representative," Jennings said, "we have a problem on our hands."

Many apparent symptoms fade with time and without counseling, mental health experts say. But if the disorder is not immediately treated, a child's ability to concentrate and learn can be disrupted, causing the child to lag in educational development while peers advance.

Left untreated, a child can also grow up less able to handle the stresses of day-to-day life, according to psychiatrist Andrew Wang of the Los Angeles Unified School District.

"It's a cumulative effect," Wang said. "The risk increases each time [the child] has a stress. Humans have a threshold when it comes to stress and when you reach a certain point, you explode."

The incidence of untreated PTSD, experts said, may be much higher in Los Angeles' burgeoning immigrant communities, where many children from war-ravaged countries have already been exposed to gunfire, and where language differences and tight budgets can deter parents from seeking counseling for their children.

"A lot of these parents simply don't have the resources to protect their kids like middle-class families do," said USC psychiatrist William Arroyo, who has counseled or helped screen about 400 children traumatized by firearms-related incidents in Los Angeles County.

"You have many families," Arroyo said, "that are minimizing the suffering of their children by adopting an attitude that says, 'Don't talk about it and maybe it'll go away.'"

Dramatic Increase

In the past, counselors and psychologists employed by the 630,000-student school district were often able to intervene when children were traumatized by violence. But with shootings on the rise and cutbacks in funding, the district has not kept pace, Arroyo and others said.

The ratio of students to counselors in the district's junior and senior high schools has doubled since 1989, to about 700 students for every counselor, records show. The district has 375 school-based psychologists, but fewer than 50 are available to counsel students who have survived or witnessed shooting incidents, said Loeb Aronin, the school district's director of psychological services.

"We are losing ground," Aronin said.

School district officials, meanwhile, have seen a dramatic increase since 1987 in the number of guns and other weapons students have brought on campus out of fear.

During the 1986-87 school year, records show, 330 students were recommended for expulsion after being caught with weapons. In 1991, there were 519 such recommendations, the majority involving sixth-, seventh- and eighth-graders.

Going Through a Combat Zone

"We've got kids now who think it's not only appropriate to bring firearms to campus, but necessary," said Marleen Wong, a licensed clinical social worker for the school district. "Even their families often feel it necessary for their kids to carry guns. That is their reality—that they are having to go through a combat zone every day."

At Hollenbeck Junior High School, officials did away with student locker privileges to limit hiding places for weapons and other contraband. Records show that as many guns were taken from students in the last half of 1991 as in the preceding four years.

At nearby Belvedere Junior High School, bullets were fired at four students or more from 1990-1992. One was shot to death in 1991 while walking home from his first day in the eighth grade.

"When one kid tells another one today, 'I'm gonna kill you,'" said Principal Victoria M. Castro, "they take it seriously."

At the Northeast Juvenile Justice Center near downtown Los Angeles, authorities see first hand the result of children's threats these days.

"The weapons available to kids in Los Angeles today are tenfold what they were 10 years ago, weapons that are unimaginable to the public," said Superior Court Judge Sherman W. Smith Jr., who recently transferred to another courthouse.

> ***"We've got kids now who think it's not only appropriate to bring firearms to campus, but necessary."***

The juvenile center has a backlog of 29 homicide cases—each one involving a firearm.

In one pending case, two 15-year-old Boyle Heights gang members are accused of beating up another 15-year-old boy in April 1992. One of the gang members allegedly held the boy in a headlock, turning him toward the other gang member, who allegedly shot the victim with a .25-caliber pistol. In another case, this one involving a .38-caliber pistol, three youths are accused of having waited for two nights in April 1992 outside a home in Culver City, then ambushing a 56-year-old man and killing him for his car.

"They didn't even mince words," said Deputy Dist. Atty. Allan Walsh. "They just shot him."

Many of the teen-age gang members prosecuted at the Northeast Juvenile Center are later supervised by Deputy Probation Officer Mary Ridgeway. She estimates that 80% have been wounded by gunfire at least once in their young lives and that perhaps 20% of the total have been shot more than once.

"It's not just the type of firepower and the easy access to guns that's changed," Ridgeway said. "It's the fact that the age of the shooters has dropped. A lot of them are 13- and 14-year-olds these days, and these kids don't care who they hit."

Authorities speculate that gang members are assigning shootings to younger members to avoid prosecution. Many are aware that the district attorney is increasingly prosecuting suspects in the mid- to late teens as adults. Moreover, records show, the number of juveniles charged with illegally carrying firearms has doubled since 1987.

"When you're 15, 16, you shoot 'em up," said one 18-year-old. "Now . . . the younger ones shoot. They're easier to brainwash. They don't know what's happening with the law.". . .

Children Hit by Gunfire

A study at Martin Luther King Jr.-Drew Medical Center found that the number of children hit by gunfire in Los Angeles began to grow dramatically in 1980. Of 34 children admitted to the medical center with gunshot wounds between 1980-1987, three died and most suffered major injuries. They included:

Age/Sex	Area of Body Shot	Shooter	Reason	Complications	Days in Hospital	Outcome
1-year-old boy	Head	Grandfather Age 46	Family dispute, stray bullet	Died 3 days later	—	Died, grandfather in prison
3-year-old girl	Rectum	Brother Age 8	Accidental, playing with gun	Colostomy	22	Home
2-year-old girl	Head	Sniper	Sniper, hit by accident	Death	—	Died
7-year-old girl	Eye	Gang member Age 17	Retaliation	Lost eye	7	Home
9-year-old girl	Head	Gang member	Retaliation	Infection, wound	6	Home

Because a disproportionate number of shootings occur in working-class areas, many residents of the county's more affluent neighborhoods consider themselves unaffected and are thus hesitant to demand change. Indeed, only 30% of Los Angeles County adults in the highest income levels say they consider their neighborhoods unsafe, compared to 60% of adults in the lowest earning brackets, the *Times* Poll found.

"If I were living in East Los Angeles or Watts, maybe I would've bought [a gun] a long time ago," said William O. Felsman, a retired aerospace engineer, "but I don't need it in Woodland Hills—there aren't many thugs here."

Gun-related violence, some authorities warn, may ultimately prove to be the great equalizer.

"It's going to continue to spread," Los Angeles County Sheriff Sherman Block said. "And if anybody in this community—and I don't care who they are or where they live—view it as happening to somebody else, they're going to wake up one day and find out they were dead wrong."

Teenage Gun Use Is Increasing

by Joseph B. Treaster and Mary B.W. Tabor

About the authors: *Joseph B. Treaster has been a reporter for the* New York Times *for over twenty years. Mary B. W. Tabor is a staff reporter for the* New York Times.

On a shadowy corner in Brooklyn, a gangly teen-ager slowly opened his jacket to give a peek at the 9-millimeter semiautomatic pistol jammed in the waistband of his jeans.

"When you've got it," he said, glancing at the weapon, "you've got the power. It doesn't matter whether you're big or small. You've got the power."

In a pizza parlor not far away, two young men said they felt naked without their guns. "It's like an article of clothing," one explained. "I put on my shoes, my pants, my shirt, my hat and my gun."

Teenagers Arming Themselves

Throughout New York City these days, there are teen-agers toting guns, armed from the arsenal of tens of thousands of pistols and revolvers, sawed-off shotguns and submachine guns that have been flooding in on the surging currents of riches and violence in the nation's biggest drug market.

But New York is not alone. Experts say that all around the country teen-agers are taking up guns. "The number of young people arming themselves and dying is reaching epidemic proportions," said Vanessa Scherzer, a spokeswoman for the Center to Prevent Handgun Violence in Washington. "It's happening in big cities and small towns."

Some of today's young gunslingers are dealers, runners and neighborhood managers in the drug trade. Some are muggers who learned quickly that one glimpse of a gun is enough to make most people turn over a wallet or a purse in a flash. But as guns have proliferated, many young people have been caught up in a vicious circle of packing weapons to protect themselves.

"You get it because you fear what is happening out there," said a teen-ager who would only identify himself by his initials, J. B. "Once you have it you feel like a god. You feel invincible."

"'It's like an article of clothing,' one explained. 'I put on my shoes, my pants, my shirt, my hat and my gun.'"

Not every young person is carrying a gun by any means. "But," said Catherine M. Abate, the Commissioner of Probation in New York City, "it's no longer the exception; it's commonplace."

Every day or so another shooting by teen-agers hits the news. Two boys on a Coney Island rooftop, test-firing a .22-caliber rifle they had just bought for $80, killed a 45-year-old woman with a single shot to the back, according to the police. A shot rang out in a a crowded corridor at a Manhattan high school and a 16-year-old protégé of the principal collapsed with a bullet in his left ankle. A flabbergasted teacher at an elementary school on Staten Island found a .45-caliber semiautomatic pistol in a fourth-grader's book bag. To everyone's relief, the gun was not loaded.

Homicide Rate Has Eased

The homicide rate in New York has eased a bit. But the more than 2,100 murder victims in 1991 was still nearly 15 times greater than the death toll for Americans in combat in the Persian Gulf war. That was an average of nearly six murders a day, more than 70 percent of them by handguns.

Since 1987, 118 youths under 16 were charged with possession of a loaded gun. The number jumped to 351 in 1988 and in 1991 vaulted to 750.

"Guns and kids are probably the most dangerous combination there is," said Peter Reinharz, the head of the Family Court Division of the city's Corporation Counsel, who serves as New York's chief prosecutor of youths under 16. "A 13-or 14-year-old holding an Uzi submachine gun has no understanding of his own mortality, let alone your mortality."

Gun Incidents Double

In the 1990-1991 school year, reports of incidents involving guns in and around the schools rose to 45, more than double the number in the previous year, said Edward Muir, the director of school safety for the United Federation of Teachers.

"The situation is desperate and it's getting worse," he said.

Halfway into the 1991-1992 school term, Mr. Muir said, 47 gun incidents have already been reported. The casualties, he said, included two parents, five teachers, a police officer and 13 students, four of whom died.

"Guns are becoming like a badge of honor with young people," said Police

Commissioner Lee P. Brown.

New York City public schools officials point out that most of the school-related incidents occurred outside the schools, some a block or two away. But by their own count, students found with guns, knives and other weapons rose 13 percent in the 1990-1991 school year, from 1,890 to 2,170. James J. Vlasto, the schools' chief spokesman, said classes are expected to begin on "gun violence and how to reduce gun violence."

Lenient States Are Warehouses

Strict laws prohibit New York gun dealers from selling handguns to anyone under 21 years of age or shotguns to anyone under 18. Every buyer must obtain a pistol license or shotgun permit from the police department. But in half a dozen states an adult can buy a pistol without a police review or any waiting period by merely showing proof of residency. And those states, law enforcement officials say, are like warehouses for gunrunners supplying New York.

All kinds of guns, from tiny, easy to conceal .25-caliber Raven semiautomatics to awesome-looking weapons in submachine gun style like the stubby Mac-10 and the snub-nosed Intratec Tec-9, are easily available to youths. "As long as you've got the money, you can get a gun," said Mark Johnson, an 11th grader in Brooklyn.

> ***"The number of young people arming themselves and dying is reaching epidemic proportions."***

In the language of teen-agers and the streets, a gun is a "piece," a "burner," a "jammie," a "tool," a "shotty," a "nine" (for nine millimeter) or, sometimes, an "istol," in a truncated version of "pistol."

A young person threatening to use his piece says he's going to "light you up," or "put you to rest," or "fat you off." A gun that has been used in a killing is said to "have a body on it."

"When a gun doesn't have bodies on it," an 18-year-old crack dealer named Mike R. said, "you can sell it. When it does have bodies you have to bury it or else they might trace it back to you."

The Arsenal Remains

New York has always had more than its fair share of illegal guns. But the cocaine and crack explosion in the mid-1980's created a huge demand for arms to protect turf and fortune. Drug experts say the craze for cocaine and crack is ebbing. But law enforcement officials say the city remains saddled with a vast armory of illegal guns, new and used, selling for as little as $40 to $1,500.

"Drugs are consumed and then they're gone," said Charles R. Thomson, the chief of the New York office of the Federal Bureau of Alcohol, Tobacco and Firearms. "But guns stay in the city until the law-enforcement agencies come across them and take them off the street."

The gunrunners serving New York vary from teen-agers in sneakers and sweatsuits to dapper businessmen in dark suits and limousines, law enforcement officials say. But their common thread is connections in the drug trade.

Until recently, Florida was the leading source of illegal guns for New York, said John O'Brien, a spokesman for the Federal firearms bureau. "That's because there were so many New Yorkers down there," he said, "and they saw how easily they could buy guns there."

But in 1988-1989, New York cocaine and crack dealers started doing business in Washington and discovered Virginia's accommodating gun shops. Now Virginia is the leader in the sale of guns brought to New York, Mr. O'Brien said.

Simply by showing a Virginia driver's license as proof of residency, Mr. O'Brien said, a person can buy two handguns from any shop there every five days with no waiting period or police review.

Popular Weapons

In neighborhood grocery stores and on bustling drug-selling corners in the grittier parts of New York, the guns fetch six or seven times their purchase price in the clubby, well-lighted gun shops in the southern and midwestern states.

"The most popular weapons are the Raven .25, the Davis .380 and the cheap 9-millimeter pistols like the Stallard and the Haskell," said Lieut. Kenneth McCann, the commander of the New York police officers on a joint task force with the Federal firearms bureau.

Teen-agers in the street say they like the Raven because it is compact, easy to conceal and relatively inexpensive, selling on the streets for $200 to $300 new. It was a Raven .25 that the police say 15-year-old Rasheem Smith used to wound Officer David Pitchon in the ankle in mid-January 1992 after bragging to friends that he was going to get back at the officer for breaking up a fistfight in which Mr. Smith was beating up another boy.

The gunrunners often travel by bus or train, sometimes in cars, but rarely through airports, where security is tighter, Mr. O'Brien said. Sometimes, he said, they take drugs from New York to sell in the other states for money to pay for guns.

"Many young people have been caught up in a vicious circle of packing weapons to protect themselves."

In mid-January 1992, in what the law enforcement officials say is a fairly typical case, officers from the joint task force arrested three young men—17, 18 and 24 years old—as they stepped off a Trailways bus from Richmond, Va., at the Port Authority bus terminal in mid-Manhattan. The 18-year-old had a black nylon carry-on bag loaded with 10 semiautomatic pistols, two James

Bondish laser gunsights and four boxes of ammunition, the officers said.

Late in 1991, the task force concluded that two students from Ohio State University, who had grown up in Brooklyn, were operating a guns- and drug-smuggling business on weekends. They would drive into New York to sell a dozen or so handguns and buy cocaine for sale in Ohio.

Increasing Violence

Arrests of people under 16 for selected felonies.
1991 figures are not complete because of court backlog.

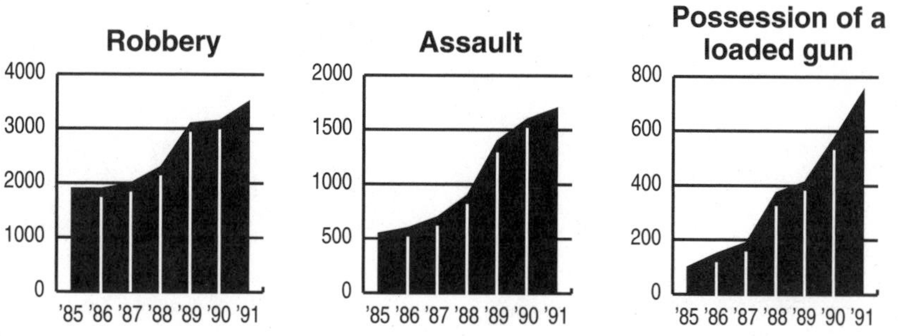

Source: City of New York Family Court

In 1990, a policeman at the Port Authority bus terminal discovered four handguns and three boxes of ammunition in a 13-year-old Connecticut girl's knapsack. Port Authority officials said they knew of only one similar case. But Mr. Reinharz said that "kids are on the buses every day working as mules, going to jurisdictions where they can pick up guns."

Police Commissioner Brown and some academics say they believe that vivid scenes of violence on television and in movies are important contributors to the rise in teen-age gunplay.

"A 13- or 14-year-old holding an Uzi submachine gun has no understanding of his own mortality, let alone your mortality."

"Some people can't make the distinction between someone getting shot on television and shooting someone," Mr. Brown said.

Terry Cooper, an eighth grader in Brooklyn, said that three friends had been shot to death and that he was hit in the arm by a stray bullet in 1989. But he said it wasn't until January 1992, when a 13-year-old boy killed a Russian immigrant near Terry's home, that he really came to grips with the idea of guns and his own vulnerability.

Terry said he heard the gun blast and ran to help. "I thought, 'It could have been me lying on the floor,'" he said. "I didn't like guns in the first place, but after that I felt worse."

Yet some teen-agers with guns talk like stone-cold killers, unmoved by their deeds, even unwilling to recognize themselves as players in the Great American Shoot-Out.

Shivering in a black T-shirt and baseball cap on a desolate street in the Bronx the other evening, Mike R. nodded knowingly as he talked about crack dealing and mugging.

Yes, he had shot at people and, yes, he thought he had hit some of them. It had been at close quarters, in stickups. But the victims had not left much of an impression. "They were just people," he said. "Just people."

The Number of Rapes Committed by Youths Has Increased

by Beth Weinhouse

About the author: *Beth Weinhouse is a free-lance writer who specializes in health topics.*

Editor's note: Names and some identifying details of rapists and their victims have been changed to protect privacy.

Jennifer Richards, 25, had been worried for much of the day about her baby's crying and fever. Late that night, she decided to take him to the emergency room, where doctors diagnosed the 19-month-old as having strep throat. Jennifer left the San Diego hospital with the baby a little after midnight. As she walked through the parking lot toward her car, a tall young man jumped out from behind a parked van. Brandishing a gun, he ordered Jennifer to put the baby onto the backseat of his van. Then, with the gun to her neck, he forced Jennifer into the front seat. As the baby cried, the stranger robbed Jennifer and raped her repeatedly, then sped down the highway for a harrowing hour and a half. Finally, he pulled over near the small town of San Juan Capistrano and raped Jennifer several times more. Then he drove back to San Diego, releasing Jennifer and her son in the same parking lot where he'd abducted them four hours earlier.

The rapist was 17 years old.

Capable of Violent Crimes

Susan Tipton, 22, is mentally retarded and suffers from cerebral palsy. She was enjoying an autumn day in her parents' yard in Washington state when John, a boy she knew from the neighborhood, suggested they go for ice cream.

Beth Weinhouse, "Young but Not Innocent," *Redbook*, April 1990. Reprinted with permission.

When Susan agreed, John lured the young woman to a secluded area where he tied her hands and one foot to a fence post. He then beat her with a stick and raped her. Afterward, he threatened that if she ever told anyone he would find her and cut off her arms.

John was 12 years old.

Children Commit Crimes

We're accustomed to thinking of childhood as a time of innocence, but as these cases—and many others like them—attest, children are capable of even the most vicious sexual assaults. For example, the highly publicized gang rape of a 28-year-old woman accosted while jogging in Central Park in the spring of 1989 was shocking not only because of the brutality of the attack but because the rapists were only 14 to 16 years old.

The frightening news is that sexual crimes—including rape—by children and teenagers are becoming increasingly common and widespread:

- According to the Federal Bureau of Investigation, boys younger than 18 account for 14 percent (4,033 in 1988) of all rape arrests in America. Approximately 5 percent (1,328) are boys age 15 and under.
- The rate of arrests for forcible rape committed by 13- to 14-year-olds in America has almost doubled over the last decade.
- Half of all gang rapes—often the most violent rapes—involve males under 21.
- Once in treatment, juvenile sex offenders admit to an average of 20 to 30 crimes committed before their arrest.
- According to crime experts, most adult rapists began their sexually deviant behavior during adolescence or even younger.

These chilling statistics can't be dismissed as simply better reporting by the victims. "For my money, it's a real increase," says Hunter Hurst, director of the National Center for Juvenile Justice in Pittsburgh. "If it were just a matter of heightened sensitivity and awareness, the *overall* number of rape arrests would be higher. Instead, the increase is concentrated among the youngest offenders." It's also important to remember that arrest rates represent only a fraction of the actual number of crimes committed. They don't include reported crimes that don't result in an arrest, unreported crimes—which many experts feel represent over half of all rapes committed—or attempted rapes.

> ***"Children are capable of even the most vicious sexual assaults."***

Until recently, society often dismissed juvenile sex offenses as examples of boys being boys. "Date rape" and rapes committed in college fraternity houses were seen as part of normal (though unacceptable) adolescent sexual mischievousness. But as the crimes become more violent and more visible, they are difficult to ignore. "We used to call these youngsters' crimes 'assault' or 'contributing to the delinquency of a minor,'" says Sharon English, assistant deputy director of Parole Services, California State Youth Authority, Sacramento. "Now we call them what they really are—rape or molestation."

Some state laws have recently changed: Illinois, for example, previously defined rape as a crime committed "by a male 14 or over." That phrase was deleted in 1985, according to Pauline Bart, Ph.D., professor of sociology at the University of Illinois, Chicago, and author of *Stopping Rape: Successful Survival Strategies*. "Nobody thought of it before, but then rape by kids younger than fourteen became more common," she says. "The state wanted to be able to define those crimes as rape and get the charge on the attackers' record."

Littlest Offenders and Littlest Victims

As shocking as it is to contemplate 14- to 16-year-old rapists, many people will find it incomprehensible that juvenile sexual offenders can be far younger. But they can: A recent case in New York City involved an eight-year-old boy who sodomized (anally penetrated) a kindergartner. A case in New Jersey a few years ago involved a group of young boys accused of sexually assaulting a six-year-old girl by putting their fingers inside her. (The charges against the boys—ages 6, 7 and 9—were eventually dismissed.) In Detroit, an 11-year-old, along with a 15-year-old, was charged with the rape of a *two-year-old* girl. Sadly, it's all too easy to find cases such as these to cite.

"Most victims of juvenile sex offenders are children."

In fact, most victims of juvenile sex offenders are children. Though youngsters' crimes against adults tend to garner the most publicity—and be the most violent—attacks by children on their peers, or on younger children, are much more common: A child can use threats, persuasion or bribery against another child far more readily than he can against an adult.

When children choose grown women as their victims, they must rely on brute force—or pick someone especially vulnerable. For example, a group of Glen Ridge, New Jersey, high school boys were charged in 1989 with sexually assaulting a slightly retarded young woman; they allegedly used a broomstick and toy baseball bat. "Unfortunately, developmentally disabled adults are targets in our society for all kinds of crime," says Gayle Stringer, director of education at the King County Sexual Assault Resource Center in Renton, Washington.

But rape crisis counselors caution against making too much of the age of the attacker; the victims' anguish is not affected by that. Says Gail Abarbanel, director of the Rape Treatment Center in California's Santa Monica Hospital, "The trauma is related to the violence and violation of the attack and the powerlessness of the victim—not to the age of the offender."

In the case of Jennifer Richards, mentioned earlier, her attacker, Erik, was quickly arrested and charged with rape, kidnapping and robbery. Erik's first trial ended in a hung jury. He and his lawyer agreed to a plea bargain—and, although Erik admits that he committed the rape, he pled guilty to just one count of kidnapping. He spent four years in the custody of the California Youth Authority, and now, at age 23, he's been paroled. Jennifer, however, is still a prisoner of her fear and depression. She seldom leaves her house after dark, and she has suicidal thoughts. (She is currently in therapy.)

"One out of three men say that, if they could get away with it, they would be at least 'somewhat likely' to rape a woman."

Susan Tipton, the retarded woman who was raped by a 12-year-old boy, was so terrified that for five months after her attack she remained silent about it. Finally, the story emerged. Her rapist was arrested, and Susan mustered the courage to testify against him. He was sentenced to three years in a juvenile rehabilitation facility.

Why Do Children Rape?

Child rapists have at least one thing in common with adult rapists—rage. "When we talk about rape, whether we are talking about adolescents or adults, we have to talk about anger, not passion," says Michael Kimmel, Ph.D., professor of sociology, State University of New York at Stony Brook. "But there are three things that are different with juvenile rapists. First, because they are so young, much of their anger is directed at older women—teachers and mothers. Second, they're very often working out issues of manhood—trying to prove they're men. Third, adolescent rape often takes place among groups of boys—street gangs in inner cities, fraternities on college campuses.

"A lot of gang rape takes place when there's one guy who wants to prove he's a man and five guys who are terrified of being thought of as less than one," says Dr. Kimmel. "Society has linked masculinity to hurting women. That's unconscionable. We have to say very clearly to adolescent boys, 'This is not acceptable. You are *not* a real man if you rape a woman.'"

Anthropologists use the expression "rape-prone" to describe communities characterized by militarism, interpersonal violence, an ideal of male toughness, and distant father-child relationships. "Our society is still very much rape-prone," says Jane C. Hood, Ph.D., a University of New Mexico sociologist. "Despite recent moves toward gender equality, our culture still equates masculinity with sexual dominance." And in such a society, she continues, it's no giant leap of logic for boys to conclude that if a woman isn't willing, rape is the acceptable alternative.

In a 1988 poll of 1,700 Rhode Island junior high school students, 25 percent of the boys said they believe a man has the right to rape a woman if he spends money on her on a date. Perhaps even more disturbing, about 16 percent of the girls agreed. Half of the students, both girls and boys, said that a woman who dresses seductively and walks alone at night is "asking" to be raped.

As kids grow older, their attitudes don't always become more enlightened. "Surveys of U.S. and Canadian college students," says Dr. Hood, "find that one out of three men say that, if they could get away with it, they would be at least 'somewhat likely' to rape a woman."

Where do children and teenagers get such disturbing attitudes about women? "Boys see females treated as objects in advertisements," says Dr. Bart. "Boys see eroticized violence in films, on television and in rock videos. The message is, 'That's what women are for.' So why should anybody be surprised when boys act on what they've seen and heard?" In case anyone doubts the connection, Dr. Bart cites an eerie detail in the case of the alleged gang rape in Glen Ridge, New Jersey. "It was reported that the boys were planning a second attack, and they wanted to get a video camera to film it."

Obviously, not every child who watches television, rock videos or even slasher films will go on to commit violent acts. "The vast majority of adolescents are able to put what they're watching into proper perspective," says Alan Morris, Psy.D., chief of the adolescent unit, Illinois State Psychiatric Institute, Chicago. "But certain individuals who are at risk may watch a movie with sadism, then go out and approximate that behavior."

At-Risk Children

What makes a child "at risk"? Experts believe that family circumstances are a major determinant. "Many juvenile offenders probably witnessed or were victims of some sort of sexual abuse and are acting out their anger," says Susan Xenarios, C.S.W., director of St. Luke's-Roosevelt Hospital Rape Intervention Program in New York City. Some therapists believe that almost all very young assailants were victims of abuse, while others doubt the correlation is quite that strong. Judith Becker, Ph.D., director, Sexual Behavior Clinic, New York State Psychiatric Institute in New York City, estimates, "Roughly a third have been sexually abused, and a higher percentage physically abused."

"Domestic violence is extremely widespread today, and children often mimic the aggressor."

"Domestic violence is extremely widespread today, and children often mimic the aggressor," says Xenarios. "If the child's father is violent, the son will often mirror his behavior." Indeed, the number of reported cases of child abuse and neglect is growing. Between 1980 and 1987, the figure nearly doubled—from 1.2 million to 2.2 million.

Jennifer Richards' attacker, Erik, was an abused child. "My father was an alcoholic who beat me so badly I once had to be hospitalized," says Erik. "My family had recently emigrated from Czechoslovakia, and my father couldn't find a job because he didn't speak English. I learned English quickly and was a straight-A student in high school. But I had to drop out to help support my family. I couldn't deal with the pressure at home."

His voice cracking, Erik describes what happened the night he raped Jennifer. "My father had been beating me. I wanted to kill him. I ran out to the car where I had a gun—I'd gotten one in case I needed it for protection against him. But when I came back to the house he had run out. I took all my things and left. I couldn't get at my father, and I was mad. I just wanted to hurt somebody."

"Almost everyone agrees that child rapists who don't receive treatment are at high risk of becoming adult rapists."

"But lots of abused youngsters would never assault another person," says Dr. Becker. One deterrent to violent behavior, according to a psychiatric journal, is for a child to have someone to talk to about his problems. Such children are more likely to develop empathy, even if they are victims of abuse. Erik, for example, says, "If I had been smart enough to ask for help when I was being abused, none of this would have happened."

However, there are no clear-cut answers. Some experts believe that genetic factors, combined with a child's environment, play a key role in criminal behavior. And in many cases, substance abuse sends a child who is already at risk over the edge. Crack, for instance, may leave users sexually aroused; when they cannot find a willing partner, they may decide to rape.

Breaking the Cycle of Violence

To some experts in the field, the issue of *what* to do with young offenders is as important as *why* they got into trouble in the first place. "We can be more productive if we look at how we can help these individuals *correct* their behavior rather than limiting our focus to 'why,'" says Alison Gray Stickrod, M.S., of the Lane County Juvenile Department in Eugene, Oregon.

Almost everyone agrees that child rapists who don't receive treatment are at high risk of becoming adult rapists. "These boys are human time bombs waiting to go off," says Elizabeth Holtzman, New York City's comptroller, who was formerly Brooklyn's district attorney. "If no corrective action is taken, they can be expected to victimize again and again."

Most experts feel that imprisonment without additional treatment is not the answer. "It would be shortsighted to simply lock up kids and then release them," says Hurst. "The relief society gains would be very temporary."

Alternatives to prison include psychiatric hospitals, residential programs oriented toward treatment and, in some cases, outpatient programs. There are currently 637 specialized treatment rehabilitation programs for juvenile sex offenders in this country—up from 346 in 1986—but unfortunately, they're not evenly distributed throughout the country. Currently California, Illinois, Michigan, Minnesota, Oregon, Utah and Washington have exemplary programs. But many states have *no* effective intervention, which sometimes results in kids' getting off scot-free.

Another factor in the lack of corrective action is that the reliability of children's testimony is often questioned; cases where both the victim and the victimizer are children are especially problematic. Also, despite the statistics, there is still some lingering denial that children can perform such terrible acts. "The public is just beginning to admit that children are committing these crimes," Stringer says. "That's why the treatment programs are fledgling at this point, but we'll develop more."

The programs that do exist for juvenile sexual offenders take a variety of approaches. Some concentrate on healing their emotional wounds. Others focus on teaching kids to replace their aggressive behavior with healthy social skills.

Treating Young Rapists

"We let the kids know that what they did was inappropriate," Dr. Becker says. "Then we try to teach them to control their behavior by letting them know which situations represent high risk for them. For instance, sixty percent of our kids report using alcohol. We tell them that when they drink or use drugs it compromises their ability to control their behavior. We also try to help them develop constructive social relationships, and we provide sex education with an emphasis on values."...

In the case of Erik, treatment appears to be working. "Erik has taken responsibility for his actions," says his parole agent. He participated in a program called Young Adults Against Crime, speaking to groups of high school students and police officers about his own experiences and about how his crime might have been prevented. He also encourages young people who are being beaten or sexually abused to seek help.

> ***"The public is just beginning to admit that children are committing these crimes."***

Efforts to stop juvenile sexual offenses, however, can't be directed at just those children who are caught and charged with a crime. To truly make an impact, experts say, we need to make broader changes. "We have to change society—change textbooks in schools, change the portrayal of women on television, include more women in political life. These changes have to be present at all levels of society," says Holtzman.

Youth Violence Is Not Increasing

by Jerome G. Miller

About the author: *Jerome G. Miller was the head of the Massachusetts youth correction system from 1969 to 1971. During his tenure, he introduced a radical social experiment. He closed down virtually all the state's large reform schools and transferred delinquent youth offenders to various community programs throughout the state. This highly controversial reform system is still used in Massachusetts and has produced no major crime wave of juvenile offenders. Today, Miller heads a nonprofit group for the humane treatment of juvenile delinquents.*

[In the Massachusetts youth correction system] we had our share of violent youngsters: Al, who axed his grandmother; Billy, who raped and killed a seventy-year-old woman; Harry, who in a holdup shot his victim in the head for eight bucks; Mark, who sexually assaulted and killed a seven-year-old boy. But, horrific as the crimes were, their perpetrators were rare in our system, even among those sent us for violent crimes.

Misrepresenting Juvenile Crime

Violent juvenile crime was a major concern of the public in Massachusetts. Not only in the state, but across the nation, violent crime had steadily increased during the fifteen years following 1956. Robbery, assault, and rape had tripled. As is the case whenever crime increases, most of the increase was attributed to an explosion of juvenile crime. But did the attribution fit?

Violent crime in the United States has always been higher than in any comparable Western country, and rises and falls in juvenile crime usually have followed the same patterns as adult crime. Though there has always been a disproportionate amount of crime among young males, particularly in the eighteen to twenty-five-year age range—and though older juveniles (sixteen and seventeen) commit more crimes than younger adolescents, there have never been self-contained dramatic increases of violent juvenile crime which did not parallel increases in adult crime. Juvenile crime rates follow adult crime rates, only a bit less so. Unfortunately, one would be hard pressed to argue this to a public primed to believe that juvenile crime is a runaway horse. Think back to the national obsession with New York street gangs and the Dracula killings in the 1950s, the Chicago street gangs of the late 1950s and early 1960s; the Philadelphia gang violence of the 1970s; and the Los Angeles juvenile gangs of the 1980s. Certainly, from time to time, there are unusual explosions of violent crime. But much of this is related to increases in the number of adolescents in the population. It isn't always clear at the time what's going on, or whether more juveniles are actually involved in violent crime than was previously thought.

"There have never been self-contained dramatic increases of violent juvenile crime which did not parallel increases in adult crime."

Juvenile Murder Rates

Though it makes up an extremely small percentage of all violent crime committed by juveniles, it is generally agreed that the most reliably reported crime is murder. Homicide rates in the United States nearly doubled between 1958 and 1972, from 4.5 homicides per 100,000 to 8.5 per 100,000. But even this unsettling surge of violence wasn't unprecedented. Homicides more than tripled between 1900 and 1914, from 2.1 to 7.3 per 100,000, and reached a high in 1933 of 9.6 murders per 100,000. As with adult homicide, the juvenile murder rate was also higher in the 1930s and 1940s than in the early 1960s. The major rise in homicides occurred between 1965 and 1970, followed by a drop between 1973 and 1975 and a rise in 1980. The national homicide rate for 1990 exceeded the 1980 rate.

In June 1988 a national newspaper, *USA Today*, ran a series of pro and con articles on whether the death penalty should be invoked for juveniles convicted of murder. In the lead article in favor of the penalty entitled "Executing Juveniles Is a Social Necessity," the head of the conservative Washington Legal Foundation began, "Nearly 20,000 murders are committed by juveniles every year, and that number is not reflected in the number sentenced to death." The fact that the statement was grossly inaccurate is less compelling than that a widely read newspaper apparently didn't question the figure before printing it on the editorial page. To be sure, many inaccuracies end up on editorial pages, but in this case, the outrageous figure of 20,000 juvenile murders was taken as unexceptional.

In 1990, for example, slightly over 23,000 murders and manslaughters were reported in the United States. Of the 20,000 persons arrested for these crimes, approximately 2,000 were juveniles. Even this figure is inflated, however, since juveniles tend to get involved in such incidents in groups and with peers. A single offense often yields multiple arrests of teenagers. In addition, due to police overcharging, charges made at the time of arrest are often lowered later, if not completely dismissed. That leaves something like 1,200 juveniles across the United States who are tried annually for murder or manslaughter. Of these, probably no more than 500 will be convicted of murder in a court of law. This is 2.5 percent of the figure which appeared, unquestioned, on the editorial pages of *USA Today*.

This kind of gap between the myth and the reality of juvenile delinquency hounded me from the beginning in Massachusetts. Each year we received no more than five or six youngsters convicted of murder. That number has remained relatively fixed for the past decade. Some years there would be as few as three; other years, as many as seven. For a while, I thought juvenile murderers were being sent to adult prisons, but they weren't. We got virtually all those under seventeen who had been convicted of murder. Then I concluded that the small numbers might have to do with the fact that juveniles in Massachusetts were subject to adult trial at age seventeen. In thirty-eight states and the District of Columbia, the juvenile court retains jurisdiction till age eighteen. In eight states, including Massachusetts, juvenile court jurisdiction is kept until age seventeen. In four states, sixteen-year-olds are handled as adults. These differences alone didn't explain the small numbers of Massachusetts adolescents arrested for murder, for when seventeen-year-olds were included in the statistics, they usually accounted for no more than two additional murders per year. But homicide is a relatively rare crime. What about the other violent offenses juveniles commit?

"Of the 20,000 persons arrested for [murder and manslaughter], approximately 2,000 were juveniles."

Less Than 5 Percent

About 25 percent of the young offenders sent to us were committed for crimes against persons. However, when these "crimes against persons" were distilled, few actually involved physical violence or even the threat of it. Nationally, about 4 percent of the arrests of juveniles are for offenses classified as violent. Violence, however, covers a wide range of behaviors. For example, a recent crime survey of victims indicated that there was no physical injury in 72 percent of offenses classified as violent and committed by juveniles. In those violent offenses in which injury did occur, it wasn't serious enough to require medical attention in 93 percent of the cases. A study of 811 Columbus, Ohio, youths with at least one violent crime on their records showed that 73 percent had neither threatened nor inflicted significant physical harm during the commission of those offenses. The same study followed a cohort of over 50,000 youth from birth to adulthood. Of this group, only twenty-two youngsters committed two or more aggravated offenses in which physical harm was threatened or inflicted.

Juveniles seldom use weapons in committing crimes. In M. E. Wolfgang's cohort study of Philadelphia boys born in 1945 and living in the city between their tenth and eighteenth birthdays, weapons were used in only 263 of 9,934 offenses known to police. A 1978 New York City study showed that weapons were present in only 17 percent of juvenile offenses classified as violent. A later victim crime survey revealed that juvenile offenders used weapons in 27 percent of violent offenses, though guns were present in less than 5 percent of those incidents. With the exception of purse-snatching, most truly violent juvenile crime is confined to peers, with young males far more likely to be victims.

> ***"Each year we received no more than five or six youngsters convicted of murder. That number has remained relatively fixed for the past decade."***

I looked assiduously for those few violent youngsters who provided the rationale for our reform schools. They were the symbol which justified the ritual of institutionalization. But despite the fact that they provided the political rationale for the whole system, they weren't so easily identified, particularly if one knew them and their offenses in detail (though I'm told that some of my successors had less trouble locating this elusive group). Youngsters defined as violent made up about 25 percent of our reform school populations. When the details of each case were known, however, less than 5 percent of the juveniles had clearly demonstrated personal violence directed at another. Here one is subject to the war stories which drive juvenile corrections: the tale of the youngster involved in a particularly lungeous and brutal act. Such juveniles exist. But while they may provide the stuff of nightly television crime news stories, they don't represent the average youth in a reform school or detention center, even one for violent offenders.

Flagrantly Dishonest

Visiting other state youth correctional systems, I felt uncomfortable hearing administrators carry on about the new violent breed of delinquents filling their institutions. I couldn't understand it. Either we had dramatically fewer dangerous youngsters in our system than they did, or I was grossly misinformed about those who peopled our institutions. It was neither. As I got to know them better, it was clear that my peers in other states knew the inmates in their institutions only dimly. They were acquainted with few personally and were uninterested in the events and circumstances which surround each offense and which are so incompletely, and usually inaccurately, represented by a rap sheet. The fact is, the number of inmates in the average youth corrections system who have a propensity for personal violence has always been extremely small.

And all too often, state administrators are flagrantly dishonest. While they hop from convention to convention bemoaning the dangerous delinquents in their youth institutions, their states are simultaneously binding over or waiving hundreds of nonviolent teenagers to adult criminal courts and adult prisons. Maryland routinely waives between eight hundred and a thousand youngsters into the adult system annually. Virginia, the same. (Recently, in preparing background in the case of a juvenile convicted of murder, I learned that, on the day of his sentencing, there was only one youngster in the whole Virginia juvenile reform school system of approximately one thousand youths who had been convicted of murder. The half dozen or so Virginia juveniles who commit murder each year must be shuttled into the adult prison system.) The pattern of sending large numbers of juveniles to adult prisons prevails in most state systems. Yet these same states also maintain large reform school systems for (presumably) serious juvenile offenders too dangerous to be in the community.

Those who run the juvenile justice system gain by defining young offenders as more violent than facts dictate. It's a kind of no-risk heroism for all concerned—judges, superintendents, institutional staff, therapists, police, and probation officers. It encourages the posturing and strutting of the I-told-you-so crowd, who make sure that, no matter what happens, no one will be accountable. This is the correctional equivalent of the old psychiatric diagnosis of "latent schizophrenia," now called "borderline personality." If the patient improves, it can be chalked up to the therapist's skill at treatment. If, on the other hand, the patient deteriorates, the therapist looks even more sophisticated, having predicted it all along. In this world it is to no one's advantage to destigmatize labels, except for those who are labeled. The process by which we label delinquents is more crucial than are its labels.

Needles in Haystacks

I eventually got to know personally the fifty or so most dangerous youth in the department. Though some had committed serious violent crimes, most were repeat property offenders who consistently placed themselves and others in potentially dangerous situations. A few were considered dangerous to themselves because of repeated escapes from detention facilities or runs from community programs. After we closed the institutions for the most violent, the number of dangerous youngsters in need of secure care, interestingly enough, decreased. We'd been defining juveniles according to the numbers of beds available for locking up the dangerous ones. Certainly there is a need for special handling of truly violent youth. But these few kids are often hidden in piles of lightweight offenders, like needles in haystacks.

The Problem of Youth Violence Is Exaggerated

by Ira M. Schwartz

About the author: *Ira M. Schwartz is a professor of social work and the director of the Center for the Study of Youth Policy at the University of Michigan in Ann Arbor. He is a former administrator of the Office of Juvenile Justice and Delinquency Prevention in the U.S. Department of Justice.*

The juvenile crime problem shouldn't be taken lightly. Every year, thousands of innocent people are injured by young law violators. Some are killed. Hundreds of thousands of others suffer from having their homes or businesses broken into or from having their property stolen or damaged by juveniles. Moreover, the fear of juvenile crime has come to affect how we view young people, where we go and at what time of day, what businesses we patronize, and even our voting habits.

The juvenile crime problem is not simply going to disappear. The development of effective juvenile crime prevention and control policies will come about only as a result of informed debate on the issue by politicians, juvenile justice officials, public interest groups, and, most important, the public. At present, the gap between the public's perception and understanding of the problem and the reality of it is as wide as the Grand Canyon. This is primarily because what debate there is on this topic is characterized by rhetoric, demagoguery, and simplistic solutions. As a result, the public is often easily led and even stampeded into supporting policies and programs that are costly and ineffective. . . .

Misleading Information

It was 10:30 P.M. on February 26, 1981. I was watching television and doing some paperwork when ABC's "Nightline" came on. Ted Koppel announced that the night's broadcast was about "crimes against the elderly." Being in the crime business, I put my work down and watched the program. I thought that the program was pretty good until a group of senior citizens from south Florida complained about all those kids who were victimizing them.

I wrote Koppel a letter in which I said that I enjoyed "Nightline" and found the program interesting and informative. I also told him that I was disturbed about the program I had seen because, contrary to belief, the characterizations regarding juveniles were inaccurate. I mentioned that the best available evidence suggests that juveniles do not commit a disproportionate amount of serious crime against senior citizens. I enclosed some material and suggested that he clarify this misunderstanding at some future time. I never received a response from Koppel. To the best of my knowledge, the inaccuracies have never been cleared up. The result was that millions of Americans were left with the impression that juveniles account for the bulk of the serious crime committed against older people.

"The public is often easily led and even stampeded into supporting policies and programs that are costly and ineffective."

Ted Koppel is a respected journalist. Although he can't control what people may say on a live television broadcast, it seems to me that he should have had a better grasp on the facts. And although the media must share some of the blame for furthering the myths about juvenile crime, the problem becomes almost insurmountable when government officials put out false and misleading information. Government statistics, whether inaccurate or not, are almost automatically considered credible in most quarters and are widely quoted.

The Juvenile Justice System

Alfred S. Regnery, administrator of the Office of Juvenile Justice and Delinquency Prevention during the Reagan administration, wrote an article entitled "Getting Away with Murder: Why the Juvenile Justice System Needs an Overhaul," which appeared in the fall 1985 issue of *Policy Review*. In the article, Regnery stated: "About 30 percent of all people arrested for serious crimes are juveniles—a total of some 1.5 million arrests per year." He also maintained that juveniles—persons under the age of 18—commit about 2,000 murders each year.

The facts are that persons under 18 years of age accounted for 592,372 arrests for Part I index or felony crimes (for example, murder, rape, robbery, aggravated assault, auto theft, larceny, burglary, and arson) in 1984. During that year, they committed 1,130 acts of murder and nonnegligent manslaughter, or about 8 percent of all such crimes.

Regnery overstated the number of juvenile arrests for serious crimes (murder and nonnegligent manslaughter, forcible rape, robbery, aggravated assault, burglary, larceny/theft, motor vehicle theft, and arson) by more than 150 percent.

He overstated the number of murders by nearly 75 percent.

Reprints of the article were distributed at government expense to elected public officials, juvenile and criminal justice professionals, public interest groups, and other interested parties throughout the country. In a "Dear Colleague" letter that accompanied the reprint, Regnery wrote: "Since being named by President Reagan to head the Justice Department's Office of Juvenile Justice and Delinquency Prevention, I have tried to call attention to the system's shortcomings and have tried to suggest improvements." He hoped the article would "be helpful to those concerned about juvenile crime, those concerned with the juvenile justice system's ability to deal with such crime, and those concerned with possible solutions."

To my mind, Regnery's article did neither. Instead, it misled people and increased the gap between the public's perception of the problem and reality.

Popular Myths

Although it is unrealistic to expect everyone to become an expert on juvenile crime, there are a number of common myths that need to be dispelled before responsible public policy can be developed in this area. Some of these are listed below.

Myth 1: The Rate of Serious Juvenile Crime Is Skyrocketing

> ***"The media must share some of the blame for furthering the myths about juvenile crime."***

In 1982, the Center for the Study of Youth Policy at the University of Minnesota's Humphrey Institute of Public Affairs commissioned a national public opinion survey on public attitudes toward juvenile crime. The survey, conducted by the Opinion Research Corporation of America, revealed that 87 percent of adults living in the continental United States believed that the country was in the midst of a serious juvenile crime wave.

The best available evidence indicates that the rates of serious juvenile crime rose significantly during the late 1960s and early 1970s. The rates stabilized during the mid- to late 1970s, declined between 1979 and 1984, and increased for the first time in six years in 1985.

The rates of serious juvenile crime are high and should not be trivialized. However, we are not in the midst of a juvenile crime wave. Moreover, although the rates increased in 1985, it is too early to tell whether this marks a watershed and a reversal in the trends. Policymakers, professionals, academics, public interest groups, and child advocates need to keep a sharp eye on the rates of serious juvenile crime in the coming years and carefully consider their meaning and implications.

Myth 2: Juveniles Account for the Bulk of the Serious Crime Committed in the United States

The proportion of serious crime accounted for by juveniles declined significantly between 1975 and 1981. Juveniles accounted for more than 40 percent of the arrests for serious crimes in the mid-1970s, and they accounted for approximately 30 percent of all serious crimes in the early to mid-1980s.

Exaggerated Problems

Myth 3: The Elderly Are More Likely to Be Victimized by Juveniles than by Adults

Whether one looks at crimes committed by individuals or by groups, the elderly are more likely to be the victims of violent crimes committed by persons 21 years of age and over than by teenagers. Less than 30 percent of the crimes against the elderly by a single perpetrator are committed by persons 20 years of age or younger. In crimes against the elderly in which there are multiple offenders, fewer than 40 percent are committed by persons under 21. Also, what evidence there is suggests that "victimizations committed against the elderly . . . [are less] . . . serious when juvenile offenders [are] involved," [according to M. J. Hindelang and M. J. McDermott].

Myth 4: The Serious Crime Rate for Girls Is Rapidly Increasing

The serious juvenile crime rates for girls increased significantly in the early 1970s, stabilized in the mid-1970s, and declined between 1978 and 1984. Like the rates for boys, they turned upward in 1985.

Myth 5: Juveniles Are More Likely to Attack Strangers than People They Know

Teenagers are more likely to commit crimes of violence against other teenagers. Nearly two-thirds of the violent crimes committed by 12- to 17-year-olds involve victims under age 18. In addition, teenagers are more likely to know or to have had some prior relationship with their teenage victims. In other words, juveniles do not generally assault people at random.

Myth 6: Violent Crimes Committed by Juveniles Are More Serious than Those Committed by Adults

"We are not in the midst of a juvenile crime wave."

The best available evidence indicates that "juvenile violence is considerably less serious in the aggregate than violence by adults. Juveniles use fewer weapons and less deadly weapons in their crimes and inflict less injury and financial loss on their victims," [according to P.A. Strasberg].

Inaccurate Data

Myth 7: Minority Youth Account for the Bulk of Serious Juvenile Crime

Minority youth do account for a substantially disproportionate number of arrests for serious juvenile crime. However, arrest statistics are only an indication of the number of people who are apprehended by police. They do not shed light on the number of crimes committed that may go undetected or unreported or that may not result in an arrest.

One of the best sources of data on delinquent behavior is the National Youth Survey, a self-report study designed, in part, to get at the extent and nature of crimes committed by young people that may not come to the attention of official authorities or result in an arrest.

"Juveniles do not generally assault people at random."

Data from the National Youth Survey indicate that minority youth, particularly black youth, do not account for a substantially disproportionate amount of serious juvenile crime. However, minority youth who commit crimes are at significantly greater risk of being arrested and charged with a Part I offense than are white youth who commit similar crimes.

Myth 8: States with Low Rates of Juvenile Crime Are States with High Rates of Juvenile Incarceration

Many elected public officials and juvenile justice professionals believe that high rates of juvenile incarceration correspond to low rates of serious juvenile crime. They feel that high rates of juvenile incarceration have a significant impact on general deterrence. Judge Peter Albrecht, one of the two juvenile court judges in Hennepin County (Minneapolis), Minnesota, recently surmised that the reason the juvenile crime rate is low in Minneapolis is that the county has a high rate of juvenile incarceration. Albrecht, in defending the county's policy of committing first-time burglars to a local youth training school, stated that the policy is designed to "nip [the problem] in the bud and give a fairly swift, relatively serious consequence on a first burglary."

The existing evidence suggests that there is little or no relationship between the rates of serious juvenile crime and the rates of youth incarceration. States with high rates of serious juvenile crime may have high or low rates of institutionalization. Conversely, states with low rates of serious juvenile crime may have high or low rates of incarceration.

Juvenile Crime Trends

The FBI [Federal Bureau of Investigation] Uniform Crime Reports are the most widely used measure of serious crime in the United States. The FBI statistics are a compilation of annual arrest figures submitted by state and local law enforcement agencies throughout the country for the eight Part I index offenses.

These FBI statistics are the best available national crime data. They are a good indicator of general arrest trends over time. However, as many who have examined these data know, FBI statistics have a number of significant shortcomings. Some law enforcement agencies fail to report their data to the FBI. Some submit data, but not for an entire year. For example, although 9,789 state and local law enforcement agencies submitted arrest statistics to the FBI for all twelve months in 1984, these 9,789 agencies covered slightly less than 180 million of the estimated 235 million people living in the United States. In other words, arrests made in police jurisdictions that include approximately 55 million people living in the United States were not included in the FBI's published statistics for 1984 because they did not conform to the FBI's reporting requirements. . . .

Also, it is important to keep in mind that juvenile arrest statistics do not reflect the actual volume of serious crime committed by young people. Juveniles "often commit crime in groups [and] the resolution of a single crime may lead to several arrests." Paul Strasberg notes that this is particularly the case with respect to robbery. Strasberg's recent penetrating analysis of violent juvenile crime trends argues that "since robbery is the most common juvenile crime of violence, and also the crime in which group offending occurs most frequently, robbery arrests contribute most to an exaggerated perception of the amount of crime being committed by juveniles." For example, there were 27,795 juvenile arrests for robbery in 1984. However, fewer than 15,000 robberies by juveniles were cleared by the police during that year. A more serious problem is the fact that arrest statistics do not account for the amount of "hidden delinquency"—juvenile crime that goes undetected or unreported or, if reported, does not result in an arrest. . . .

Informing the Public

The juvenile crime problem is an issue that has managed to escape close public scrutiny. What debate there is on the topic tends to be dominated by rhetoric, a remarkable absence of hard facts, and politicians advocating for the "quick fix" or whatever happens to be the most politically expedient. Consequently, a large proportion of the billions in tax dollars that go into subsidizing the juvenile justice bureaucracy (for example, law enforcement, prosecutors, public defenders, juvenile courts, detention centers, probation and parole services, training schools, halfway houses, group homes, residential treatment centers) is wasted.

The greatest challenge to developing sound juvenile crime prevention and control policies lies in the development of an informed citizenry. Public interest groups, civic organizations, child advocacy groups, criminal and juvenile justice watchdog agencies, and interested professional associations need to launch aggressive campaigns to get the juvenile crime issue on the public agenda at the state and local levels. They need to educate and mobilize citizens to pressure policymakers to take an honest and objective look at the juvenile crime problem, to carefully examine how juvenile justice system resources are being allocated and whether they are being allocated wisely.

Violent Youth Crimes Are Not a Serious Problem

by Charles Patrick Ewing

About the author: *Charles Patrick Ewing, a clinical and forensic psychologist and attorney, is professor of law and associate professor of clinical psychology at the State University of New York at Buffalo. Ewing, the author of* Crisis Intervention as Psychotherapy, Battered Women Who Kill: Psychological Self-Defense as Legal Justification, *and editor of* Psychology, Psychiatry and the Law: A Clinical and Forensic Handbook, *has examined many homicide defendants and testified as an expert in numerous murder trials.*

They called him the "Iron Man." Standing five feet, ten inches tall and weighing 240 pounds, Craig Price pleaded guilty to mass murder. He told a Rhode Island judge that he broke into two homes in the summer of 1987 and murdered four neighbors: two adult women and two girls, ages ten and eight. The victims were beaten and stabbed—one woman was stabbed fifty-eight times. After hearing Craig Price's plea, the judge sentenced him to the stiffest sentence allowed under Rhode Island law: incarceration for five years and seventeen days.

Teen Murderers

Craig Price fell through one of the cracks in Rhode Island law. Already on probation for assault and burglary, he committed one murder when he was thirteen and three others just weeks later when he was fourteen. By the time he pleaded guilty to the four killings, Craig was just seventeen days shy of his sixteenth birthday. Under Rhode Island law, no one under the age of sixteen may be tried as an adult, even for murder, and no one tried as a juvenile may be locked up beyond his or her twenty-first birthday.

Craig Price will walk out of the Rhode Island Training School a free man on October 11, 1994. Leaving the courtroom after being sentenced, Craig seemed well aware that he had beaten the system. Greeted by a rowdy throng of his high school friends who had come to see him off, Craig told the crowd, "When I get out of here, I'm going to smoke a bomber (a marijuana cigarette)." Then, as the Training School van pulled away, he bid his friends a trite teenage goodbye: "Later."

For almost his entire life, seventeen-year-old Dale Whipple was physically, psychologically, and sexually abused by his parents. Dale often sought help from school guidance counselors but no one ever did anything to stop the abuse. Finally, Dale decided he could take no more. The Indiana youth lured his mother into the garage and hacked her to death with a rusty, double-edged ax. Dale then went back into the house and did the same to his sleeping father.

Charged with two counts of murder, Dale claimed self-defense, saying he killed his parents to protect himself from his father's increasingly severe beatings and his mother's recent sexual advances. Although the judge concluded that "fear of future physical abuse was a factor essential to these crimes," he refused to allow the jury to consider Dale's plea of self-defense.

After the jury found Dale guilty but mentally ill, the judge handed down two concurrent sentences of forty years in prison. Explaining why he made the sentences concurrent rather than consecutive, the judge said he was impressed by the evidence that Dale had, in fact, been severely abused by his parents for years. Dale Whipple must serve at least twenty years in prison before he is eligible for parole. . . .

A Rare Breed

Every year at least 1,000 and often more than 1,500 American youngsters under the age of eighteen intentionally take the lives of others and are arrested for murder or manslaughter. Some of these killings are crimes of premeditated violence motivated by greed, lust, or a desire for revenge. Others are crimes of passion: impulsive overresponses to provocation by the victim or to some explosive drive within the killer. Still other cases seem utterly senseless.

Who are these kids who kill? To begin with, kids who kill are really a rare breed. While homicides committed by children and adolescents fascinate the public and generate a great deal of media attention, these killings are actually quite infrequent. People younger than eighteen constitute roughly one-quarter of the total resident population of the United States. Yet annually for the past decade or so, consistently fewer than 11 percent of all individuals arrested in the United States for murder or intentional manslaughter have been under the age of eighteen.

"Who are these kids who kill? To begin with, kids who kill are really a rare breed."

In 1988 . . . there were 16,326 murder and intentional manslaughter arrests in the United States. Only 1,765—roughly 11 percent—of those arrested were under eighteen years of age. To put it another way, fewer than five juveniles in every 100,000 were arrested for intentionally killing someone—approximately half the adult arrest rate for these same crimes.

The homicide rate for younger juveniles is even lower. The vast majority (most years more than 85 percent) of juveniles who kill are fifteen, sixteen, or seventeen years old. Annually for the past decade or so, fewer than 1 percent of those arrested for murder or non-negligent manslaughter have been under the age of fifteen. And during this same time period, only a handful of those arrested for these homicide crimes have been younger than ten years old. For example, in 1988, only seven (.6 percent) of the 1,765 juveniles arrested for murder or manslaughter were nine years old or younger.

"Fewer than 11 percent of all individuals arrested in the United States for murder or intentional manslaughter have been under the age of eighteen."

Arrest data undoubtedly underestimate the number of very young children who kill since at least some of these youngsters are probably never formally arrested. Indeed, in most jurisdictions, children under the age of seven are automatically deemed incapable of criminal conduct. Still, there is little doubt that extremely few homicides are committed by children under the age of ten. . . .

Like age, gender is also a factor in juvenile homicide. Juvenile homicide, like most crimes at all ages, is much more likely to be perpetrated by boys than girls. Just as younger juveniles rarely kill, girls of any age are extremely unlikely to kill. At all ages under eighteen, the vast majority of those arrested for murder or non-negligent manslaughter are boys.

Factors and Variables

In 1988, 93 percent of the juveniles arrested for intentional homicide crimes in the United States were boys. That figure, while striking, is consistent with statistics on homicides committed by adults. On an annual basis, men consistently comprise nearly 90 percent of *all* individuals arrested for murder or non-negligent homicide. In 1988, 87 percent of all adults arrested for these crimes were men.

Not only do girls kill much less frequently than boys, but their victims are different. FBI data on juvenile homicide indicate that while girls almost always kill family members or acquaintances, boys are more likely to kill acquaintances or strangers.

Race and ethnicity are also important variables in juvenile homicide. Black youths are vastly overrepresented among juveniles arrested for murder or non-negligent manslaughter. While roughly one-sixth of all Americans under the age of eighteen are black, in recent years approximately one-half the juveniles arrested for these homicide crimes have been black. Indeed, in 1988, over 57 percent of the juveniles arrested for these offenses were black. Hispanic youths are similarly overrepresented among juveniles arrested for murder and manslaughter. Although approximately 8 percent of the U.S. population is Hispanic, Hispanic youths account for almost one-quarter of all juvenile arrests for homicide crimes.

Undoubtedly, these racial and ethnic disparities reflect discrimination in the criminal justice system. It is widely acknowledged that blacks and Hispanics are more likely than whites to be arrested for the crimes they commit. Yet, even allowing for such discrimination, it is evident that black and Hispanic youths commit a vastly disproportionate share of juvenile homicides.

Suffering Mild Disorders

Available data also shed light on other characteristics of kids who kill, such as the extent to which these youngsters are emotionally disturbed, mentally ill, mentally retarded, learning disabled, neurologically impaired, behaviorally disturbed, or simply "normal" youths who commit extremely abnormal acts. Homicides committed by children and adolescents are so rare and often so apparently inexplicable that people tend to assume that any youngster who kills must be emotionally disturbed, if not mentally ill. Thus, it is not surprising that most juvenile killers are examined by psychologists, psychiatrists, or other mental health experts. Nor is it surprising that, like most people referred for psychological or psychiatric evaluations, most juveniles who kill wind up with one diagnostic label or another applied to them. What may be surprising, however, is that most of these youths are diagnosed as suffering only relatively mild disorders.

Chapter 2

What Causes Youth Violence?

The Causes of Youth Violence: An Overview

by Dean E. Murphy

About the author: *Dean E. Murphy is a staff writer for the* Los Angeles Times *daily newspaper.*

Dwayne Wright was 17 when he spotted Saba Tekle on a highway in northern Virginia, decided he wanted to have sex with her and pumped a bullet into her back when she tried to run away. Wright, now 19, awaits execution on Virginia's Death Row.

Five New Jersey teen-agers, two of them 14, allegedly strangled a pesky classmate with an electrical cord as he recited the prayer Hail Mary in his car. Three of the boys admitted to the murder and will testify against the others.

Two Pasadena [California] juries in 1992 found teen-agers David Adkins and Vincent Hebrock guilty of murder in the shotgun slayings of three girls—including Adkins' girlfriend—during a party at one of the girls' homes. A witness says Hebrock, who was 17 at the time, boasted to Adkins, who was 16: "Yeah, dude, we smoked 'em all."

Children are killing more than ever. The number of juveniles arrested for homicide between 1981 and 1990 increased 60% nationwide, far outpacing the 5.2% increase among adults, according to recent FBI crime statistics.

Record Number of Killings

Although juveniles are still far less likely to kill than adults, an unprecedented 2,003 youths were arrested for murder and non-negligent manslaughter in 1990, according to federal statistics. In 1981, one in every 10 people arrested in the United States for murder was under 18; by 1990, it was one in six.

"Ten years ago, it was a rarity to have kids in Juvenile Hall charged with murder," said Rod Speer of the Orange County [California] Probation Department, which has recorded a 130% rise in juvenile homicide arrests since 1982. "Now it is not so."

In Los Angeles County, murder charges were filed against 357 juveniles in 1990, compared to 171 in 1983, when statistics included murder and attempted murder. In 1991, the number of juvenile murder cases dropped to 301 countywide, but law enforcement officials attribute the downturn to a change in reporting procedures, not a lessening of the bloodshed.

Neither local nor federal statistics differentiate between gang-related and other juvenile homicides, but authorities say some of the nationwide increase can be explained by an explosion in gang- and drug-related violence in large metropolitan areas, including Los Angeles.

But the numbers go far beyond the problem of urban gang violence, many law enforcement officials and psychologists say. The escalating juvenile murder rate reflects a widespread—and perhaps more disturbing—penetration of violence into the lives of young people from all walks of life, they say.

Child abuse, television and movies, pop youth culture (the Ice-T album that features the controversial "Cop Killer" song also includes the tune "Momma's Gotta Die Tonight") and the prevalence of handguns have made violence and images of violence staples in the diet of many young Americans, they say.

"I have a real grim outlook on this," said Charles Patrick Ewing, a clinical and forensic psychologist in New York who has studied the subject extensively. "I don't see it getting any better. Kids learn to kill. They learn to be violent." And they learn, he said, from their adult abusers.

A Jump in Youth Violence

The skyrocketing juvenile murder rate is all the more alarming, some psychologists say, because it mirrors an overall increase in violent crime by adolescents. Forcible rape by juveniles rose 28% between 1981 and 1990, while aggravated assaults jumped 57%, according to the FBI statistics. Throughout the period, the number of Americans under 18 decreased.

"Homicide is not only bad in itself, it is an index for the aggressiveness of a particular group," said Dewey Cornell, a psychologist at the University of Virginia who conducts clinical evaluations of violent youths. "For every juvenile arrested for homicide, there are about 50 arrested for other types of violent crime. After all, often the difference between a homicide and an assault is how quickly the [paramedics] arrive or how well the youth aimed the weapon." . . .

> ***"The skyrocketing juvenile murder rate is all the more alarming, some psychologists say, because it mirrors an overall increase in violent crime by adolescents."***

In suburban New York City, police have been unable to come up with a clear motive for the ritualistic strangulation of Robert A. Solimine, 17, except to say that Robert's teen-age friends grew tired of his pestering.

Margaret Yakal Chircop, Robert's mother, blames the boys' parents as much as the teen-agers.

"What are 14-year-olds doing out with 18- and 17-year-olds? What are they doing out at 11 o'clock?" asked Chircop, of Clifton, N.J. "This is a lot about parents not giving a hoot about their kids, just wanting to get rid of them."

Several recent studies of adolescent killers point to family influences among the possible causes of the violence. By and large, the studies dismiss the widespread popular belief that juvenile murderers are usually psychotic or kill because of bizarre mental health problems, concluding instead that many young murderers have been victims themselves.

A psychiatric study published in 1988 of 14 juveniles condemned to death found that 12 had been "brutally, physically abused" in their homes and five had been sodomized by older male relatives. The physical abuse ranged from being hit on the head with a hammer to being placed on a hot stove top.

The study, based on psychiatric tests and interviews with the youths, also showed that all but one of the condemned killers had grown up in households rife with violence. One father beat his pregnant wife, and a stepfather "preferred hunting men to animals." The parents also had histories of alcoholism, drug abuse and psychiatric treatment.

"Of 72 youths charged with murder, . . . more than one-third had alcohol and drug abuse problems, and most of them had parents who were divorced."

"Not only did older family members fail to protect these adolescents, but they also often used the subjects to vent their rages and to satisfy their sexual appetites," concluded the study, which was prepared for the American Academy of Child and Adolescent Psychiatry.

A separate study of 72 youths charged with murder in Michigan found that only five were psychotic when they committed the crime, but more than one-third had alcohol and drug abuse problems, and most of them had parents who were divorced.

Elissa P. Benedek, the center's director of research, said the 1987 study revealed that youngsters who kill are not all alike. For some, murder was the culmination of years of criminal acts, while for others, killing came as an uncontrolled impulse during a heated family argument.

Violence Is Everywhere

More and more kids are solving problems through violence, Benedek said. "There are more guns, more violence in our society in general, more child abuse, more violence on TV and in movies, more drugs and more people inured to violence."

Paul Mones, a Santa Monica [California] attorney who specializes in parricide cases, said his experience has shown that most adolescent murderers learn about—and become desensitized—to violence in the home. Mones, who recently wrote a book on parricide, *When a Child Kills*, has been involved in about 200 parricide trials.

> ***"Many children who kill have learned about violence by watching their parents, aunts, uncles and siblings."***

The violence does not necessarily have to be directed against the child, Mones said. Many children who kill have learned about violence by watching their parents, aunts, uncles and siblings. In the case of Dwayne Wright, the teen-ager on Virginia's Death Row, the boy's mother testified that her son began having behavior problems shortly after his older brother was fatally shot.

Wright, who also has been convicted of murder and attempted murder in Maryland, showed little emotion during the Tekle trial but reportedly broke into tears when his mother discussed his despair over his brother's death.

"When kids are born there is this giant jar of morality and respect for fellow human beings," Mones said. "In a good family, that giant jar is filled to the top and a lot of good things are done to kids to keep the level up there. The single greatest factor that puts fissures in that giant jar, and makes it leak out, is violence in the home."

Robert F. Horan Jr., who prosecuted Wright in the Tekle murder, was less inclined to search for answers in Wright's troubled family than in the availability of handguns and the prevalence of violence on TV and in movies.

Wright killed Tekle during a two-day rampage that left two people shot to death and one seriously injured. Wright has admitted to occasional drug dealing—he claims one of the shootings was related to a deal gone sour—but prosecutors believe that his outburst of violence was random—and made possible primarily by his ability to possess (albeit illegally) a handgun.

"Fifteen or 20 years ago, juveniles fought with their fists, or sometimes with a stick," said Horan. "But the notion of tracking someone down and going after them with a gun, that was a very seldom thing. Nowadays, it is perceived as macho in a lot of circles to be armed."

The Prevalence of Guns

A recent study of homicides in Washington, D.C., by the federal Office of Criminal Justice Plans and Analysis found that 18 of 19 youths serving time for murder in the city had carried guns before their arrest.

While the study may be skewed by the realities of life on the city's toughest streets, other research supports the contention that guns are widely available to youths everywhere.

A survey of high school students nationwide by the Centers for Disease Control found that one in 25 students had carried a gun in 1990, while a study published in the *Journal of the American Medical Association* in June 1992 found that 34% of urban high school students perceived handguns to be easily accessible.

In an editorial accompanying the study, and several others on violence in America, the medical journal said the studies "paint a grotesque picture of society steeped in violence, especially by firearms, and so numbed by the ubiquity and prevalence of violence as to seemingly accept it as inevitable."

Many law enforcement officials and academicians who have taken an interest in juvenile killers see a strong—if unproven—relationship between the influences of handguns and television and movie violence.

Horan, the Virginia prosecutor, and others blame television for blurring the distinction between justifiable violence and violence for violence's sake. Cornell, the University of Virginia psychologist, said Hollywood no longer "sanitizes" violence or tries to balance it with other messages. "Just compare Rambo to any of the John Wayne characters," Cornell said.

"Violence used to be for a just cause," he said. "To defeat the Nazis, or protect the women and children from the Indians. Now the distinction between good guys and bad guys is passe."

There is a broad consensus in the scientific community that exposure to television and movie violence increases the physical aggressiveness of children, but there has been less agreement about whether that aggressiveness translates into increased violence, let alone a greater likelihood to commit murder.

Ewing, who has written two books on adolescent killers, said television violence alone will not turn a child into a murderer. While the vast majority of children watch television regularly, he said, only a fraction commit homicide. Family influences—perhaps reinforced by a steady dose of violence on television—are the real culprit, he said.

> ***"We have kids growing up who treat violence as if it is an ordinary fact of life, from Ninja Turtles to Arnold Schwarzenegger movies."***

"Violence on TV or in movies doesn't make kids violent, but it makes them more willing to accept violence from other people, and that is more frightening in a way," Ewing said. "We have kids growing up who treat violence as if it is an ordinary fact of life, from Ninja Turtles to Arnold Schwarzenegger movies."

A Lack of Traditional Family Structure Causes Youth Violence

by Karl Zinsmeister

About the author: *Karl Zinsmeister is a writer living in upstate New York and an adjunct scholar with the American Enterprise Institute, a conservative research organization in Washington, D.C.*

Crime does not wash over all Americans equally. It especially terrorizes the weakest and most vulnerable among us. Three quarters of America's 64 million children live in metropolitan areas, a fifth live in low-income households, at least a tenth come home after school to a house containing no adult, and all are physically immature and incompletely formed in character. These are the people who suffer most when law and order decay. Children need order. Aside from love and sustenance, there is nothing they need more than order.

Foundations for Children's Well-Being

Law enforcement is often presented as a conservative issue, but today there is a powerful bleeding-heart justification for getting tough on crime: to protect child welfare. Physical safety and psychological security are the foundations—the essential preconditions—for a child's health, education, and overall development. A good school, an accessible doctor, a rich library, a 15 percent increase in the Head Start budget—these are of little use to a child sharing an apartment with his mother's abusive, violent, drug-selling boyfriend, or to a child who fears the very sidewalks, or to one who cannot find a safe haven even in the classroom. In failing to insulate our children from criminal activity, we are jeopardizing the future of millions of American youngsters.

Yet none of the established children's-defense organizations has emphasized public order as an issue of supreme importance to the young. Why have those

Karl Zinsmeister, "Growing Up Scared," *The Atlantic*, June 1990. Reprinted with permission.

who claim to speak in behalf of children made no outcry for tougher laws, no-nonsense sentencing, more police officers, more prisons, safer schools, and less drugs? Why have they initiated no campaign for putting the full weight of public protection on the side of babies and schoolchildren, instead of on the side of mothers who poison their own offspring with crack, and gang members who bring guns into classrooms?

Stress Crime Reduction

The present state of affairs is intolerable. It is time to compile a new list of "children's issues," and to put crime reduction at the top.

In May of 1987 the mayor of Washington, D.C., visited an eighth-grade science class for gifted students at a public school in a poor neighborhood. The mayor posed a question. "How many of you know somebody who's been killed?" There were nineteen students in the class. Fourteen hands went up. The mayor went around the room: How were they killed? The answers began like this: "Shot." "Stabbing." "Shot." "Shot." "Drugs." "Shot." These were thirteen-year-old children. Given that they were in the gifted class, one can assume that they were from more privileged backgrounds than most of their schoolmates.

Over a four-month period in Detroit at about the same time, 102 youngsters age sixteen or under were shot, nearly all of them by other children. There was so much violence in the public schools that the whole system had to be shut down for two days. In October of 1987 *The Wall Street Journal* ran a front-page story that chronicled three months in the life of a twelve-year-old Chicago boy named Lafeyette Walton. That life included almost daily gun and submachine-gun battles in his housing project, beatings and maimings of relatives and friends, rapes, gang recruiting, cocaine-running by a nine-year-old female cousin, and several murders.

Our failure to curb such mayhem must be blamed on tolerance, not ignorance. Anecdotes like the ones above have been piling up for years. There is no shortage of quantitative evidence either. Researchers at the University of Maryland School of Medicine, in Baltimore, recently completed a study of 168 teenagers who visited an inner-city clinic for routine medical care. The teenagers were questioned about their exposure to various kinds of violence. A stunning 24 percent had witnessed a murder; 72 percent knew someone who had been shot. These teenagers had themselves been victims of some type of violence an average of one and a half times each and had witnessed an average of more than five serious criminal episodes. One out of five had had their lives threatened, and almost one out of eleven had been raped. The doctors who collected the information point out that because of the nature of the clinic popula-

> ***"It is time to compile a new list of 'children's issues,' and to put crime reduction at the top."***

tion, some 80 percent of the respondents were female. Among a sample of adolescent males many of these measures of exposure to violence would be higher.

Social Warfare

"What I think is going on in the inner city is warfare—social warfare," one psychologist in Boston says. Lawrence Gary, the director of the Institute for Urban Affairs and Research at Howard University, says, "This kind of violence is a new phenomenon in America. We've always had murder and violence, but not like this. We don't know what the long-term impact is going to be."

Young people are not only increasingly exposed to violence; they are also increasingly the perpetrators of violence. In the most troubling cases we are seeing a pattern of extreme remorselessness. The Central Park "wilding" attack is an infamous example; those accused of raping and nearly killing a young jogger in 1989 said afterward that "it was fun." In an earlier case, in Washington, D.C., a group of youths robbed, raped, and brutally murdered a middle-aged mother named Catherine Fuller while singing and joking. In another instance in Washington an eighteen-year-old shot a cab driver in the head because he "wanted to try out a gun." In another, two teenagers killed a third who passed them on the street because they wanted his "boom box."

"In Washington an eighteen-year-old shot a cab driver in the head because he 'wanted to try out a gun.'"

"I had a kid who shot a guy twenty-seven times," one juvenile-court supervisor reports. "What kind of anger is that?" Even the murder victim's girlfriend, he says, showed no emotion when informed of the crime. In Brooklyn three teenagers methodically set fire to a homeless couple in 1987. When rubbing alcohol wouldn't ignite the pair, the youths went to a local service station for gasoline, which worked. Hundreds of similarly disturbing cases exist. Investigators say that juveniles are often found laughing and playing at homicide scenes.

From 1983 to 1988 the number of minors arrested for murder increased by a startling 31 percent (to 1,765), even though the number of people age twelve to seventeen actually decreased by eight percent over those five years. The jump in murder arrests of children age fourteen or younger (up 28 percent, to a total of 201 over that same period) is especially troubling. Victor Herbert, the executive director of New York City's Division of High Schools, says a new breed of young people "who are very reckless, very carefree, and, we believe, very dangerous" has arrived on the scene. "There's real fear among young people about each other," he reports.

Homicide is now the leading cause of death among children in many American inner cities, and about half the assailants are other youths. Extrapolations from death-certificate and FBI statistics show that approximately 2,000 minors were murdered in 1988—twice the number killed in 1965, when there were 6.5 million more people under age eighteen in the country. Among blacks the destruction is particularly disturbing. More than 1,000 black children fell victim to homicide in 1988, a 50 percent increase over the toll in 1985. The murder and drug epidemics sweeping black communities are now so serious as to have actually reduced the average black lifespan. From 1970 to 1984 steadily improving medical technology and diet, rising income, and other factors pushed black life expectancy up from 64.1 years to 69.7 years. The progress stopped right there. While white longevity has continued to rise, the average black lifespan has decreased since 1984 by nearly four months—a development without parallel in the postwar period.

> ***"The most important source of violence by and among children is family breakdown."***

The Roots of the Problem

The most important source of violence by and among children is family breakdown. More than 60 percent of all children born today will spend at least some time in a single-parent household before reaching age eighteen. That kind of collapse of family structure is historically unprecedented in the United States and possibly in the world. For many black teenagers, according to a report by one child-welfare organization, marriage is "now an almost forgotten institution."

There is a great difference of opinion over the cause of this family decay. On one side is, let us say, the Charles Murray school, which argues that perverse government policies lie behind the collapse of family responsibility. In opposition is what we might call the Daniel Patrick Moynihan school, which argues that the causes are a mystery (but probably involve culture) and that government intervention offers the best hope for a solution. But despite the deep split over causes and solutions, there is broad agreement—at last—that family disintegration is at the root of many of the social and economic problems that worry us most.

At Risk: Kids in One-Parent Homes

To say that family structure is now the principal conduit of class structure is not to deny that plenty of children in intact families have problems, or that many youngsters from single-parent homes will grow up to be happy and successful. There are children being raised in Beirut today who will turn out fine too; nonetheless, growing up in Beirut is not to be recommended. The point is, having only one parent's time, energy, and earning and teaching power is a serious blow from which a child recovers only with effort. Lack of male direction is an additional problem for many such children.

That is not personal prejudice. A major study of children from one-parent families, conducted by the National Association of Elementary School Principals, has found that 30 percent of the two-parent elementary school students surveyed ranked as high achievers, compared with only 17 percent of the one-parent children. At the other end of the scale, 23 percent of the two-parent children were low achievers—versus 38 percent of the one-parent children. There were more clinic visits among one-parent students, and their rate of absence from school ran higher. One-parent students were consistently more likely to be late, truant, and subject to disciplinary action. One-parent children were found to be more than twice as likely to drop out of school altogether.

Monetary Aid to Families

The Bureau of Justice Statistics reported not long ago that 70 percent of the juveniles in state reform institutions grew up in single-parent or no-parent families. One recent study of seventy-two adolescent murderers found that three quarters came from single-parent homes. Most street-gang members, it has been shown, come from broken homes. . . .

One of the depressing lessons we have learned in the past quarter century is how unamenable the problems of the broken family are to monetary solutions. It is not that we haven't tried to make compensation for the withering of the nuclear unit. Two thirds of all people in female-headed families with children under eighteen now get benefits from a welfare program (Aid to Families with Dependent Children, General Assistance, Supplemental Security Income, Medicaid, food stamps, rent assistance), the Census Bureau tells us. Of all never-married mothers, more than 80 percent are receiving some kind of government check. The federal government spends more than $100 billion every year on means-tested assistance to families. Yet this aid has not even come close to providing those households with the kind of existential security that most intact families enjoy.

Given family integrity's essential importance, one might have expected society-wide efforts to support and encourage two-parent families when signs of rot were first detected, in the 1960s. That didn't happen. For the past quarter century American public policy has shied away from the idea that certain family forms are more desirable than others. There is no attempt to promote childbearing within wedlock. There is little penalty attached to child abandonment. There is scant recognition of the social benefits of marriage, or of the social contributions of those who devote themselves to conscientious childrearing. There is no reward from our public programs for standing by kith and kin.

"One recent study of seventy-two adolescent murderers found that three quarters came from single-parent homes."

Television Violence Promotes Youth Violence

by Deborah Prothrow-Stith

About the author: *Deborah Prothrow-Stith is an assistant dean at the Harvard School of Public Health in Cambridge, Massachusetts. She is a former Massachusetts commissioner of public health.*

Researchers have established that years of ingesting television's violent repast may promote aggression. And no wonder! Look what television teaches: *Good guys use violence as a first resort. Any amount of killing is all right, so long as one's cause is just. Violence is a hero's way to solve problems.* In a world permeated with violence, these dangerous lessons learned during a decade or more of watching may be the incendiary cap that ignites a confrontation. And instead of walking away, two hot-headed young men, armed with deadly weapons, may choose to stay and fight.

No reasonably alert observer could doubt that there is a great deal of violence in our popular arts, but what does that mean? Some would say that the violence in our mass media, particularly television, merely reflects the violence in our society. Is that the case? Or does the violence in our mass media *promote* violence in our society? Does heavy television watching, for example, cause children to behave more aggressively than they might otherwise?

The Most Powerful Mass Medium

We are focusing on television because of its preeminence. Almost since its inception, television has been the most pervasive and powerful mass medium. The availability of new ways of watching television—subscribing to Cable, for example, or hooking up to a VCR—has only increased television's cultural dominance. Network television, meantime, remains the conduit for our national culture. Day-time and prime-time network dramas shape how Americans view conflict between individuals. Network news programs define the way most

Excerpted from Deborah Prothrow-Stith, *Deadly Consequences*. New York: HarperCollins, 1991. Reprinted with permission.

Americans view the world. The networks broadcast our sports and our great public spectacles, such as inaugurations and state funerals. Network television even broadcasts our movies, although in recent years, many viewers have been switching to Cable for movies and for music, especially the hard rock broadcast on the Music Television Video (MTV).

"Two Surgeon Generals have publicly supported the thesis that an overdose of media violence can trigger aggressive behavior."

For most children, television in its several guises is as much an influence as school or church—maybe more so. Most American children spend more hours watching television than they spend on any other waking activity, including going to school. From preschool until around seven years of age, the average young child watches between two and three hours of television a day. By the age of eight most children are watching four hours of T.V. daily—that's twenty-eight hours a week. Later, in mid-adolescence, viewing declines by an hour or so a day. Of course, some children watch less television than the average, and others, most often those growing up in poverty, watch much more.

Lack of Parental Control

Many adults view television as what psychologist Ron Slaby calls "a children's medium," and, I might add, a good babysitter. Rarely do parents control what children watch or how much they watch. In families with two televisions, parent and child often do not watch together. Nor do parents talk to children about what they see. Experts say this is especially unfortunate as watching together and talking can help children understand and interpret what is broadcast.

For decades critics have been saying that the twenty, twenty-five, or thirty hours a week our children are spending in front of the television is damaging them and undermining our society. Violence, as every parent knows, is not the only problem. I myself am particularly concerned with the time-consuming aspect of television. Children who are watching T.V. are not playing ball, practicing the piano, or doing their homework. Nor are they reading books! One Canadian study documented the impact on children's reading skills when multichannel television arrived at their remote mountain town in the 1970s. Within a year the reading comprehension of the children had declined. Children who are watching *Three's Company* are not reading books.

Also, there is the issue of violence. A rancorous debate has surrounded the question of television's impact on aggression for thirty years. Television executives have used all their energy and resources to prove that television-viewing does not teach children to behave violently. Scores of psychologists and university professors, on the other hand, have produced a huge body of research concluding that a causal connection does indeed exist between violent behavior and television. They believe, and the evidence seems to indicate, that some of the violence today would not take place were violence to disappear from the airwaves.

While the case is not air-tight, two Surgeon Generals have publicly supported the thesis that an overdose of media violence can trigger aggressive behavior. This view has also been championed by the American Medical Association, the American Pediatric Association, the American Academy of Child Psychiatry, and the American Psychological Association. I, too, believe that violence on television is one of the factors that causes some young people to behave violently. I base my opinion not only on research but also on common sense. For me the issue of television's impact on children's behavior was settled when my own son and daughter were old enough to prefer one pair of blue jeans to another. Each pair of pants was made of 100 percent cotton denim, each had the same stitching, the same snaps; but they had different labels. One brand had been advertised on television, the other had not. Of course, my kids wanted the jeans they had seen advertised on television. Manufacturers spend hundreds of millions of dollars a year advertising their products on television because of T.V.'s impact on behavior. If television did not have an impact on the behavior of consumers, manufacturers would use other advertising media. . . .

Copycat Violence

Most of the time when we think about the impact of media violence, we think about cases in which disturbed young people are "inspired" to commit violent acts by what they see on the large or small screen. Researchers have established that copycat events are not an anomaly. Statistically-speaking, they are rare, but predictable, occurrences. Television shows, movies, novels—all can trigger copycat violence. Sensational news stories also may be copied. In the weeks after a major prize fight, for example, the homicide rate all over the country temporarily rises. Following the suicide of Marilyn Monroe, 300 Americans committed suicide who were statistically predicted to remain alive.

It's not just movie stars that can "inspire" people to commit violence against themselves. My friend Dr. Mark Rosenberg, of the federal Centers for Disease Control in Atlanta, tells the story about a woman in Atlanta who committed suicide by shooting herself. Inside her purse next to her body was the story of another woman in Atlanta who had shot herself to death. The clipping revealed where the first victim had bought the gun she turned on herself. The second victim had gone to the same store to buy a gun.

> ***"Television shows, movies, novels—all can trigger copycat violence."***

We are a suggestible species. We learn how to behave from each other. When we see one of our species act, their act becomes a model for us to emulate. In this way, we sometimes make the unthinkable thinkable, the undoable doable. We can learn how to kill a president from a movie. We can learn how to commit suicide from each other. We can also learn how to commit mass murder. The Northeastern University researchers Jamie Fox and Jack Levin have studied the phenomena of mass murder. They looked at incidents during the past three decades in which assailants opened fire, usually in crowded public places—schools, offices, restaurants—killing large numbers of people. These incidents, they discovered, have increased significantly over the years. In the past they were rare occurrences. Now two to three mass murders happen each month.

No one knows all the reasons why these incidents are becoming so common, but Professors Fox and Levin believe the publicity that surrounds them is one of a series of reasons. The attention focused on mass murder may make this crime seem like a glamorous and powerful way to demand the world's attention and to exact retribution for wrongs, real and imagined. And then there is the copycat aspect; one act encourages another. Publicity alone does not "cause" a person to commit mass murder. Perhaps, however, constant exposure to information about violence and mass murder can plant and legitimate the idea that killing one or more persons is an acceptable way to avenge oneself. Deviance, like other human phenomena, exists within a social framework. In a very peaceful society, even the angriest and most seriously disturbed people will behave non-violently most of the time. A few rare violent incidents will occur. In a very violent society like ours many angry and disturbed people are prompted to behave violently.

"The leading predictor of how aggressive a young male would be at nineteen turned out to be the violence of the television he preferred at age eight."

A Psychologist Studies the Effects of Television

The teenager dressed like Rambo who slaughters his family will get an avalanche of publicity. Reading about this crime we may be filled with fear and a sick feeling that our modern, technological life is slipping out of control. That does not make Rambo lookalikes the primary or even the secondary cause of the nation's rising homicide rate, however. The scores of psychologists who study television violence have interests that go far beyond the relatively small sensational homicides that dominate the headlines. These academics seek to discover the impact of video violence on the more than 20,000 homicides that occur each year, on the millions of assaults and on the tens of millions of American children for whom television is a daily habit. Their work is of particular interest now, when the first generations of young people reared on a heavy diet of television have come of age.

Leonard D. Eron is the researcher whose name is most associated with this effort. Eron and his numerous collaborators have carried out a series of long-term studies investigating aggression in school children. Hundreds of young people have been followed for thirty years at ten year intervals, beginning at age eight. The authors' most illuminating finding is that aggression tends to be a stable characteristic, one that is established early and remains in effect unless some form of intervention is successfully applied. In other words, the 8-year-old who gets in trouble for bullying has a disproportionately great chance of growing into the 19-year-old who robs and mugs and the 30-year-old sentenced to a lengthy prison term for assault, or even murder.

> ***"Following the violent program the children's play is invariably more aggressive."***

Affinity for Television Violence

Eron and his colleagues established a quantifiable link between television watching and aggression. Among the hundreds of boys who were followed, a preference for T.V. violence turned out to be a key warning sign of later trouble. In fact, the leading predictor of how aggressive a young male would be at nineteen turned out to be the violence of the television he preferred at age eight. This does not mean that years of viewing violent television will make a 19-year-old behave violently, but there is reason to believe that television can be a key factor. Eron himself has written that what a child watches can make the difference between a child who strikes out at others and one who does not. So convinced is he of the negative impact of violent television that he lists massive exposure to violent television programs ahead of parenting practices as a factor in the creation of antisocial young adults.

Another interesting element of Eron's research relates to church-going. Retrospectively, Eron and his colleagues searched for the factors that seemed to inoculate children against trouble in later life. They looked at the aggressive 8-year-olds who did *not* grow up to have trouble with the law. Church-going turned out to be a significant factor. Aggressive 8-year-olds who were taken to church were less likely to grow up to have trouble with the law than those who did not go. As the wife of a minister, this finding makes perfect sense to me. The way I see it, religious services and Sunday school provide a setting for children to learn non-violent conflict resolution. If they are Christian, they are taught to turn the other cheek. Whatever their religion, however, they are taught to set high moral and ethical standards for themselves.

A Learned Behavior

I share the view of Eron and most non-Freudian psychologists that aggression is a learned behavior, one that can be unlearned. Like many psychologists I believe that the family and social environment can teach children to use violence to solve problems. The basic set of ideas that describe how this learning takes place is called social learning theory. The underlying assumption in this theory is that children learn how to behave from their social environment.

According to social learning theory, children learn how to behave aggressively by watching others use violence to their advantage and then imitating what they have seen. This process is called "modeling." Parents who have seen their three- or four-year-old watch a newcomer at the playground and then later reproduce the newcomer's unpleasant habit—throwing sand at other children, for example—know how powerful a learning tool modeling is. Modeling is only part of the picture, however. The modeled behavior will become a part of the child's standard repertoire only if it is reinforced. That means if the child gets some sort of reward—control of his brother's truck, say—when he exhibits a new behavior, he will use that new behavior often. How to sit still in the classroom. How to comfort a crying baby. How to talk to adults and other children. How to hit and punch to get what you want. These are all "skills" that children develop by the subtle interaction of modeling plus reinforcements.

The social learning process operates regardless of whether the observed behavior is seen on T.V. or in person. Through research in the field, psychologists have repeatedly shown how this process works. In numerous experiments based at pre-schools, researchers have observed children at play before and after seeing violent television programs. Following the violent program the children's play is invariably more aggressive. They are much more likely to hit, punch, kick, and grab to get their way. In other words, television teaches children how to use aggression for personal gain. The environment, then, reinforces this behavior. Moreover, in follow-up studies, researchers have learned that the greater the amount of violent television a child watches, the more violent his or her interaction with peers is likely to become, and these effects linger.

"Children who watch a great deal of violent T.V. are desensitized to the wrongness of what they are seeing."

Television's Positive Messages

It ought to be noted, however, that not all of television's lessons are violent ones. Social learning does not just involve the modeling of negative behaviors. Researchers have shown that positive behaviors can be modeled, too. The people who produce *Sesame Street* and *Mr. Rogers* do a great job of providing models of desirable social behavior for young kids to emulate. Concern for others. The willingness to delay gratification. The capacity to compromise. All these behaviors and many more are made available to small children who watch these programs. These lessons will not become patterns of behavior, however, unless home and schools provide reinforcement. When a child sees another child sharing on *Sesame Street* and then tries sharing at home, parents need to be vigilant. Positive behavior needs reinforcement or it will not reoccur. It is not enough for parents to say all the don'ts. "Don't hit your brother." "Don't take his toys." They must provide positive praise. "Gee, that was good sharing." "You did a good job helping your brother." "I know it's hard to share, but I can see you are really trying." The kind words, a friendly pat, and a smile reinforce and help cement the child's fledgling efforts to be a good citizen.

Kids Desensitized to Violence

If you show a 20-year-old male a romantic movie and then ask him about a rape, he will probably empathize with the rape victim. But if you show him a violent movie—*The Texas Chainsaw Massacre*, say—and then ask him about a rape, he is likely to tell you that the rape victim deserved what she got. She was a vicious tease. She was asking for it. The process at work is called disinhibition. Repeated exposure to real life or fictional violence can make violence seem normal and acceptable.

Similarly, children who watch a great deal of violent T.V. are desensitized to the wrongness of what they are seeing. Television tells them that violence is an everyday occurrence, a justified form of self-defense. Teens who live in communities where violence is endemic are particularly vulnerable. T.V. reinforces the seeming ordinariness and rightness of the violence that confronts them daily. The violence these children see on television tells them that the violence in which they live is expected and normal—when in fact it is neither.

People who watch a great deal of television violence are more fearful than other people, and they overestimate the amount of violence in their environment. George Gerbner, Director of the Annenberg School of Communications at the University of Pennsylvania has studied the worldview of heavy television viewers. Rich or poor, young or old, those who watch four hours or more of T.V. a day share a common disillusionment. Gerbner calls this phenomenon the "mean world syndrome." This affliction, he says, besets heavy television watchers, who in time cease to differentiate between the world portrayed on television, where half the inhabitants are police officers and the other half are violent criminals and news stories about crime are replayed endlessly, from the real world. Those suffering from the "mean world syndrome" are filled with feelings of danger, mistrust, intolerance, gloom and hopelessness. They erroneously assume that the perverse and violent world portrayed on commercial television accurately reflects reality. When asked by researchers to describe the dimension of the

> ***"Young males growing up in poverty, in homes that lack non-violent male role models, are the most vulnerable to television's violence-promoting message."***

crime problem, they grossly overestimate the incidence of crime and violence. The mental universe heavy T.V. viewers inhabit is the sensational, predatory, lowest-common-denominator world portrayed on "the tube." The world they look out upon is perpetually framed by television's version of human events.

Gerbner has also done interesting work with children. He discovered that children are especially vulnerable to the underlying assumptions television makes. Years before children are capable of making moral judgements, television provides them with a view of how the world is and how the world should be. Even when children understand that the plots of television dramas are fiction, they tend to accept as real the rest that television portrays—the relationships, the material wealth, the settings. How should people treat each other? When should violence be used? What kind of car and house and clothing must a person have to be happy? How long does it take to get what you want in life? Who is a hero? Who is a chump? These are the kinds of sophisticated questions television answers. Our children watch, and they learn.

"Some children are more vulnerable than others to television's violence-promoting message."

The Children Most at Risk

Television's portrayal of violence as a glamorous, successful, and entertaining method of resolving disputes is a problem for most children and most parents. All of our children are being dosed, overdosed I would say, by these messages. But some children are more vulnerable than others to television's violence-promoting message. Boys and men who are poor, who are urban, and who have witnessed or been victimized by violence in their families are more at risk for the dangerous lessons television teaches.

At a conference in Philadelphia which I attended, one of the participants, a probation officer, shed some light on those at greatest risk. He suggested and I agree with him that young males growing up in poverty, in homes that lack non-violent male role models, are the most vulnerable to television's violence-promoting message. Boys like this may never get to see an adult man restrain his own anger or control his own violent impulses. They may never experience non-violent discipline. They may never have the chance to see an adult man, or a woman, resolve disputes effectively and assertively, using non-violent strategies. Boys living in these circumstances are the ones most susceptible to television's message that heroes use violence to serve their purposes.

Emmett Folgert, a youth worker in Boston's Dorchester Youth Collaborative who is close to scores of young, poor fatherless males has elaborated on this thought. Boys without fathers who grow up in impoverished, female-headed households, Folgert believes, identify with the violent heroes on television to a degree that other young boys do not. Folgert, trained as a social worker, labels this kind of identification "clinical." The imaginary relationship such boys have with their T.V. heroes has great emotional meaning. Desperately hungry for fathering, such boys transform their television heroes into imaginary fathers. They talk to these pretend fathers. They make up long stories about what their T.V. heroes would do if they lived in Boston in a poor neighborhood. They ask their imaginary heroes for advice. What should they do? How should they handle themselves? Folgert says the answer they receive is always the same. Their heroes tell them to be tough. Their heroes tell them to fight.

We teach our children to kill, and some children are more vulnerable than others to this deadly lesson.

Child Abuse Can Cause Youths to Become Violent

by Charles Patrick Ewing

About the author: *Charles Patrick Ewing is a clinical and forensic psychologist and a law professor at the State University of New York at Buffalo.*

Juveniles who kill often seem to come from broken families in which one or both parents are disturbed, neglectful, or abusive. Although many youngsters may grow up in homes broken by parental separation or divorce, the percentage of broken homes is much greater among those who kill—at least among juvenile killers who have been the subjects of nearly half a century of published research.

Much of the research on juveniles who kill also indicates that many have parents who are alcoholic or mentally ill. The single most consistent finding regarding juvenile homicide, however, is that kids who kill, especially those who kill family members, generally have witnessed or have been directly victimized by domestic violence. The most common form of domestic violence witnessed by juveniles who kill is spouse abuse (one parent assaulting the other), but being directly victimized by child abuse is even more common.

The extremely high incidence of child abuse victimization among juveniles who kill has been widely documented. For example, among the fourteen juvenile death row inmates examined by Dr. [Dorothy] Lewis and her associates, twelve had been "brutally" abused physically, and five had been sodomized by older family members. Similarly high rates of child abuse victimization have also been found in other multisubject studies of juvenile killers. . . .

Makings of a Juvenile Killer

Homicide, like most behavior, is learned. It is a function of both person and circumstance. We are all capable of killing under some circumstances, and none of us kills under all circumstances. Killings occur only when certain people with certain learning experiences find themselves in certain situations.

Juvenile homicide is no exception. Juvenile killers are not born but made. Although there are as many specific recipes for creating juvenile killers as there are juvenile killings, there is also a general recipe for turning kids into killers. Not every case has every ingredient. In fact, we do not know all the ingredients or their precise proportions, but we do know the major ones. Whatever else may go into the making of a kid who kills, virtually all juvenile killers have been significantly influenced in their homicidal behavior by one or more of just a handful of known factors: child abuse, poverty, substance abuse, and access to guns.

"Some children who are abused or witness abuse of loved ones learn to be violent; their abusive parents are powerful, negative role models."

The good news is that we know what these factors are and could do something to reduce their prevalence. The bad news is that we are doing very little. Perhaps the worst news is that, as a result, both the annual number and rate of juvenile homicides have been increasing, will continue to increase, and will probably reach record high proportions before the turn of the century.

Kids Who Kill: Case Studies

Seventeen-year-old Heath Wilkins was sentenced to die for robbing and brutally shooting a convenience store clerk as she begged for her life. Abandoned by his mentally ill father when he was three years old, Heath was raised by his drug-abusing mother who often beat him.

Fourteen-year-old Shirley Wolf, with help from fifteen-year-old Cindy Collier, hacked an eighty-five-year-old woman to death with a butcher knife. From the time she was an infant until she turned fourteen, Shirley was sexually abused by her father, uncle, and grandfather. Cindy was beaten and raped repeatedly throughout her childhood.

With help from his older sister, Deborah, sixteen-year-old Richard Jahnke ambushed, shot, and killed his father—a man who had beaten Richard and sexually abused his sister for most of Richard's life.

Robert Lee Moody shot and killed his father after repeatedly seeing him beat Robert's mother. After hearing of the abuse Robert's father inflicted upon his family over the years, a judge publicly denounced the dead man as "the scum of the earth" and sentenced Robert to probation.

The abuse suffered by Heath Wilkins, Shirley Wolf, Cindy Collier, Richard and Deborah Jahnke, and Robert Lee Moody is not uncommon among juveniles who kill—regardless of who they kill. The single most consistent finding in juvenile homicide research is that juveniles who kill have generally witnessed or have been directly victimized by family violence.

The correlation between child abuse and juvenile homicide makes sense.

Some children who are abused or witness abuse of loved ones learn to be violent; their abusive parents are powerful, negative role models. Other abused children suffer psychological or physical trauma that leads to the kinds of neurological or psychological problems often associated with juvenile homicidal behavior. Still other abused children kill in direct response to the abuse they suffer—they kill their abusers.

An unknown but probably large amount of child abuse goes unreported. At the same time, however, the majority of reported cases of child abuse are unsubstantiated. An unsubstantiated report does not mean that the reported abuse did not occur; it means only that the authorities, for whatever reasons, were unable to find the kind of substantiating evidence the law requires to justify state intervention. These problems make it difficult to determine just how much child abuse there really is and whether child abuse is, as many claim, not only increasing but reaching epidemic proportions in the United States.

Child Abuse Statistics

The best, indeed the only, nationwide data available on child abuse are reporting statistics. Despite their obvious limitations, these data make one thing absolutely clear: there has been a tremendous and steady increase in the number of reported cases of child abuse over the past decade. The American Association for Protecting Children (AAPC) surveyed all fifty states, the District of Columbia, and the U.S. Territories and estimated the annual number of child abuse and neglect reports for the years from 1976 through 1987. The AAPC's estimates, derived from these surveys, are shown in the table.

> ***"Increases in the incidence or severity of child abuse will undoubtedly be followed by corresponding increases in the number and rate of juvenile homicides."***

Although these data do not establish that *substantiated* cases of child abuse are increasing, testimony given before the U.S. Senate Judiciary Committee in May 1989 indicated that there was a 64 percent increase in the number of *confirmed* child abuse cases in the United States between 1980 and 1986. Other data indicate that child abuse is not only increasing in frequency but also in severity. The clearest indicator that child abuse is becoming more violent and more physically damaging is the recent dramatic increase in child abuse fatalities.

Between 1985 and 1987, there was a 25 percent increase nationally in the annual number of children who died as a direct result of child abuse. In 1988, the number of recorded deaths from child abuse reached 1,225—an increase of 5 percent over the national total for 1987. Between 1986 and 1987, child abuse deaths almost tripled in Utah and virtually doubled in Virginia and North Carolina. During fiscal year 1988, Illinois experienced 97 child abuse deaths, an 80 percent increase over fiscal year 1987. In California, 96 children died in 1988 as a result of child abuse, a 15 percent increase over 1987.

National Estimates of the Number and Rate of Child Abuse and Neglect Reports, 1976-1987.

Year	*Number of Reports (and percentage change)*	*Rate per 1,000 Children (and percentage change)*
1976	669,000	10.1
1977	838,000 (25.26%)	12.8 (22%)
1978	836,000 (–0.24%)	12.9 (0%)
1979	988,000 (18.18%)	15.4 (19%)
1980	1,154,000 (16.80%)	18.1 (17%)
1981	1,225,000 (6.15%)	19.4 (7%)
1982	1,262,000 (3.02%)	20.1 (4%)
1983	1,477,000 (17.04%)	23.6 (17%)
1984	1,727,000 (16.93%)	27.3 (16%)
1985	1,928,000 (11.64%)	30.6 (12%)
1986	2,086,000 (8.20%)	32.8 (7%)
1987	2,178,000 (4.40%)	34.0 (4%)

Given the correlation between child abuse and juvenile homicide, increases in the incidence or severity of child abuse will undoubtedly be followed by corresponding increases in the number and rate of juvenile homicides. If, as many contend, the United States is experiencing an epidemic of child abuse, this epidemic will undoubtedly affect the incidence of juvenile homicide for years to come.

Rock Lyrics May Contribute to Youth Violence

by Hannelore Wass, M. David Miller, and Carol Anne Redditt

About the authors: *Hannelore Wass and M. David Miller are professors emeritus of education at the University of Florida in Gainesville. Carol Anne Redditt was a doctoral student in education counseling at the university at the time this article was published.*

In previous studies we found that approximately a fifth of the adolescents attending school listed among their favorites rock music with destructive themes (explicitly advocating and promoting Homicide, Suicide, or Satanic practices in Rock music [HSSR]). We also found that race, gender, school environment (urban, rural, suburban, parochial schools), and parents' marital status were factors predicting whether or not an adolescent was an HSSR fan: whites were more likely to be fans than blacks, boys more likely than girls, adolescents attending a public school more than those attending a parochial school, and adolescents whose parents were never married or remarried more likely than those of married parents. In addition, we found that HSSR fans spend more time listening to rock music and watching music television, more often said they like the words as much as the beat/rhythm of the music, and more often knew the words of their favorite songs. HSSR fans more often felt young children should be allowed to listen to rock music with destructive themes and more often were convinced that under no circumstances are young people influenced by rock lyrics to commit suicide, homicide, or satanic acts.

The Influence of Violent Themes

Violent themes in rock music, especially in contemporary heavy metal and punk rock, and their influence on children and adolescents have been of con-

Hannelore Wass, M. David Miller, and Carol Anne Redditt, "Adolescents and Destructive Themes in Rock Music: A Follow-Up," *Omega: The Journal of Death and Dying* 23 (3): 199-206, © 1991 Baywood Publishing Co., Inc. Reprinted with permission.

cern for several years. A number of professionals, their representative organizations such as the American Academy of Pediatrics and the National Education Association, various child advocacy groups including the Parents Music Resource Center, and others have suggested that such lyrics promote destructive and suicidal behavior in adolescents. Representatives of the entertainment industry and rock stars say such concern is unfounded: young people only like the sound and rhythm of rock music, do not listen to lyrics, do not understand their meaning, and at any rate, only a very small fraction of the music contains such lyrics and only a very small minority of adolescents is interested. With some concerned groups demanding censorship or stricter regulation and the industry and artists asserting their constitutional right to free expression, the debate inevitably has a political dimension as well. Most recently, several states have begun to introduce or consider record-labeling legislation, which apparently has prompted the Recording Industry Association of America to announce plans of voluntary warning labeling for records with sexually graphic and violent lyrics.

> ***"It is possible . . . that destructive lyrics, combined with other factors, . . . do lead to antisocial and destructive behavior."***

The Rock Lyric—Destructiveness Link

While our findings and those of others provide evidence contrary to the industry's and artists' assessments, they do not answer any questions about the link between preference for music with destructive themes and destructive behavior. Such links, however, have been reported in anecdotal case studies and in the national news. Recent statistics are not reassuring: the rates of adolescent suicide and suicide attempts have increased sharply in the past years. The most recent statistics also show increases in youthful violence.

While the negative influence of televised and filmed violence on children's behavior has been well established empirically, very few systematic studies have been focused on the effects of rock music and music television. It is reasonable to assume, however, that destructive lyrics in rock music and music television, similar to aggressive themes in television drama and film, do have a negative impact on behavior. A simple cause-effect relationship between exposure to destructive rock lyrics and subsequent destructive behavior is probably impossible to determine and based on current knowledge of behavior, is unlikely.

It is possible, however, that destructive lyrics, combined with other factors such as dysfunctional families, substance abuse, and problems in school, do lead to antisocial and destructive behavior. It is also possible that such themes function as a trigger for such behavior impacting those who are already "at risk" and those who exhibit antisocial or destructive behavior. If destructive rock lyrics do contribute to destructive behavior, or if they reflect such behavior, then we can expect that the proportion of HSSR fans among juvenile offenders would be larger than that of typical adolescent populations. The major purpose of this follow-up study was to determine if this is the case with residents in youth detention centers. In addition, we wanted to explore possible differences between HSSR and non-HSSR fans in attitudes toward rock music with destructive themes.

Survey of Adolescent Offenders

The sample consisted of 120 adolescent offenders in two youth detention centers located in a southeastern state. These youths are in the custody of the State Department of Health and Rehabilitative Services. The centers provide a short-term restrictive environment following adjudication pending disposition, or pending court action, transfer, or relocation.

The adolescents ranged in age from thirteen to eighteen years and in grade levels from grades six to twelve; 27 percent were school dropouts; 77.5 percent were boys; and 67.5 percent were white.

> ***"[Our] finding suggests a strong relationship between antisocial or destructive behavior and a preference for rock music with destructive themes."***

The questionnaire, consisting of Likert-type, categorical, and open-ended items used in the previous two studies, was administered to volunteers in a large group setting. Loglinear and multiple regression analyses were used to determine the relationships between demographic variables, HSSR status and other music-related behaviors and attitudes.

HSSR fans were participants who listed any combination of at least four bands, individuals, albums, or singles with explicit lyrics that advocate homicide, suicide, or satanic practice. We also collected data on adolescents' religious affiliation and parents' marital status and occupation.

Of the 120 students, ninety-one reported being rock fans. Of these forty-nine (53.8%) were HSSR fans. . . . Only students' race and grade had significant effects on HSSR status. Consistent with the earlier studies, blacks were not HSSR fans (0.00%), but many whites were (58.02%). Grade was classified into three categories—dropouts, middle school (grades 6-8), and high school (grades 9-12). Dropouts were more likely to be HSSR fans (59.38%) than adolescents attending high school (30.99%). Middle school students were about equally likely to be HSSR fans. Of the participants 35 percent did not report their religious affiliation. As a result, we excluded this variable from the analyses. . . .

There were no differences in what students liked best in the music (beat/rhythm, or words). When asked whether it is all right for children under the age of ten to listen to HSSR music, HSSR fans said yes (69.77%) more often than did non-HSSR fans (40.91%). When asked if adolescents would commit destructive acts as a result of listening to HSSR music (suicide or killing), most HSSR fans thought they would not (76.60%), while non-HSSR fans were divided in their views (50.00% yes, 45.31% no, 4.69% unsure). In addition, more blacks (62.96%) than whites (28.21%) thought that destructive acts result from HSSR music.

[The results] . . . showed no significant differences by HSSR status, gender, race, and grade in knowledge of the words of rock songs, in agreement with the words, nor in time spent watching MTV. However, HSSR fans and whites spent more time listening to rock music, and high school students were less influenced by rock music than dropouts or middle-school students.

Data Links Violent Behavior and Destructive Themes

Data we previously reported were collected from students in public and parochial schools. Those collected in this study closely paralleled the earlier one, except that the participants in this study were delinquent adolescents in state custody for antisocial or destructive behavior, and the data were collected one year later. In our judgment, no major shifts in rock music nor in adolescents' attitudes toward rock music have occurred in the intervening period. Therefore, we attribute the differences in results to differences between adolescent offenders and typical adolescents in public and parochial schools. However, if such shifts did occur, these changes may, in part, explain the results.

> ***"Mental health workers [should] consider adolescents' music-related behaviors and orientations as a useful indicator for psychological assessment."***

There were two major differences in results between this study and the previous one. First, the proportion of HSSR fans is much higher for the delinquent youths. In the earlier study, less than one-fifth of the rock fans were HSSR fans (17.5%). In this study, the proportion was three times as large (53.8%). This finding suggests a strong relationship between antisocial or destructive behavior and a preference for rock music with destructive themes. Two other studies seem to support this interpretation. In a survey of 700 Canadian high-school students, J. Tanner found that compared to fans of mainstream, popular rock, and other music, heavy metal fans scored higher on a measure of delinquent behavior. Tanner also reported that heavy metal fans scored lower on a measure of commitment to school, supporting the present finding that more dropouts were HSSR fans than adolescents who attend school. Lawrence C. Trostle discovered a positive relationship between a group of self-proclaimed "stoners," a Los

Angeles juvenile gang presumably engaging in animal sacrifices and grave robbings, and their preference for heavy metal rock groups and belief in black magic and witchcraft.

Second, the youthful offenders were more similar in their attitudes and behaviors toward music whether they were HSSR fans or not than in the earlier study. Previously, we found that HSSR fans differed from non-HSSR fans on six of the eight measures of music-related attitudes and behaviors; in this study, they differed in only three. A higher proportion of HSSR fans thought it is all right for children under the age of ten to listen to HSSR music, assumed that adolescents would not under any circumstances commit suicide or kill someone as a result of listening to HSSR music, and spent more time listening to rock music. These significant differences, however, were consistent with the results of the earlier study. They seem to suggest that while rock music plays a more important part in the lives of HSSR fans, typical or delinquent, these fans consider destructive rock themes as harmless. Non-HSSR fans in the two groups, on the other hand, more often hold views similar to those of concerned professionals and parent groups.

"Killing someone or practicing satanism might stand for power, whereas self-destruction might stand for depression and a sense of isolation."

Finally, while being a youthful offender seems to be a good indicator of being an HSSR fan, parents' marital status and gender were not. One might speculate that antisocial and destructive behaviors are found in children of intact as well as one-parent or reconstructed families, and that the structure of the family is probably less significant in shaping behavior than other variables such as child-rearing and patterns of interaction. It is interesting, given the traditional differences in the socialization of boys and girls, that girls in the offender group more often share music preferences and attitudes of boys than do girls in the more typical population.

As in the earlier study, HSSR fans were primarily white. So too, are most of the musicians in heavy metal and punk groups. Blacks may not see these as suitable role models. We also believe that, in general, black adolescents tend to prefer more melodious forms of rock and blues. It would be interesting to see what effects the increasingly popular rap groups, especially black rappers, have on black and white adolescents.

Destructive Themes as Metaphors

One might speculate that destructive themes in rock music should be understood metaphorically rather that literally. For example, killing someone or practicing satanism might stand for power, whereas self-destruction might stand for depression and a sense of isolation. It is possible that, for some adolescents, death themes in rock music, including those advocating destructive acts, are actually therapeutic. Often parents avoid discussing death with their children. Death-related topics are seldom a part of the public schools' curricula either. Rock lyrics may in some instances provide the modality for dealing with issues of death and for managing the anxieties they create. We suggest that counselors and mental health workers consider adolescents' music-related behaviors and orientations as a useful indicator for psychological assessment. As previously, we also recommend that the efforts of professionals and advocacy groups should continue to inform parents and to appeal to the social responsibility and self-restraint of the entertainment industry and artists.

Greed Causes Youth Violence

by Mercer L. Sullivan

About the author: *Mercer L. Sullivan is a senior research associate at the New School for Social Research Graduate School of Management and Urban Policy in New York City.*

Editor's note: In this study, the author surveyed adolescents from three neighborhoods in the New York City borough of Brooklyn. Actual neighborhood names were changed by the author. "Projectville," "La Barriada," and "Hamilton Park" are black, Puerto Rican, and white neighborhoods, respectively.

Although [my] book focuses on the crimes that high-risk youths commit for money, whether nonviolent or violent, it is necessary to consider the other patterns of violence which characterize their neighborhoods in order to comprehend the standpoint from which they perceive the costs of engaging in violent crimes for money. Their willingness and ability to employ violence for economic gain, both initially and over time, cannot be understood apart from the context of the noneconomic functions of violence in their neighborhoods.

Street Fighting Precedes Economic Crime

The most prominent pattern of noneconomically motivated violence in the lives of the study respondents was that of fighting with age peers. Some reported episodes of family violence, but most did not report being seriously abused as children, and the scattered instances of family fights in our data stand in contrast to adolescent street fights in both number and severity. Nearly all respondents, excluding only those labeled "punks" (weaklings) or "*patos*" (Spanish slang for effeminate males) by their peers, reported fighting in both individual and gang confrontations. The fighting was often quite severe, frequently involving weapons. Many had seen companions killed. This adolescent street fighting chronologically preceded involvement in systematic economic crime in most respondents' biographies and provided some of them with experience in the techniques of violence, which they then applied to the systematic pursuit of income.

Patterns of adolescent street fighting differed from patterns of systematic economic crime in two important respects. First, although most respondents in the field study reported both income-motivated crimes and fighting, peak involvement in fighting generally preceded periods of peak involvement in economic crime. Second, although street fighting frequently involved disputes over property, its basic motivations concerned status and territory rather than income. Those respondents who became involved in systematic economic crime generally did so after earlier involvement in individual or group confrontations with other adolescents.

> ***"All economic crimes—burglary and drug dealing as well as . . . street robberies—involved the potential for violent confrontations."***

The economic crimes characterizing these neighborhoods varied in the role and amount of violence they involved, but all economic crimes—burglary and drug dealing as well as more overtly violent crimes such as street robberies—involved the potential for violent confrontations. By the time respondents became involved in economic crimes on a systematic basis, they had experienced street fights and knew how and when to fight or run and how to procure and use weapons.

We found some variations between study neighborhoods in the social organization of adolescent street fighting, but all three were essentially similar in that any male youth growing up there found it necessary to establish a place for himself in the configuration of adolescent cliques and territories. From the early teens on, the young males in each neighborhood spent much of their time together outside their parents' houses and recognized some sort of attachment to a territory or "turf." Smaller children and adults might pass through unchallenged, but youths from other areas who passed through without invitation or an appropriate display of deference would be assumed to be provoking confrontation. . . .

First Explorations into Economic Crime

Noneconomic adolescent violence in the form of street fighting provided early socialization into illegal behavior and the techniques of violence, which some individuals then went on to apply to systematic economic crime. Sustained involvement in economic crime resulted in patterns of behavior which were shaped by neighborhood-specific illegal markets, criminal organizations, and environments of social control.

Early explorations of economic crime, in contrast, were typically undertaken without accurate knowledge of the associated risks and rewards and also typically undertaken at an age at which the individual had little experience with generating a flow of income of any sort. Under such circumstances, these youths' expectations concerning the returns from economic crime differed considerably from the expectations they developed later on when they experienced a need for more sustained income and had developed a more realistic perception of the varied legal and illegal income opportunities open to them. More sustained involvements in economic crime were shaped by the structure of both illegal and legitimate economic opportunities within the individual neighborhoods.

A few respondents cited as their first economic crimes incidents of stealing fruit or candy from stores before they were yet teenagers, but most, even though they had committed such acts, did not consider them significant crimes. Those who had become involved in systematic economic crime tended instead to cite incidents that occurred when they were fourteen or fifteen years old as their first experiences with gaining illegal income. These were generally nonconfrontational acts of theft such as picking pockets, stealing car parts, or, most commonly, burglaries of factories or apartments; they were usually conceived and carried out very close to their own familiar territory by pairs or groups of age peers. Violent confrontations at these ages were still almost always fights with other youths for status and territory rather than for economic gain. During their early teens, none of the respondents was willing to risk violent confrontations with adults, even though fighting with other youths was common.

"During their early teens, none of the respondents was willing to risk violent confrontations with adults, even though fighting with other youths was common."

Respondents varied considerably, both within and between study neighborhoods, in the degree of emphasis they attributed to economic and noneconomic motives for engaging in their first crimes for money or property. Their accounts of these experiences differentiate them both from street fights, including those in which radios or other personal items were seized, and also from later and more sustained involvements in economic crime. Such statements as "that was about fighting, not stealing" in accounts of street fights clearly downplay the economic motive. In contrast, the accounts of sustained involvements in economic crime include constant evaluations of the risks and benefits of particular types of crime in relation both to other types and to legitimate jobs.

The Thrill Factor

Between these two extremes, accounts of first explorations of economic crime typically emphasized a certain amount of explicitly economic motivation combined with a search for excitement and the desire to establish a reputation among peers. This admixture of noneconomic motives in early economic crimes is evident in the field material from all three neighborhoods. A Projectville respondent who later became a frequent economic offender described his first experiences with shoplifting and purse snatching when he was fourteen.

> *Ben Bivins:* I used to be with guys a little older than me and we would go stealing.
>
> *Interviewer:* What was that like back then? What did you want the money for?
>
> *BB:* It wasn't so much the money then. It wasn't till I got older, say 'bout seventeen, and I wanted to buy clothes and impress females, that's when I started caring about the money. Back then, it was more like the excitement of it, plus, you got to make that reputation for yourself. . . .

The income motivation during early economic crimes appears to have been generally undeveloped; the excitement of doing the crime was at least as important as the profit to be gained from it. This early emphasis on thrills, despite the fact that most of these youths came from poor families, is not surprising when one considers their situation at the ages of fourteen and fifteen. At this point in their lives almost none of them had experienced earning a regular flow of income, legal or illegal. Even the Hamilton Park youths, whose parents were somewhat more affluent and who would themselves have access to a considerable amount of part-time work in their later teens, had not yet had much work. Nor were they expected to provide regular income to support basic subsistence. Even the youths from the poorest households in Projectville and La Barriada depended on their parents for food and shelter; though they knew need and deprivation, they experienced them as the children of impoverished parents.

Theft as Recreation

Under these circumstances, their initial economic crimes must be seen as responses to poverty in a dual sense. First, the income that they did derive was used to satisfy those personal needs beyond basic subsistence for which their parents could not provide. In fact, most of their early income, from whatever source, was spent on clothing and recreation. Second, the actual doing of the crime constituted a kind of recreation in environments with few recreational facilities and lots of boredom. Crime in the early teens was undertaken not as an easier or more lucrative income alternative to employment (which in any case was often unavailable) but rather as an alternative to hanging out day after day with no money at all.

> ***"Crime proved a viable way to make money at the same time that they were beginning to perceive a need for more regular income."***

The undeveloped nature of these youths' economic motivations is evident not only in their own evaluations of why they first committed thefts but also in the way they handled the proceeds. Many stole initially in order to enjoy direct use of the stolen objects. Stealing that took place in adolescent street fights, for example, usually involved the appropriation of youth culture consumer items—radios, bicycles, sneakers, coats—which were then as likely to be used directly as to be sold. Initial experiences with stealing cars were often for the purpose of joyriding. Some youths who snatched gold jewelry on the streets and subways did so initially in order to wear it themselves. Because they were usually unaware at this stage of the true worth of what they had stolen, they received only a fraction of what it was worth, even on the black market, if they did sell the merchandise.

"Youths found that they could sell the products of criminal enterprise with ease and virtually no risk."

After the first few experiences with economic crime, however, their motivations began to change. Few encountered serious sanctions as a result of their initial ventures. Crime proved a viable way to make money at the same time that they were beginning to perceive a need for more regular income. With continued involvement, the income motivation became steadily more important. Stealing for direct use gave way to conversion of stolen goods into cash. Once they learned what prices to expect for stolen goods, the risks and rewards associated with specific criminal opportunities were weighed against those associated with opportunities for other types of crime or for legitimate work.

At this point, the specific opportunity structure of each neighborhood environment began to channel exploratory criminal behavior into very distinctive patterns. Although the movement from stealing for thrills to stealing as part of a more sustained search for income was a common process in all three neighborhoods, both the extent of more sustained involvement and the particular types of criminal activity undertaken in each neighborhood were shaped by the local environment.

The Transition to Systematic Economic Crime

The variations between neighborhoods in opportunities for legitimate employment were one set of factors influencing the extent and type of developing involvements in economic crime. The greater availability of employment for the white youths of Hamilton Park was associated with lesser involvement in systematic economic crime, especially during the middle teen years. The Hamilton Park youths who did commit economic crimes tended not to commit the highly exposed and risky predatory street crimes in which many of the Projectville and La Barriada youths became involved.

Although neighborhood variations in employment opportunities influenced the propensity of local youths to engage in income-motivated crime, their actual participation derived from features of their local environments which combined to produce neighborhood-specific structures of illegal opportunity. The following neighborhood characteristics influenced the types and sequencing of opportunities for income-motivated crime, as reflected in the neighborhood-specific crime patterns of local cliques of youths.

Ecology. The physical ecology of the local neighborhoods defined a certain set of possibilities for and limits on illegal income opportunities for local youths. Since youths tend to commit crimes fairly close to the area with which they are familiar, especially during their earlier stages of involvement, ecology had a direct effect in terms of the sheer physical availability of crime targets—factories, stores, crowded shopping areas, unprotected pedestrian routes to and from transportation—and of empty lots and abandoned buildings to conceal stolen goods or car-stripping and drug-selling operations.

Ecology also reflected the social isolation of poor neighborhoods. The same residential areas that contained high proportions of burned-out blocks and abandoned buildings or were located near noxious industrial and transportation facilities were also characterized by a lack of services and of effective neighborhood organization to demand services. This isolation from municipal government and services affected the ability of local residents to control crime in their areas.

Local Markets for Illegal Goods and Services. Physical opportunities for economic crime do not elicit criminal behavior apart from a social atmosphere that validates and supports economic crime. The most pervasive social supports for youthful economic crime in the study neighborhoods were the markets for the illegal goods and services supplied by youths. Such markets played a crucial role in channeling exploratory ventures into more systematic economic crime. When youths found that they could sell the products of criminal enterprise with ease and virtually no risk, this discovery provided an early and crucial connection between their individual acts of income-motivated crime and a wider, reinforcing social context.

"Youths who worked for adults started off doing the riskiest jobs but faced the possibility of advancing to more sheltered and lucrative criminal roles."

Illegal Marketplaces

The organization of underground markets varied from one neighborhood to another, however, and this variation contributed to the specificity of local structures of illegal opportunity. Neighborhoods varied in how openly drugs and stolen goods could be sold on the street and in their particular combinations of diffuse and specialized markets. Some neighborhoods contained specialized fences for gold, auto parts, and other goods; all neighborhoods contained diffuse markets, based primarily on personal networks, in which youthful suppliers could sell illegal goods and services to ordinary residents buying for their own use. Certain neighborhoods or sections of a particular neighborhood were also known as marketplaces for stolen goods, drugs, gambling, and prostitution, attracting a large number of both suppliers and purchasers. These relatively open marketplaces were in some cases located on the borders of a residential area in which such activities could not be carried out so openly but which supplied clientele to the adjoining market areas.

Recruitment into Economic Crime

Social Organization of Criminal Operations. Few of the income-motivated crimes reported by youths in the study were carried out by one individual alone. Most youths operated with others in some kind of structured relationship, however rudimentary. Several aspects of the social organization of the actual criminal operations had significant implications for the types and sequencing of illegal opportunities within each neighborhood environment.

First, there were different *patterns of recruitment.* The major distinction was between recruitment by the adolescent peer group and recruitment by older or more established criminal entrepreneurs. Most youthful stealing was conceived within peer cliques and did not involve older people except as buyers of stolen goods. Involvements in such youthful predations lasted from a few weeks to two or three years but rarely continued unchanged once the participants reached their twenties. The pattern frequently reported was one in which youths in their middle teens learned from slightly older youths how to rob and steal just as the older youths were about to decrease or end their own involvement.

Though most youths were recruited into economic crime initially by other youths, some respondents did report being recruited by adults. This kind of recruitment characterized certain types of crime—specifically auto theft, drug selling, and organized gambling—and had much different implications for the career possibilities of the youths involved.

Second, associated with the difference in being recruited by peers or adults were differences in the importance of *vertical and horizontal lines of organization.* Youths working primarily with each other, though they might assume differentiated roles at some points, all faced roughly the same high level of risk and were forced to decrease or discontinue their predations as risks and sanctions mounted. In contrast, youths who worked for adults started off doing the riskiest jobs but faced the possibility of advancing to more sheltered and lucrative criminal roles. Horizontal relationships were also important at higher levels of criminal enterprise, as in the case of drug sellers who shared sources, clients, and information.

> ***"All these neighborhoods were characterized by patterns of noneconomic violence, and most males . . . knew how to use force."***

A third aspect of the social organization of crime is the *transmission of skills*. Although crimes committed by youths tend to be relatively unskilled and unspecialized, some individuals from each neighborhood clique emerged as more successful than their peers at types of crime that many of them had attempted. The more successful individuals could attribute their success to special abilities and cite specific reasons for the failures of their peers.

Criminal Skills

Two broad categories of skills were significant: manual skills, which are important in burglary and car theft, and social skills, which are important in drug dealing and in working with others generally. Those who claimed such skills also acknowledged learning them from older or more experienced individuals. Skill acquisition was particularly important in criminal operations that included vertical lines of organization and possibilities for career advancement. Those who aspired to such advancement displayed a keen awareness of the need to learn the requisite skills.

A fourth aspect is *the role and management of violence*. Since the ability to employ violence is a third kind of criminal "skill," both the propensity of an individual to engage in a crime and his ability to continue engaging in it had much to do with that crime's requirements for the use of violence. The kind of crime that a local neighborhood would tolerate also had a great deal to do with the type and amount of violence involved: robbery, which automatically involves the use or threat of violence, was the most universally unacceptable crime in each of the study neighborhoods. Larceny and burglary, however, also involve the potential for violent encounters with the police or with a victim. Some youths started selling drugs because doing so did not involve violent predations, yet the potential for violent encounters with predators or competitors is very high with protracted involvement in the drug world. As noted earlier, all these neighborhoods were characterized by patterns of noneconomic violence, and most males in these neighborhoods knew how to use force. The role of violence in the types of economic crime they undertook and their ability to manage it, however, were crucial factors in determining how long they could continue to be involved in systematic economic crime. The indiscriminate use of violence led inevitably to arrest or retaliation; the ability to employ it effectively without upsetting business required nerve and judgment that most often came with experience. Older individuals who had acquired such experience thus had a broader range of opportunities for economic crime.

Drug Use Can Cause Youth Violence

by James A. Inciardi

About the author: *James A. Inciardi is a professor and the director of the division of criminal justice at the University of Delaware in Newark. Inciardi is the editor of the 1991 book* The Drug Legalization Debate.

Given the recent concerns over the perceived rising rates of drug-related violence in many inner-city neighborhoods across the nation, this analysis focuses on the various types of violence associated with crack use and crack distribution in Dade County (Miami), FL. The data are drawn from a National Institute on Drug Abuse (NIDA)-funded study of adolescent drug users conducted from 1985 to 1988, with followup interviews during 1989 with crack users and dealers in Miami's inner-city communities.

Serious Delinquents and Drug Abuse

In 1985, few people nationally had ever heard of crack cocaine, but it was already a problem in Miami and Dade County. Awareness of this problem permitted crack to be included in the drug history section of a planned interview schedule for a street study of adolescent drug use and crime. The focus of the research was not crack per se but rather the drug-taking and drug-seeking behaviors of some 600 Miami youths who were "seriously delinquent." *Serious delinquency* was defined as having committed, during the 12-month period prior to interview, no less than 10 FBI "Index" offenses [homicide, rape, assault, robbery, burglary, larceny/theft, motor vehicle theft, and arson], or 100 lesser crimes. A second criteria for inclusion in the study was the regular use of one or more illegal drugs at any time during the 90-day period prior to interview. *Regular drug use* was defined as use at least three times a week.

One of the rationales for the study, which is of particular importance for this technical review on drugs and violence, is that most systematic studies of delin-

From James A. Inciardi, "The Crack-Violence Connection Within a Population of Hard-Core Adolescent Offenders," in *Drugs and Violence: Causes, Correlates, and Consequences.* NIDA Research Monograph 103. National Institute on Drug Abuse, U.S. Department of Health and Human Services, 1990.

quency have focused on representative populations of either adolescents in general or juvenile offenders in particular. Although these investigations have provided the research community with important data on issues relating to drugs, delinquency, and youth crime, little has been generated that is descriptive of the extremely hard-core populations of adolescent drug-using criminals. This study was specifically designed to reach a segment of that population. Moreover, it is in such a population that high levels of drug-related violence are most likely.

Demographics of Hard-Core Adolescents

Research subjects were located through multiple-starting-point "snowball sampling" techniques in Miami and Dade County neighborhoods where drug use and crime rates were high. During the data collection phase of the study, a total of 611 youths meeting the selection criteria were contacted and interviewed. Some 83.6 percent were males, and 16.4 percent were females; 41.4 percent were white, 42.2 percent were black, and 16.4 percent were Hispanic. Although blacks (who make up 15 percent of the Dade County population) are overrepresented in the sample, and Hispanics (44 percent of the Dade County population) are considerably underrepresented, this racial-ethnic distribution is not unlike that found in other studies of the Miami drug scene. These 611 youths had a mean age of 15 years, with the largest proportion in the 16-to-17-year cohort. Although 71 percent were still attending school at the time of interview, 537 or 87.9 percent had been either suspended or expelled from school at least once, with such disciplinary actions typically resulting from drug use or drug sales on school premises. Finally, whereas only 1.3 percent of these youths were living alone, 521 or 85.3 percent were living with one or more members of their own family.

All of the youths interviewed had extensive histories of multiple drug use with identifiable patterns of onset and progression. They began their drug-using careers at [mean] age 7.6 years with alcohol experimentation, followed by their first alcohol intoxication more than a year later. Experimentation with marijuana began at age 10.4 years, with the regular use (three or more times a week) of both marijuana (100 percent of the sample) and alcohol (53.7 percent of the sample) within a year thereafter. Experimentation with cocaine, speed, heroin, and prescription depressants occurred during the 12th year, with 93.3 percent moving on to the regular use of cocaine by age 13. Their first use of crack cocaine occurred at a mean age of 13.6 years, and, by age 14, 85.6 percent of the sample considered themselves to be regular users of the drug.

> ***"All of the youths interviewed had extensive histories of multiple drug use."***

It would appear from the data that the criminal careers of these 611 youths emerged more or less in tandem with their drug-using careers. Their first crimes occurred at a mean age of 11 years. Notably, more than 90 percent had engaged in drug sales and thefts before age 12, and 64 percent had participated in a robbery by age 13. In addition, 90 percent had histories of arrest and 45.5 percent had been incarcerated; however, only 13.4 percent reported any substance abuse treatment.

Current Drug Use and Crime

All of the youths in this population were daily users of at least one drug. Marijuana was used three or more times a week by 95 percent of the sample, 64.2 percent used some form of cocaine daily, and all but 9 percent used at least one coca product (powder cocaine, crack cocaine, or coca paste) three or more times a week. By contrast, the use of speed or heroin was relatively uncommon. Only 3.9 percent of the sample reported using heroin daily.

[There are] a number of interesting insights into the criminal activity of these youths. Unquestionably, their criminal involvement is considerable. They reportedly perpetrated some 429,136 criminal acts during the 12-month-period prior to interview—an average of 702 offenses per subject. Although this figure might seem astronomical at first glance, analysis indicates that the majority of offenses are clustered in what are often referred to as "drug related" and other "less serious" crime. For example, some 59.9 percent were "drug business" offenses—the manufacture, transportation, and sale of drugs. Manufacture typically involved the small-scale production of crack for either personal use or for street-level sale. Transportation involved the delivery of drugs (typically crack) from dealers and crack houses to customers, the steering of customers to dealers, or the communication of customers' orders to dealers and crack houses. Sales were almost exclusively in small rather than bulk amounts. In addition, some 10.2 percent of the offenses involved prostitution or pimping, 11.6 percent were individual incidents of shoplifting, and 11.1 percent were stolen-goods offenses. As such, a total of 92.8 percent of these 429,136 offenses involved drug law violations, vice, shoplifting, and dealing in stolen property.

> ***"Some 88.4 percent of the sample reported carrying weapons most or all of the time, and more than half of these carried handguns."***

This should not suggest, however, that these youths do not commit serious crimes. The sheer volume of their criminal acts suggests that they do. They were responsible for some 18,477 major felonies. Among these felonies were 6,269 robberies and 721 assaults. Although the majority of these robberies were purse snatches, a significant number were armed robberies in homes, shops, and on the street. In fact, some 88.4 percent of the sample reported carrying weapons most or all of the time, and more than half of these carried handguns.

The general relationship between drugs and violence within this population can be examined within the context of P.J. Goldstein's (1985) conceptual framework of the psychopharmacological, economic compulsive, and systemic models of violence.

> ***"It doesn't seem to matter whether you're on or off crack . . . you're crazy both times. . . . A lot of people been cut just because somebody looked at them funny."***

Psychopharmacological Violence. The psycholopharmacological model of violence suggests that some individuals, as the resut of short-term or long-term use of certain drugs may become excitable, irrational, and exhibit violent behavior. Of the sample, 5.4 percent reported involvement in this form of violence at least once during the 12-month period prior to interview. Interestingly, only 4.6 percent reported being the victims of psychopharmacological violence during this same period. In either case, the impatience and irritability associated with drug withdrawal or the paranoia and edginess associated with stimulant abuse were the typical causes of this behavior. During mid-1989, a 17-year-old daily crack user summed up both situations:

> It doesn't seem to matter whether you're on or off crack . . . you're crazy both times. If you're high, you think someone's goin' ta do something to you, or try an' take your stuff. If you're comin' down or are waiting to make a buy or just get off, you seem to get upset easy . . . A lot of people been cut just because somebody looked at them funny or said somethin' stupid.

Economic Compulsive Violence. The economic compulsive model of violence holds that some drug users engage in economically oriented violent crimes to support their costly drug use. 59.1 percent of the sample (n=361) participated in 6,669 robberies during the 12-month period prior to interview, the majority of which were committed to purchase drugs. In addition, whereas 24.1 percent of the sample indicated that they had robbed drugs from users or dealers, 39.9 percent reported that they had been the victims of a drug robbery.

Systemic Violence

Systemic Violence. The systemic model of violence maintains that violent crime is intrinsic to involvement with any illicit substance. Systemic violence refers to the traditionally aggressive patterns of interaction within the systems and networks of illegal drug trafficking and distribution. According to this definition, 9.0 percent of the sample reported being victims of systemic violence, and 8.3 percent were perpetrators of such violence. Typically, violence emerged in this population from fights resulting from territorial disputes, the sale of poor quality drugs, and "messing up the money." To this can be added the execution in 1987 of two crack user-dealers in Miami's Liberty City community who were suspected to be police informants. As the reported perpetrator of these homicides indicated:

> I'm not sayin' when I did it, how I did it, or where I did it. But I will say why. Because they were cheatin', lyin'—, takin' money from cops and sellin' out . . . So I was told to teach 'em a good lesson, and make a good example of 'em.

. . . [There is] a clear relationship between a youth's proximity to the crack market and his or her overall position in the street worlds of drug use and crime, *including violent crime*. It would appear, for example, that the more involved a youth is in crack distribution, the younger he or she first committed a crime, was first arrested, and was convicted and incarcerated. For example, whereas youths with *no* involvement in the crack business first used drugs at a mean age of 12.6 years, committed their first crime at 11.7 years, experienced their first arrest at 12.8 years, and were first incarcerated at 14.2 years, the corresponding mean ages for these same events in the dealer+ group were 10.6, 10.3, 11.1, and 12.8, respectively. Moreover, the nearer the proximity to the crack market, the higher the likelihood of an early history of a first arrest resulting in incarceration.

The Crack Business

In terms of the extent of criminal involvement during 1 year prior to interview, once again, those more involved in crack distribution had greater levels of crime commission. As indicated in [the] table, for example, greater proportions of those closely tied to the crack business were involved in major felonies and property offenses than those more distant from the crack trades. The major exception to this pattern involved the vice offenses, due primarily to the extremely small proportions of females in the sample.

The most important items in the discussion of [the] table relate to violence—robberies and assaults. In this regard, those more proximal to the crack distribution market were more involved in violent crime. Moreover, those in the dealer and dealer+ [drug manufacturers, smugglers, or wholesalers] groups committed more violent crimes on a per capita basis than those in the "none" and "minor" groups. Specifically, the mean number of robberies committed by the four groups were as follows: none (6.8), minor (5.6), dealer (13.9), and dealer+ (18.2).

> ***"Those more proximal to the crack distribution market were more involved in violent crime."***

These data address a number of points about the relationships between crack, crime, and violence in Miami and perhaps elsewhere. In particular, recent media reports appear to be correct in their assessment of the involvement of youth in crack distribution and violent crime as significant trends in some locales. These reports, however, may be overreporting some aspects of the crack-violence connection while underreporting others, yet, at the same time, profoundly underestimating the significance of the whole crack-crime connection.

Crack and Criminal Activity

Criminal activity during the 12-month period prior to interview among Miami and Dade County hard-core adolescent offenders (percentage involved).

Offense	Crack Business Involvement None (n=50)	Minor (n=20)	Dealer (n=138)	Dealer+ (n=46)	Total Sample (n=254)
Major Felonies	44.0	65.0	87.7	95.7	78.7
Robbery	12.0	40.0	66.7	73.9	55.1
Assault	4.0	0.0	8.0	17.4	8.3
Burglary	24.0	25.0	70.3	91.3	61.4
Motor Vehicle Theft	30.0	35.0	57.2	73.9	53.1
Property Offenses*	94.0	95.0	100.0	100.0	98.4
Shoplifting	90.0	95.0	100.0	100.0	97.6
Theft from Vehicle	34.0	30.0	75.4	84.8	65.4
Pickpocketing	2.0	5.0	13.0	10.9	9.8
Prostitute's Theft	8.0	5.0	20.3	4.3	13.8
Other Larcenies	4.0	0.0	0.7	0.0	1.2
Con Games	6.0	5.0	53.6	63.0	42.1
Forgery (any)	10.0	5.0	60.1	73.9	48.4
Stolen Goods	76.0	85.0	94.9	97.8	90.9
Property Destruction	16.0	0.0	35.5	34.8	28.7
Other Crimes	0.0	0.0	0.7	0.0	0.4
Vice Offenses	18.0	5.0	33.3	17.4	25.2
Prostitution	18.0	5.0	22.5	6.5	17.3
Procuring	4.0	5.0	30.4	15.2	20.5
Drug Business (Any Drug)	86.0	100.0	100.0	100.0	97.2

*Forgery (any) = checks, credit cards, and prescriptions; stolen goods = selling, trading, and buying to resell; property destruction includes arson but is almost entirely vandalism.

First, whereas media reports suggest that homicide is a concomitant of crack distribution among inner-city youths, this may not be the case in Miami and Dade County. Moreover, much of the current focus on crack-related violence may be more the result of a media event than an emergent trend. . . .

Although crack distribution by hard-core adolescent offenders in Miami may not reflect the gang-related violence that has been suggested in Los Angeles, it is nevertheless highly criminogenic. As the data in this paper have demonstrated, young crack dealers commonly violate not merely drug laws, but also those protecting persons and property.

Youth Gangs Cause Violence

by Léon Bing

About the author: *Léon Bing, a former fashion model, is a journalist and the author of* Do or Die, *an insider account of teenage gangs in Los Angeles.*

He is seventeen years old, and he is homeless. I met him through one of his homeboys on whose couch he has been sleeping for the past week. This is how he lives, from couch to couch, or in a sleeping bag, or in the back seat of a parked car. A couple of days in one place, maybe two weeks in another. He does not remember the last time he went to school, and he does not know how to read or write. He is as close to invisibility as it is possible to be.

The reason he's talking is because his friend has vouched for me. We are in my car because I have to run some errands, and I want to save time, so I have decided to take this kid—Faro—along. He sits next to me, looking out the window. His mouth is slightly open, and I can see that his teeth are small and straight. The tip of his tongue is almost, but not quite, the exact shade of raspberry sherbet. His hair has been sectioned into a myriad of tiny braids, each with a blue rubber band at the tip. He is wearing shabby sweats and busted-down Nike high-tops. He is very thin; the bones of his wrists stick knobbily out of the elastic cuffs of his hooded jacket, which is at least two sizes too small for him.

We ride in silence for a while, and then I ask him about his family. It takes him a long time to answer, and when he does, his voice is soft, controlled.

Senseless Deaths

"My mother, she died from a drug overdose. I got a grandmother, but she gonna go the same way—she just wanderin' the streets day and night, lookin' for handouts so she can fix herself a pipe. My brother got killed in a holdup three years ago."

I ask which end of the gun his brother was at, and Faro looks at me in surprise. It is the first time we have made any kind of eye contact. He has sixty-year-old eyes set down in that seventeen-year-old face. Graveyard eyes.

"Most people think he was holdin' the gun." He almost smiles; it is a pained expression. "He wasn't but eight years old. He was lookin' at comic books in a 7-Eleven and some dude come in to rob the place." He turns away to look out the window. "The homies give him a nice funeral. I used to have a picture of him, laid out, in my scrapbook. It got lost.". . .

"We was in a car, all homies, and I was like, 'Let's pop this dumb nigger, let's empty the whole clip in him.'"

We pass a group of little kids, five- and six-year-olds, walking in line behind their teacher. As they get to the corner, the teacher raises both arms in readiness to cross the street, signaling for the children to do the same. All of them lift their arms high over their heads, like holdup victims, following the teacher to the other side.

"I watch out for the little kids in my neighborhood. So gangs who we don't get along with"—he names several sets, both Bloods and Crips—"don't come in and shoot 'em up. All them I just named, they come in and shoot us up, then we catch one of 'em slippin' and it's all over for them."

He is looking at the children as he talks. His voice is soft, but somehow it is not calm.

"Like there was this fool, this enemy nigger from our worst enemy set, and he was with his wife and his baby. They was walkin' down there near Vermont, where he had no business bein'. He was slippin' bad and we caught him. We was in a car, all homies, and I was like, 'Let's pop this dumb nigger, let's empty the whole clip in him.'" Faro turns to look at me, as if he wants to make sure I understand what he is saying. "We had an AK—two-barrel banana clips, two sides—and I just . . .". He hesitates only for an instant. "I just wanted to make him pay."

Killing an Enemy

Careful to keep my voice as soft as his, I ask him what it was he wanted the guy to pay for.

"For all our dead homeboys. For bein' our enemy. For slippin' so bad." He is warming to his subject, his voice is coming alive now. "You gotta understand—enemy got to pay just for bein' alive." He is quiet for a moment, then he gives a little hitch of his shoulders, like a prizefighter, and he goes on. He is animated now, reliving the event for me. "I was like 'fuck it, Cuz—I'm gonna strap this shit to the seat and I'm just gonna *work* it.'" He twists around to face the passenger door and mimes the action of holding and aiming an AK-47 rifle. "So I strapped it to the seat, like this, and we circled around and pulled up on this nigger from two blocks away, crept up on him slow like, and I just gave it to him." Faro begins to jerk and buck there in his seat as the imaginary weapon in his hands fires automatically. "*Pah-pah-pah-pah-pah-pah-pah!* You know, just let him have it. Just emptied the whole . . .". He is wholly caught up in his recollection, inflamed with it, drunk with it. "I lit his ass *up!* I killed him—shot his baby in the leg—crippled his wife!" He is facing me again, his eyes fixed on some point just to the left of mine. "She in a wheelchair now, I heard, wearin' a voicebox, 'cause one of the bullets caught her in the throat." Then, in afterthought, "The baby okay."

We are silent for a moment; when Faro speaks again his voice is a fusion of bad feelings: despair, remorse, a deep, biting resentment. "I just lit his whole family up and. . . ." He sucks in air, holds it a couple of seconds, puffs it out. "It was like, damn, Cuz—I killed him, that was my mission, but still—his whole family." He shakes his head several times, as if he cannot will himself to believe his own story. Then he places the tip of one index finger on the glass next to him and taps it in a nervous, rhythmic beat. "That's a crazy world out there, and we livin' in it."

"If people in yo' family is just dyin', if the person you love the most, the person who love* you *the most be dead, then what else* do *you got to live for?"

"Dying in it, too."

The finger stops tapping.

"If you die, you die. Most gangbangers don't have nothin' to live for no more, anyway. That why some of 'em be gangbangin'."

He seems to sense what it is that I'm thinking.

"I ain't just talkin' 'bout myself, either. I'm talkin' for a lotta gangbangers. They mothers smokin' dope. Or somebody shot somebody else's mother, and that person figure if they gangbang they got a chance to get 'em back." He is silent again for a beat or two. Then, "People don't have nothin' to live for if they mother dead, they brother dead, they sister dead. What else they got to live for? If people in yo' family is just dyin', if the person you love the most, the person who love *you* the most be dead, then what else *do* you got to live for?"

"Yourself."

It's as if I hadn't spoken; he doesn't even hear me.

"I tell you this—you see enough dyin', then you be ready to die yourself, just so you don't have to see no more of death.". . .

Hard Lessons in Gang Class

"Okay—this is Gang Class. There's no sidebusting in here. Anything said in this room stays here. There will be no disrespecting anyone else's neighborhood. No sign-throwing. O.G.'s [a respected gang member] will help new members." A.C. Jones is speaking; he presides over this course, Gang Class, which is held once a week at Camp Kilpatrick [a Los Angeles juvenile detention camp]. The boys assigned to the class are considered hardcore gang members, and tonight there are nineteen students in the room. G-Roc [Gangster Roc, an interviewee] is one of them.

Jones moves across the room to pull down the shades at the windows and over the pane of reinforced glass cut into the door. This classroom is like the others I have seen: the desks are brightly painted and unscarred by graffiti; there are posters of the solar system, a chart of the human body, and large drawings of the four food groups on the walls. Books are neatly arranged on the bookshelves and, on a ledge under the windows, there are glass tanks that contain some of the wildlife indigenous to the area: a couple of lizards, a land tortoise, a tarantula.

Gang Class is a ten-week course in which each boy must accumulate two hundred merit points. Homework is assigned each week, and every completed task is worth twenty points. Last week the students were told to write their own obituaries along with a letter to their mothers explaining why it was necessary for them to die for their gangs.

When a boy has successfully completed Mr. Jones's class, he is allowed to make the choice of leaving it or staying on as an O.G. If he decides to stay, he is expected to act as an unofficial counselor for the newer kids in the class. There are five of these O.G.'s here this evening.

"Because he said somethin' wrong and now you gotta smoke him for it, right?"

Mr. Jones picks up a piece of chalk and writes, in large block letters, a single word on the blackboard: KILL.

The room goes very quiet; the only sound you can hear at this moment is the muted shuffling of feet under the desks. Mr. Jones faces his audience and waits for complete silence before he speaks.

Why Gang Members Kill

"Okay, y'all know what that word means. Now I want each of you to give me a real good reason to kill somebody."

The words are barely out of his mouth when hands begin to jab the air. Jones nods at one of the kids.

"For the fuck of it."

Jones turns back to the blackboard, writes those words. "Okay, 'for the fuck of it.' Let's have another reason."

"Put in work for the 'hood."

Jones writes again. "Okay, that's a good reason. Next?"

" 'Cause he's my enemy."

"Yeah, that's righteous." Jones prints quickly. "An enemy."

"For revenge."

"Yeah, let's get that one down, that's a good one. Revenge." The chalk screeches against the board.

"If y'all can kill for something, y'all better be ready to die for it."

" 'Cause he said somethin' wrong."

"You mean like dis' you?"

"Naw. Just wrong—like, you know, *wrong*."

"Yeah, okay. Because he said somethin' wrong and now you gotta smoke him for it, right?"

"Ye-eeeeeeeeeh." The kid slouches back in his chair, grinning. He is clearly well pleased with himself for having made his thoughts so perfectly understood. Jones writes the words on the board, then turns back to face the kids. "Come on—let's get some reasons up here. Y'all supposed to be such tough dudes. Let's go."

Gang Members Respond

Now the answers begin to come quickly.

" 'Cause he look at me funny, give me that mad-dog look."

" 'Cause I don't like him."

" 'Cause he asked me where I was from."

" 'Cause he wearin' the wrong color."

" 'Cause he gonna hurt a member of my family."

"For money."

Jones is nodding his head, scribbling furiously on the blackboard.

"So I can jack somebody for dope."

" 'Cause he give me no respect."

" 'Cause he a disgrace, he a buster."

"For his car."

" 'Cause he try to get with my lady."

" 'Cause he a transformer [a spy] in my 'hood."

"In self-defense."

" 'Cause he try to jack you—take yo' shit."

"For a nickel."

"For the way he walk."

"If he got somethin' I want and he don't wanna give it to me."

" 'Cause I'm a loc."

"For his association."

" 'Cause he called me a baboon—dis' me."

" 'Cause he fucked with my food—you know, like took one of my French fries or somethin'."

" 'Cause I don't like his attitude."

" 'Cause he say the wrong thing—he wolf me."

" 'Cause I'm buzzed—you know, all like, high and bent."

"Just playin' around."

" 'Cause he fucked up my hair in the barber shop."

Jones chuckles as he writes down this one. "Fucked up your hair, huh? Well, I can understand that."

And still the reasons to kill keep coming.

" 'Cause he a snitch."

" 'Cause he hit up my wall, crossin' out names and shit, writin' R.I.P."

"If a lady don't give me what I want. You know—the wild thing."

" 'Cause they ugly."

" 'Cause he try to run a drag [a con] on me."

All of the reasons are up on the board now, in three neatly lettered rows. Mr. Jones steps back, surveying the list for a moment, nodding his head. Then he turns to look at the kids again.

Reasons to Die For

"Okay. Now. Which of this shit would you die for?" There is a beat of utter silence; the air seems to shimmer with the combined stares of shocked students. Jones stands quietly, staring back at them. "Oh, come on, now. If y'all can kill for something, y'all better be ready to die for it. So let's hear it: which of these reasons you gonna die for?"

> ***"It isn't just killing another person for the hell of it that is the subject here."***

One of the kids pipes up. "Hell, you can erase *all* that shit."

"No, let's go point by point, see what we got here. Okay, who's gonna die 'for the fuck of it'?"

Five hands go up. An Essay [Hispanic] kid, he's one of the newest members of the class, wants to talk about it. "It would be like when you play Russian roulette, you know? Like if I got nothing else to do, because I'm bored."

Mr. Jones does not hesitate to put a finer point on it, "But that would be suicide, killing yourself, wouldn't it?"

The kid doesn't see it that way—the original premise was "reasons to *kill*"—"it didn't say nothing about who." Now, surprisingly, it is one of the other students, one of the five kids who also raised his hand to defend this reason to kill someone, who argues with the Essay kid, telling him how wrong he is.

"We ain't talkin' about killin' yo'self here, fool—we talkin' about smokin' somebody else just for the fuck of it. You got the heart to kill somebody else?" The Essay kid assures him that he does. Now Mr. Jones interrupts to explain that it isn't just killing another person for the hell of it that is the subject here.

He reminds the students that in killing the stranger, they must also die. That's the deal in this instance. You kill—for whatever reason—you die. The five hands that were raised go back down. The words "for the fuck of it" are erased from the blackboard.

Wearing the Wrong Color

As are the other reasons. There are some arguments, of course: "Putting in work for the 'hood" and "revenge" get some people yelling. But as Mr. Jones reads the reasons aloud, one by one, the show of hands gets smaller. Until he gets to "wearing the wrong color." Then every hand in the room thrusts into the air. Every kid here is willing to die for red or blue—the Essays are adamant about this one too.

We are at the heart of gangbanging.

Jones holds up both hands for silence. "Okay, I want y'all to listen hard and go along with this: I'm a madman with a fully loaded 'gauge. You all naked, sittin' there in yo' chairs with nothin' on. But they's some clothes *under* the chairs—three pairs of pants to choose from: pair of blue pants, pair of red pants, pair of white pants. Now—anyone puts on any color but white"—he hoists the imaginary shotgun, squints down the barrel—"Booyah! You dead." He turns, aiming dead center on a kid's chest. "What color pants you gonna put on?"

The kid's eyes move quickly around the room—everybody is waiting. He licks his lips, "Red pa . . ."

"Booyah!" Jones swings toward another kid.

"Bl . . ."

"Booyah!" Jones shakes his head. "Maybe y'all didn't hear me. I'm a madman, I don't care about no loyalty. I just don't like any color but white, makes me mad if somebody don't like it, too. Mad enough to kill you." He nods at a kid who has his hand up. It's G-Roc.

"But if I choose the white pants instead of my set's color, that make me a buster."

The other boys nod their heads vigorously. Jones smiles sweetly.

"And if you put on the blue or the red, what does that make you?"

> ***"Every kid here is willing to die for red or blue."***

G-Roc shrugs.

"Make you dead for no other reason but a madman's whim. You R.I.P. because he like white pants. Now, how many of you gonna die for that?"

The kid persists. "Yeah, but if I do put on yo' color, I'm just a punk."

"No. I just like white. I don't care about no blue, no red, no pink, no green. I just like white."

G-Roc shrugs. "Okay. I'll put on the white." But he's not happy about it; you can see it all over his face.

"Anybody else gonna die for the red or the blue?"

No hands.

Jones erases the words "wearing the wrong color." Then he turns back to look at the kids again. "Lemme tell you somethin'—you can be down for your 'hood, you can go to jail for your 'hood, you can die for your 'hood. And if you do, if you die, you know what happens? *Nothing.* Nothing changes. The beat goes on. All your dead homeboys? Even *they* don't mean diddly. Because nothing changes."

"Everybody—even you—are afraid of abnormal people. Abnormal just don't make it."

Jones reads off the rest of the reasons that are still on the board. There is no show of hands, until he gets to the words "for his association." This was G-Roc's reason, and he is implacable now: he will kill and he will die because he does not approve of another person's allegiance. When Jones attempts to reason with him, he simply shakes his head, over and over. He remains unmoved even in the face of argument from a couple of the O.G.'s. The only thing that he will say is, "Y'all don't know me."

Finally only three reasons to kill—and to die—are left up there on the blackboard. There is "for his association," with one vote next to it, and there are "for my family" and "self-defense," both of which got a unanimous show of hands.

Now Jones clears the board entirely. Then he puts another word up there: IRRATIONAL.

"Who's heard this word? Irrational."

No hands. Jones writes again, two words this time. NORMAL. SPRUNG.

"How about these?"

Some hands go up. Jones gives the nod to one of the O.G.'s.

"Normal means like regular."

"That's right. And 'sprung'?" He points to another kid.

"It mean nutty."

"Right. And that's what that first word means—irrational. Irrational means sprung." Jones leans back against the desk, crossing both arms against his chest. "Most normal people have a kill-die equation. What that means is if your mother prays at church every Sunday at the Ebenezer Tabernacle and somebody threatens her children, she will kill or die for them. Fathers too. That's what protecting the family is about. Self-defense and protecting your family is a normal kill-die equation. "

Gangs Induce Public Fear

The kids are listening hard now; Jones goes on. "At the beginning of class we were some abnormal, sprung motherfuckers." A mild laugh ripples through the room. "That's what people think about gang members—they will kill people for any damn thing. That's what people look at. If you decide to be normal, you have to be willing to kill only for that thing you are willing to die for. If you get to that point, you gonna make it—you won't be the kind of person whose numbers are so fucked up that I want him in the penitentiary forever. Forever. Because his numbers are too fucked up."

One of the younger kids—the one who was ready to kill the barber for a less than satisfactory haircut—pipes up.

"How many numbers was up on that blackboard?"

"Y'all gave thirty-seven reasons to kill."

The kid shakes his head. "Thirty-seven's a bigass number."

"Yeah, it is. And if you got more than two for two, then you're the kind of person other people are afraid of. People are afraid of you if you're abnormal."

Jones nudges his head forward a fraction. "Want to get respect? You don't gotta kiss nobody's ass, you don't have to smack, you don't have to talk white. Just be a normal motherfucker. Because everybody—even you—are afraid of abnormal people. Abnormal just don't make it."

The kid who thought that thirty-seven was a bigass number nods his head solemnly. "It don't make no sense."

"That's right. It don't make no sense."

Bigotry Causes Youths to Commit Hate Crimes

by Los Angeles County Commission on Human Relations

About the author: *The Los Angeles County Commission on Human Relations is an agency that works to improve community human relations by reducing prejudice, as well as discrimination based on race, religion, sex, age, and other factors.*

In March 1989, copies of a survey on school hate crime were distributed to all schools in Los Angeles County. This project was a joint endeavor by the Los Angeles County Commission on Human Relations and the Los Angeles County Office of Education, and was designed to assess the level of interethnic conflict and hate crime on K-12 campuses.

Of the 1,570 surveys distributed, 956, or 61 percent were returned. Of these, 354 schools responded that they had had incidents of hate crime, and 602 responded negatively. Overall, 37 percent of these schools responding to the survey had incidents of hate crime during the school year.

Hate Crime

The victims of school hate crime and related incidents differ from their adult counterparts, as described in the Commission's *Hate Crime in Los Angeles County* reports. In the adult population, Blacks were far and away the largest number of ethnic targets. This contrasts with school incidents, which show slightly more anti-Latino incidents than anti-Black incidents. Anti-White incidents were the next most prevalent group reported by schools, which occur very infrequently in the adult population.

Immigrant students were also at substantial risk, accounting for almost one-quarter of all incidents. And, if the students were Asian or Latino, the risk was even greater: about one-half of all anti-Asian incidents and one-third of all anti-Latino incidents were described as anti-immigrant in nature. Gay and Lesbian

From Los Angeles County Commission on Human Relations, *Intergroup Conflict in Los Angeles County Schools: Report on a Survey of Hate Crime*, October 1989. Reprinted with permission.

students and Jewish students also accounted for a significant number of victims.

Differences also occurred between the types of incidents directed against school employees and those against students, as well as among the types of discipline invoked for such acts. Hostility among students occurred more frequently than against employees. Racial slurs were the most common student actions, followed by physical violence and, much further down the scale, graffiti, destruction of property and miscellaneous other acts.

"Overall, 37 percent of . . . schools responding to the survey had incidents of hate crime during the school year."

Against employees, racial slurs and name-calling were also most frequently reported, followed by graffiti and destruction of personal belongings. Physical violence against school employees, while reported by a substantially lower number of schools than that directed toward students, was still reported by a surprisingly high 22 schools.

Perhaps because incidents against school employees were viewed as being an attack on authority as well as bigotry-related, they tended to receive more severe penalties than those between students. . . .

Survey Findings

1. Surveys were sent to all 1,570 schools in the County, and 61 percent of all schools responded. Of those schools responding, over one-third reported incidents of hate crime against students and employees.

2. Junior high schools and middle schools were somewhat more likely to be the site of hate crimes than high schools. Elementary schools had the lowest reported incidence of all sites.

3. An analysis was done of hate crime incidents both to determine the total number committed against specific groups and number of schools reporting incidents against a group. Anti-Latino incidents were the greatest in number; anti-Black incidents occurred at the greatest number of schools. Whites were the third largest victim group.

4. Nearly one-third of all anti-Latino incidents and one-half of all anti-Asian incidents were attributed to anti-immigrant sentiment. This is in contrast to the adult population, where proportionately few anti-immigrant incidents are reported. This finding reinforces the Commission's perception that adult immigrants are frequently the victims of hate crime, but it goes unreported.

5. Gay and Lesbian students were at substantial risk. Even given their relative invisibility, there were still 65 individual incidents directed toward them.

6. Individuals associated with hate groups themselves commit a relatively low percentage of hate crimes (4.5 percent). Their presence, however, seems to indicate (or contribute to) a more intolerant environment: of the schools that re-

ported incidents of hate crime, 14 percent had seen evidence of White supremacist groups on their campus, as opposed to the schools with no incidents, of whom only 5 percent had experienced the presence of such groups.

7. In the majority of instances where students were the victims of hate crime, perpetrators were counseled and returned to class. In the majority of instances where a school employee was the victim, perpetrators were suspended. For both groups, subsequent referral to parents, followed by referral to law enforcement, were the next most common actions taken.

8. Hate crime against school employees does occur. However, it occurred at only 6.3 percent of responding schools, indicating that it is less prevalent than incidents between students. . . .

Reason for the Survey

In 1980, the Los Angeles County Commission on Human Relations began compiling statistics on criminal acts motivated by racial and religious bigotry. Now, in addition to annually collecting data and publishing a report to the Board of Supervisors, the Commission investigates individual cases, provides victim referrals, and develops preventive programs in connection with all forms of "hate crime."

Throughout the years, the Commission has received a limited number of reports of school-based hate crime, usually perpetrated by an outside adult. In recent years, however, reports of increased conflict between students themselves have begun to surface.

> ***"Currently, public awareness of hate crime perpetrators is expanding to include adolescents and young adults."***

Currently, public awareness of hate crime perpetrators is expanding to include adolescents and young adults, with much recent news coverage focused on interethnic conflict on college campuses. Yet, little or no information is available on incidents at the primary and secondary level, where the attitudes are formed that will manifest themselves later in adult behavior.

Given this lack of information, the Commission approached the Los Angeles County Office of Education in November 1987 about the feasibility of a joint project. The Office of Education, sharing the Commission's concern about the need for better information and resources, enthusiastically embraced the program and dedicated substantial amounts of personnel and time to the project. . . .

The Commission on Human Relations defines hate crime as any criminal act, committed against an individual or institution, motivated by bigotry based on race, ethnicity, religion, or sexual orientation. This definition is shared by most local law enforcement agencies and other organizations which respond to hate crime. Thus, the use of racial slurs and name calling, although reprehensible, is not a hate crime. However, because such acts occur so frequently on campuses, because they often reflect serious intergroup tension, and because they may lead to vandalism or assault, the Commission includes these acts in this report of hate-related incidents.

Who Are the Victims?

Racial. Across the board, more schools reported anti-Black incidents than any other type (168 schools). The second largest number of individual incidents was also directed against Blacks (624), exceeded only by anti-Latino incidents.

These findings are disturbing in light of the relatively small number of Black students enrolled in Los Angeles County schools. In 1988, Blacks accounted for only 13.8 percent of County-wide school enrollment, yet they were the victims of about 29 percent of the individual incidents. Or, in other words, they were victimized at a rate of more than double their representation.

Latinos closely followed Blacks in the number of schools reporting (144) and exceeded their number in actual incidents directed against them (651). The per capita impact was less severe, in that Latinos account for 46.7 percent of the 1988 enrollment but about 30 percent of the victims. However, there is a disproportionate representation of Latinos as a victim group in the "Anti-Immigrant" category (see below).

Whites accounted for the third largest victim group, with 91 schools reporting a total of 337 individual incidents. Thus, Whites, who account for 28.9 percent of the County schools population, accounted for 15.8 percent of the individual victims, or a rate of about one-half their representation.

Asians and Pacific Islanders were also disproportionately represented as victims of hate incidents. Anti-Asian incidents were reported by 91 different schools, for a total of 309 incidents. They account for 14.5 percent of the victims but only 8.6 percent of the population, ranking their victimization at almost double their representation. Like Latinos, they were more frequently the targets of anti-immigrant incidents than other ethnic groups.

> ***"Blacks accounted for only 13.8 percent of County-wide school enrollment, yet they were the victims of about 29 percent of the individual incidents."***

Arab and other Middle Eastern students were the next most prevalent victim group, with 34 different schools reporting a total of 107 incidents. And, like Latinos and Asians, they were frequently the focus of anti-immigrant sentiment. Filipinos, American Indians, and the "Other" classification all totaled less than a hundred incidents at less than 20 schools (65, 4 and 23, respectively).

Figure 1 illustrates the percentage of hate crime incidents directed toward four major ethnic groups in Los Angeles County schools.

Figure 1. Percentage of Incidents Against the Student Population

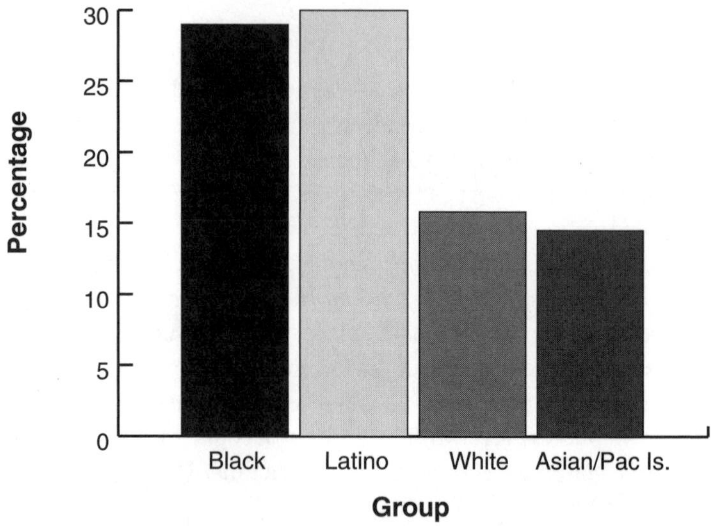

Religious. There were markedly fewer religious incidents reported than racial ones, and fewer than in the adult population. However, like their adult counterparts, Jewish students were the majority of anti-religious victims, with 40 incidents reported at 20 schools.

The next most common incidents were in the "Other" category (defined by respondents as Mormon, Buddhist, and Jehovah's Witness), in 6 schools for a total of 17 incidents. These were followed closely in number by anti-Christian incidents, of which 17 occurred at 4 schools. Anti-Islamic/Muslim incidents were reported by 2 schools, for a total of 5 incidents.

Gay/Lesbian. Anti-Gay and Lesbian incidents were also substantial in the school-age population. Anti-Gay violence was the sixth most common type of reported violence, with 65 incidents occurring at 24 schools.

Immigrant. A substantial portion of incidents directed against students was reported to be anti-immigrant in origin. Over 22 percent of the student racial incidents were categorized as anti-immigrant, for 471 incidents at a total of 82 schools.

These statistics deviate substantially from those reported for the adult population, where only an insignificant number of racial incidents appear to be motivated by anti-immigrant sentiment. This disproportionate number of responses in the school population, as observed and recorded by school administrators, bears out what the Commission had long suspected: there is a high probability that there are numerous immigrant hate crime victims in the County population who, for various reasons, do not report their victimization to authorities.

It is in this category that a large percentage of anti-Latino and anti-Asian incidents occur. Latinos, the most prevalent victim group, accounted for 227 incidents at 55 schools. This indicates that more than one-third of all reported anti-Latino incidents were rooted in anti-immigrant sentiment.

Even more disturbing, Asian anti-immigrant incidents—reported at 42 schools for a total of 144 incidents—accounted for over half of all anti-Asian incidents. Since Asians are the second largest immigrant group in Los Angeles County, and since relatively few adult anti-Asian incidents are reported to the Commission, it may be assumed that they also suffer from underreporting in the County at large.

School Levels Responding

Overall, 956 County schools responded to the survey, or 61 percent of those to whom a questionnaire was sent. Of these, 642 elementary schools responded, accounting for a little more than two-thirds of the respondents. Of these, 216 (34 percent) reported that they had hate crime, and 426 (66 percent) reported that they had not.

Of the junior highs and middle schools responding, 64 schools, or 47 percent, had experienced hate crime incidents and 73 schools had not. Of the senior high schools responding, the "yes" response rate was 42 percent (69 schools), and the "no" rate was 58 percent (96 schools).

In comparing the responses of differing school levels, there seems to be a slightly higher probability of incidents occurring in the junior high school population.

Types of Hostility

Racial slurs and name calling were the most prevalent type of hostility reported against students. Such incidents were almost three times more likely to occur than any other type of hostility, with 275 schools reporting 1,346 incidents, or 47 percent of the total incidents in this category.

> ***"There are numerous immigrant hate crime victims . . . who . . . do not report their victimization to authorities."***

The next most common manifestation of conflict was physical violence, which occurred almost 25 percent of the time. 140 schools reported 566 individual acts against students and, while there was no question on the survey regarding "multiple act" incidents, it must be assumed that at least some of the incidents of physical violence began with racial slurs or name calling and escalated.

Graffiti was the third most common occurrence and was reported at 16 percent of all schools in this category, with 88 individual campuses having a total of 365 incidents. This was closely followed in frequency by destruction of property or personal possessions, which was reported at 12 percent of these schools (306 incidents on 72 campuses).

Percentage of Incidents Against Students by Type

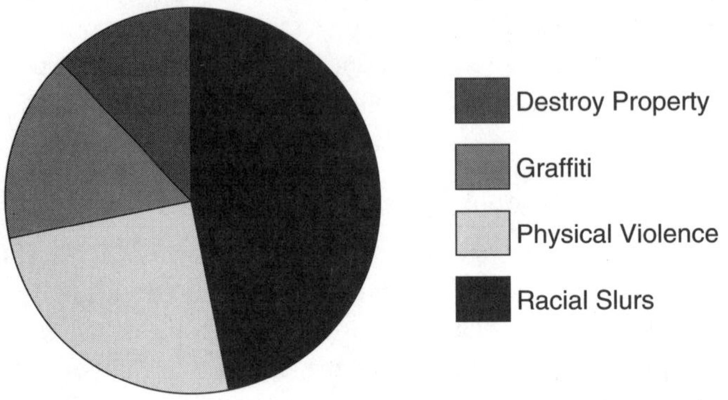

White supremacist groups had 103 individual incidents attributed to them, out of a total of 2,265 incidents for all schools and all categories. Of these, the most were attributed to skinheads (62 incidents), followed by the White Supremacy, "SWP," or "WSP" groups (14 incidents), Neo-Nazis (14 incidents), and the Ku Klux Klan (13 incidents).

In addition to the above, 14 additional groups were associated with incidents in this category. While some of the names were unknown to the Los Angeles County Probation Department's Gang Unit, several were able to be identified for racial/ethnic composition. Of these, 13 incidents were attributed to Black gangs (Bloods, Crip Killers), 6 to Latino gangs (Compton Barrio Segundo, Inglewood 13, L.B. Suicidals, South Side Longos), and 5 to a Jamaican gang (Posse).

It must be noted here that there is a substantial difference between White supremacist or "skinhead" gangs and gangs in the traditional sense of the word, as noted above. While gangs such as Crips or Bloods draw upon their own ethnic group for their affiliations, their primary reason for existence is not to promote racial solidarity but to provide social support and (illegal) economic rewards. In addition, most of these gangs usually victimize others of their own ethnicity. In the case of White supremacist groups, however, their primary activity is to threaten, intimidate, or physically assault non-Whites under the rubric of "racial superiority" and "White pride."

It must also be noted that while the number of incidents directly connected with hate groups is relatively small, their presence seems to indicate (or contribute to) a more intolerant environment. Of the 354 schools that reported incidents of hate crime, 48, or 14 percent, had seen evidence of hate groups on their campus. For schools reporting no incidents, the number was much lower at 31 observations out of 602 responding campuses (5 percent). . . .

Incidents Against School Employees

Violence and hostility toward school administrators, teachers and other employees occurred much more infrequently than intra-student violence. However, the numbers were still surprising, with 61 schools reporting 454 incidents against employees. Of these, it was estimated that in 80 percent of the schools, less than a quarter of the incidents were directed toward teachers. 35 percent of all schools reported none against teachers whatsoever.

The most common occurrence was racial slurs or name calling, reported 218 times at all 61 schools. Next most common was racist, anti-religious, or anti-Gay graffiti, reported by 32 schools for a total of 101 incidents. Destruction of property and personal belongings was the third most frequent occurrence, reported by 29 schools for 90 separate incidents.

And, last but by no means least, 22 different schools reported 45 acts of physical violence against employees. . . .

Profile of Schools at Risk

Schools which participated in the survey were promised confidentiality of their responses. Accordingly, 2 samplings of Schools were selected by the County Office of Education and provided to the Commission with their names deleted. The first was from schools which reported no incidents of hate crime whatsoever, and the second was from schools which had reported a high incidence of hate crime. In each sample, schools were grouped in 10 percent ranges according to the ratio of the student body represented by their largest minority ethnic group.

Comparisons that were done suggest that schools are more likely to have a high incidence of hate crime when at least one minority ethnic group exceeds 10 percent of the student population. By contrast, the largest single group of schools reporting no hate crime (36 percent of the sample) fell into the category in which the largest minority group in the school made up less than 10 percent of the student body. Although further study is needed to substantiate this finding, it can be hypothesized that schools whose minority ethnic composition exceeds 10 percent for any one group are at increased risk for hate crime.

> ***"The [second] most common manifestation of conflict was physical violence, which occurred almost 25 percent of the time."***

Another issue raised by the survey has troublesome implications in that one traditionally associates hate crime with incidents which are perpetrated by Whites against non-Whites. However, given the tremendous ethnic diversity of the schools that participated in this survey, it is probable that at least some of the incidents reported in the survey were perpetrated *by* students of color *against* other students of color, Gay and Lesbian students, immigrant students, and White students.

> ***"While the number of incidents directly connected with hate groups is relatively small, their presence seems to indicate . . . a more intolerant environment."***

The samples provided by the County Office of Education were also used to determine whether a relationship exists between socioeconomic status of students in Los Angeles County and the incidence of hate violence in these schools. The percentile rank for socioeconomic status that was assigned to schools as a part of the California Assessment Program was used to measure this variable. The median percentile rank for socioeconomic status was compared at three grade levels (6th, 8th, and 12th) for schools with a high incidence of hate crime versus those reporting no hate crime. The analysis did not show any clear relationship between the socioeconomic status of students and the incidence of hate acts in the County schools.

Resources in Use

Of the schools responding that they had had incidents, 57 percent are using curricula materials dealing with human relations or multicultural issues. For the schools responding negatively, only 35 percent used such resources. This leads the Commission to speculate that either such resources are being used reactively, i.e., after some interethnic tensions have surfaced, or that such resources are viewed by those in more tranquil schools as being unnecessary. . . .

A number of schools reported the DARE (Drug Abuse Resistance Program) as a resource for dealing with interethnic conflict. Equal numbers of other schools reported "self esteem training" and "social sciences curriculum" in the resources section.

Only a small number of the schools sampled reported using specific multicultural education materials. Those reported were the National Conference of Christians and Jews' "Green Circle" program, and the Anti-Defamation League's "A World of Difference" curriculum. There seems to be a clear need to increase awareness of the resources available and encourage their integration into the curriculum, rather than relying on generalized approaches.

Chapter 3

What Measures Can Reduce Youth Violence?

CURRENT CONTROVERSIES

Reducing Youth Violence: An Overview

by Ronald Henkoff

About the author: *Ronald Henkoff is an associate editor for* Fortune *magazine.*

The children who killed 12-year-old Amanda Simpson seared a hole in the American Dream. Just after midnight on April 28, 1991, while Amanda and her mother were sleeping, a group of youngsters broke into their Dayton home and stole a microwave oven. A short while later, some of the juveniles reentered the house, this time with a can of gasoline. They doused the kitchen floor and set the fuel alight. "Fuck 'em, let 'em burn!" the ringleader, a 15-year-old boy, exclaimed. Smoke and flames raced through the tiny structure. Amanda died five days later. Her mother, Judith, was seriously injured, but survived.

Violent Deaths

Amanda Simpson was only one victim in a raging epidemic of violence against children. You have heard and read a great deal about guns and gangs and ghettos. But this onslaught of childhood violence knows no boundaries of race, geography, or class. Amanda Simpson, a white parochial school student in a medium-size Midwestern city, was killed by a spontaneously organized throng of white children—a bunch of kids loose on the street, unrestrained by their parents, their peers, or their community.

Six boys and two girls, ages 12 to 16 at the time of the crime, were convicted or pled guilty in connection with Amanda's death. The child they killed was an animal lover, a saxophone player, a computer buff, and a volunteer at a local nursing home. One year she sold more than 1,000 boxes of Girl Scout cookies, enough to win a week at the summer camp to which her mother, a single parent, could not afford to send her.

An ever-increasing number of youngsters are caught up in violence—as victims, as witnesses, as perpetrators. The number of children under the age of 18

Ronald Henkoff, "Kids Are Killing, Dying, and Bleeding," *Fortune*, August 10, 1992, arrested each year for murder has jumped 55% in the past decade, to 2,674 in 1990. Juvenile arrests for aggravated assault and forcible rape are rising dramatically. Says Colonel Leonard Supenski of the Baltimore County police department: "There are a whole lot of disaffected, alienated youth out there who use violence, and use it with no remorse."

For too many children, there are no safe havens. They are victimized at home, at school, on the street. An astonishing number of youngsters are beaten, maimed, molested, and murdered by parents, relatives, or baby-sitters. The National Committee for the Prevention of Child Abuse (NCPCA), using reports filed by all 50 states, calculates that 2.7 million kids—some 4% of American children—suffered from abuse or neglect last year; that's an increase of 40% just since 1985. An estimated 1,383 children (half of them under the age of 1 year) died from maltreatment in 1991, the worst year on record. If anything, says Deborah Daro, the NCPCA's research director, these figures understate the problem.

"An ever-increasing number of youngsters are caught up in violence."

Among older children, the numbers are even bleaker. More adolescents die from violence—especially gun violence—than from any illness. According to the National Center for Health Statistics, homicide by firearms is now the second-leading cause of death (after motor vehicle crashes) for 15- to 19-year-old whites. For African Americans in that age bracket, homicide is *the* leading cause of death. Altogether, 2,771 children, ages 10 to 19, died from homicide in 1989, up 48% from 1984. Another 2,245 in that age group died from suicide, now the third-leading cause of death among adolescents.

A Public Health Emergency

Teenage violence mostly affects urban African Americans (except for suicide, a predominantly white problem). But it is beginning to spread. Under pressure from big city police departments, gangs are stashing their guns and dope in the suburbs and recruiting high school students as pushers. Says Captain Richard Kozak, chief of intelligence for the Illinois State Police: "We're seeing gang activities in places where they didn't exist two years ago. The gangs are playing off the fact that law enforcement in the suburbs is not prepared to deal with them."

But is *anybody* really prepared to deal with this escalation of childhood violence? In a word, no. The grim trends tell us—or ought to—that our entire approach to the problem has been misguided. We are constantly acting after the fact, trying to mend bodies after they have been broken.

When children are burned or stabbed or shot, we bury them, or we deliver them to overstretched hospitals, shelters, and foster homes. When youngsters commit violent crimes, we send them into an antiquated juvenile justice system that rarely punishes them sufficiently and almost never rehabilitates them. When teenagers kill themselves, we have groups to console their bereaved parents, but we have very few programs to identify and help potentially suicidal kids before they pull the trigger.

> ***"The most pressing task is to get guns away from children."***

"We believe violence in America to be a public health emergency, largely unresponsive to methods thus far used in its control," declared a recent editorial by two physicians in the *Journal of the American Medical Association*. The authors, former surgeon general C. Everett Koop and journal editor George Lundberg, are right. We must address violence against youth the way we treat other public health threats like smoking, drunken driving, or drug abuse: We must focus our efforts on prevention.

The most pressing task is to get guns away from children. The widespread availability of firearms makes it far too easy for kids to kill and be killed. Guns figure in more than 75% of adolescent homicides and more than half of adolescent suicides. Should we really be surprised that so many children are infatuated with firearms? There are more than 200 million privately owned guns in America, and half of all households have at least one. Movies, TV programs, and popular songs are saturated with gun-toting heroes and villains. A five-year study by the American Psychological Association found that the average child has witnessed 8,000 murders and 100,000 other acts of violence on television by the time he or she has completed *sixth* grade.

Guns and Violence

An astounding number of children either own a gun or know how to get one. Says Baltimore County's Colonel Supenski, whose suburban jurisdiction surrounds Baltimore but excludes the city itself: "For youth today, I don't care where you live, what class you are, or whether you're white, black, or Hispanic, it's cool to carry a gun. Owing to a lot of things, primarily the entertainment industry, it's a macho thing to do."

The teenage arms race shows no signs of abating. A national survey of high school students in 1990 by the Centers for Disease Control found that 4% had carried a gun at least once in the past month. In a more recent study of 11th-graders in Seattle, 6% of boys said they had actually brought a gun into the school building. And these pieces aren't just for show: One-third of the gun-owning students in Seattle reported that they had fired their weapons at another person.

Given the proliferation of guns, it's not surprising that kids say they need to carry one to protect themselves. But the line between "protection" and "aggression" is often so thin that it disappears. At the Henry Horner Homes, a mostly

African American housing project on Chicago's West Side, some teenagers view popping a person as a noble act, a matter of honor and pride. Says David Powell, a counselor at Better Days for Youth, an antigang program: "These kids think if someone is messing with their girlfriend and they shoot him, that's not violence. They see what happens on TV. If the hero has a problem, he shoots. And the hero shows no remorse."

Guns are surprisingly easy to get. In the Seattle study, 34% of the students said they had easy access to a handgun. In Chicago, where handgun sales have been banned since 1982, an inner-city youngster can take delivery of the weapon of his choice in under two hours. All it requires is a few bucks and a brief chat with the guys hanging out on his front steps. For $20 he can buy a used .22 caliber pistol. For as little as $200 he can own a brand-new, semiautomatic 9-millimeter pistol.

No Remorse

And it takes no skill at all to become a juvenile murderer. The increasingly popular 9-millimeter semiautomatic weighs about 2½ pounds. A teenager can conceal the muzzle in the waistband of his pants and cover up the handle with his sweatshirt or warm-up jacket. The gun's magazine can spew out 15 bullets in less than nine seconds. When one magazine is spent, the shooter can quickly snap on another. This is a point-and-shoot weapon. Aim it at another person and you are likely to inflict great damage, as this writer (who had never used a handgun) discovered when he trained the weapon on a human-shaped firing range target.

> ***"The kids are all on edge. Brush against them, and they're ready to fight."***

James Love knows all about 9-millimeter pistols. When he was 15, he used one to murder a 22-year-old. He also wounded the young man's teenage brother. Now 20, Love, who was tried and convicted as an adult, is serving a life sentence in the Maryland Penitentiary in Baltimore—eligible for parole in 14 years. As a teenager in an East Baltimore housing project, Love ran a small-time drug ring that netted big money, as much as $10,000 a day. Love says his two victims owed him $15,000. When they didn't pay, he shot them.

"When you shoot someone, you don't think about the consequences," says Love, a muscular young African American man dressed in shorts, a T-shirt, and a Nike Air cap. Love now expresses some regret for what he did: "I wish it never would have happened. It ain't worth taking nobody's life for no money."

That message is not getting through to the streets. Teenagers are not only shooting one another, they are also killing, wounding, and terrorizing their younger brothers and sisters. The steady popping of guns can inflict lasting psychological wounds. Children can become withdrawn, mistrustful, fatalistic, defensive, and violent. Says Sharon Brown, a director of programs for children at the Lutheran Social Services center at Cabrini-Green, a housing project on Chicago's North Side: "The kids are all on edge. Brush against them, and they're ready to fight."

Listen to the children of Cabrini-Green describe their world. Says 10-year-old Derrell Ellis: "You can't come outside. You got to duck and dive from the bullets. They be shooting most every day." Eleven-year-old Rachella Thompson used to hurry away from her fifth-floor window when gangs began gunfights in the courtyard of her building. Now, she says, "I don't care. I just sit there and play Nintendo. If they're going to shoot, they're going to shoot. Ain't nobody going to stop them."

Children exposed to a single violent event can suffer anxiety and depression for years. Psychologist James Garbarino, coauthor of a book called *Children in Danger*, has studied children in the war zones of Mozambique, Northern Ireland, Kuwait, and Israel's Occupied Territories, as well as the children of the war zones of American cities. Says he: "We haven't begun to address the issue of kids who see violence every day."

Response to Home Life

These kids don't see violence just in the streets. All too often they witness it in their homes—the result of an altercation between people who know each other. Says Dr. Carl Bell, head of Community Mental Health Council, a psychiatric center on Chicago's South Side: "It's not gang related or drug related or crime related. It's just people getting mad at each other and going off on each other."

This kind of violence sends a powerful message to the children who witness it. Says Bell: "Everyone talks about violence on TV. But they forget that a personal endorsement of violence from someone who is loved, trusted, and respected carries the most weight in the world." African American children are not only more likely to witness violence at home, they are also more likely to be victims of it.

Dayton resident Delrine Edwards, a 27-year-old African American woman, knows this only too well. Her second-youngest child, Demetri Green, died at the age of 3, strangled by her husband, Lorenzo, who said he was high on drugs at the time. Lorenzo, who was not Demetri's father, pleaded guilty to involuntary manslaughter and is serving nine to 25 years in prison. Says Delrine Edwards, who has three other children: "Demetri was a child, so I know he's in heaven. At least I don't have to worry about him like I do the others."

"There are no easy answers to the complex problem of childhood violence."

There are no easy answers to the complex problem of childhood violence. Because a disproportionate number of its victims are poor and African American, the issue overlaps with many other social problems: youth unemployment, welfare, racism, failing schools, sick hospitals, rotten housing, alcoholism, drug abuse, teen pregnancy, and single-parent households.

Our current approach is a de facto policy of containment. While middle-class neighborhoods are still relatively safe, violence festers in the homes, schools, and communities of the 18% of American children who live in poverty. Says Garbarino: "You cannot write off one-fifth of your society for free." The price is more jails, more foster homes, more crime, more deaths, more fear.

> ***"Although anger is a basic human emotion . . . many children never learn how to deal with it nonviolently."***

Nor is there any guarantee that juvenile violence will stay put. Says Commander Robert Dart, a beefy ex-Marine who heads the Gang Crime Section of the Chicago Police Department: "In some cases we eradicate gangs. In some cases we push them. I was born in Chicago, I live in Chicago, and I work for Chicago. If I have to push the gangs somewhere else, that's what I'll do." That somewhere else may be your home town.

Beyond eliminating poverty or shoving crime from one jurisdiction to another, there are several workable and affordable steps we can take to reduce our children's exposure to violence:

• *Help parents be parents.* The best place to begin is at the beginning of a child's life. Hawaii's Healthy Start program, funded by the state, intervenes from day one. A case worker interviews new parents in the hospital shortly after their baby is born. The aim is to identify parents at risk of abusing their children: teen mothers, alcoholics, drug users, welfare recipients, or people who have themselves been abused, either by their own parents or their spouses.

Assisting Parents

Parents who fall into the high-risk category are offered, at no charge, the services of a home visitor. The visitors are paraprofessionals, typically high school graduates who grew up in stable households. A home visitor may counsel a family for as long as five years. Parents are not compelled to enroll in the program, but only a handful refuse the service.

The home visitors, who work for private social service agencies under contract to the state, act as all-purpose advocates for the family. They show parents how to feed and nurture a baby. They ensure that children get regular preventative medical care, including inoculations. In some cases they help parents secure jobs, housing, and, when eligible, welfare and Medicaid.

Healthy Start shows healthy results. Without intervention, some 20% of high-risk parents can be expected to mistreat their children, a figure borne out by research in other states. Among the 1,204 families served by Healthy Start between 1987 and 1989, there were just three cases of abuse and six of neglect—less than 2%. Once the program expands to cover all at-risk families in the state, the total annual cost will be about $16 million. That's substantially less than the $40 million a year Hawaii spends on post-abuse protective custody and foster care.

Healthy Start is also likely to have a salutary effect on crime later in life. Abused children are walking evidence that violence begets violence. A Denver study of first-time juvenile offenders, for example, concluded that 84% had been abused before the age of 6. Says Gail Breakey, the director of the Hawaii Family Stress Center, the leading provider of Healthy Start services: "Child abuse is actually the root cause of so many social problems."

The National Committee for the Prevention of Child Abuse, using a $1 million grant from the Ronald McDonald Children's Charities, is campaigning for the establishment of home visitor programs nationwide. It hopes to have Healthy Start programs in place in 25 states by 1995.

Alternatives to Violence

• *Teach children how to manage anger.* Although anger is a basic human emotion, beginning with a wailing infant's insistent demand for nourishment, many children never learn how to deal with it nonviolently. At the Roth Middle School in Dayton, which is nearly 90% African American, several hundred students take part in a program called Positive Adolescents Choices Training (PACT). Developed by psychologists at nearby Wright State University and incorporated into the middle school's health education classes, PACT aims to defuse violence by teaching African American students how to talk instead of fight.

"We need to reassert the principles of parental and community responsibility."

PACT participants use role playing to reenact the kinds of real-life disputes that can escalate into violence. For example, an adolescent boy confronts a friend who has been spreading false rumors that his sister is pregnant. Instead of cussing his friend out, the boy asks if they can talk, says something positive about their friendship, states what he is angry about and why, tells his friend what action he'd like him to take, asks if he understands, and thanks him for his time. If they can't reach an agreement on the first boy's terms, they try to negotiate a compromise.

Hard as it is to teach kids surrounded by violence to cool their emotions, preliminary studies show that students trained by PACT are less likely to get suspended from school for fighting and more able to handle themselves peaceably in tough situations.

The PACT students who have shown the most progress are those whose parents have enrolled in Impact, a companion program to help them deal with *their* anger. Says Willa Cotten, a parent participant: "I used to get into total screaming matches with my daughter. This program helped me understand all the peer pressure these kids are going through." Cotten now tries to make 13-year-old Wilhemina understand that if she breaks the rules, she won't be shouted at or beaten, but that she will lose privileges.

Parental Responsibility

PACT, like Healthy Start, stresses a most important concept that has eroded in many families: parental responsibility. Says Michelle Hassell, coordinator of the program: "These parents yell at their kids, throw things at them, and threaten them, but they don't discipline them. If you don't discipline your kids, you set them up to fail, because no one is going to love them the way you do."

There are many school-based violence prevention programs, but no one has attempted to evaluate their long-term effectiveness. Cautions Rodney Hammond, PACT's project director: "These programs are not a panacea. The absence of social skills is not the prime reason for violence. But if our society refuses to deal with the big variables that contribute to violence, like poverty and the easy availability of guns, then we as psychologists need to minimize the casualties as best as we can."

• *Keep guns away from kids.* We cannot control juvenile violence without controlling guns. Requiring manufacturers to build child-resistant features into firearms could be a small first step. Trigger restraints and other devices would help prevent very young children from accidentally shooting themselves or someone else. But these mishaps are only part of the problem. Says Stephen Teret, director of the Johns Hopkins University Injury Prevention Center: "What we need to do is gun-proof children rather than child-proof guns."

In 1989, Florida became the first state to make adults partially responsible for the use of guns by children. Any adult who fails to keep a loaded gun safely away from a child under age 16 can be charged with a felony if the child uses the gun to shoot somebody. Laws similar to the Florida act are now on the books in ten states and three cities.

> ***"If you don't discipline your kids, you set them up to fail."***

These laws, while helpful, are mere dams erected to stop a tidal wave. Every year about four million new guns are manufactured in the U.S. for civilian use; nearly 1.4 million of those are semiautomatics. Municipalities like Chicago and Washington, D.C., ban the sale of handguns, but the laws are of limited use when firearms can be bought legally just a few steps outside the city limits.

We need action at the federal level, and we need it fast. The public is ahead of politicians on this issue. A 1991 Gallup poll found that 68% of Americans feel that laws covering the sale of firearms should be "more strict." A resounding 93% favored imposing a mandatory seven-day waiting period on anyone trying to buy a gun, the so-called Brady Bill now languishing in Congress.

But the Brady Bill, if it passes, would primarily stop convicted felons and mentally ill people from buying firearms. With 200 million guns in circulation, we need to do much more to stanch the flow. Says Dr. Katherine Kaufer Christoffel, professor of pediatrics and community health at Northwestern University's medical school: "The solution is to ban the manufacture, sale, and private possession of handguns." We can start by outlawing assault weapons, like the 9-millimeter semiautomatic pistol, that are wreaking so much havoc on our children.

Stopping the Crime

Violence against children undermines the very foundation of our nation. Opponents of gun control who cite the Second Amendment to the Constitution should pay more heed to the preamble, especially the phrase about insuring "domestic tranquillity." We the People have created a most untranquil society for our children, where the right to bear arms has been used to sanction a buildup of lethal personal weaponry unprecedented in human history. We cannot "secure the blessings of liberty to ourselves and our posterity" if we continue to allow the slaughter of our offspring.

Beyond controlling guns, we need to reassert the principles of parental and community responsibility. Our children's future is etched in the wan face of Judy Simpson. Amanda Simpson's mother is a frail woman. She is 34 but looks many years older. When she speaks of Amanda, her entire body convulses. Her pain is so palpable that it fills the room. The arsonists who killed her only child left her too ill to work, forcing her to rely on the limited largess of her retired parents and the caring counseling of the victims advocates at the Montgomery County prosecutor's office.

Imbedded in Judy Simpson's anguish is a seething rage, a mission, a purpose: "They took my lovely child from me. I can't do anything to get Amanda back, but I need to get her story out, for the sake of other parents and other children. For too many juveniles, crime seems to be a game. This has to stop."

"For too many juveniles, crime seems to be a game."

We owe at least that much to the memory of Amanda Simpson and Demetri Green. We owe it to the frightened kids of Cabrini-Green. They are all our sons. They are all our daughters. They are all our responsibility.

Crime Prevention Programs Reduce Youth Violence

by The Milton S. Eisenhower Foundation

About the author: *The Milton S. Eisenhower Foundation, founded in 1981, is an organization dedicated to reducing crime in inner-city neighborhoods. This organization researches ways that communities can implement programs to improve the lives of disadvantaged youths.*

Over twenty years ago, the bipartisan President's National Advisory Commission on Civil Disorders (the Kerner Commission) concluded, "Our nation is moving toward two societies, one black, one white—separate and unequal."

Shortly thereafter, the bipartisan National Commission on the Causes and Prevention of Violence (the Eisenhower Violence Commission), surveying the carnage in many American cities in the wake of the ghetto riots and rising crime rates of the late 1960s, concluded that "safety in our cities requires nothing less than progress in reconstructing urban life."

Results of a Ten-Year Study

As the private sector recreation of the commissions, the Milton S. Eisenhower Foundation has worked since the early 1980s to carry out their agendas—by reducing urban violence through youth empowerment, community revitalization and grass-roots action.

In this report, we summarize the results and lessons of our demonstrations during the last decade, describe our resulting next generation of national private sector ventures and propose national inner-city policy based on our practical experience in day-to-day street-level implementation.

Through trial and error over the last decade in places like the South Bronx, East Brooklyn, Liberty City in Miami, Dorchester in Boston, Washington, D.C., and Newark, we learned as much from local program failures as from successes.

From *Youth Investment and Community Reconstruction*, a publication of the Milton S. Eisenhower Foundation, Washington, D.C. Reprinted with permission.

As a result, there now are some answers to seemingly intractable questions. How effective are specific anti-crime and anti-drug tactics, like neighborhood watch, in the inner city, whatever their popularity in the media? What are the relative roles of minority nonprofit community organizations and the police? Of private organizations and public sector agencies? What are the uses—and limitations—of volunteers? Can wise policy invest simultaneously in both individual high-risk youth and the neighborhoods where they live? What is the cost? Is it cheaper than prison building? Is an inner-city youth empowerment and community reconstruction policy now feasible politically, as rhetoric over a "peace dividend" again is heard, even if muted by post-cold war Persian Gulf politics?

Community-Based Programs Work

Our central conclusions are hopeful. For example, community-based organizations *can* create effective strategies to reduce crime and drug abuse in inner cities. But effective programs cannot be developed "on the cheap." Our experience tells us that these inner-city ills require comprehensive solutions, not piecemeal, hit-and-miss efforts. The most successful programs reach well beyond the immediate symptoms of crime or drug abuse to address the deeper problems of the surrounding community, and particularly the multiple needs of disadvantaged youth.

Dr. David Hamburg, President of the Carnegie Corporation of New York, has concluded:

> We'll never know as much as we like, as evaluations are difficult and can direct resources away from the strategies themselves, but we know enough to act and we can't afford not to act.

As the 1990s begin, we now know enough to act on the common principles that so often spell success for inner-city youth and communities.

On the national level, our response to the continuing—indeed increasing—problem of crime and violence in the cities was largely reactive. We poured substantial amounts of scarce resources into "hardware"—including armored equipment whose value was questionable at best. We began steadily to put more and more people behind bars—in the nation's prisons and in local jails. Expenditures for criminal justice in the 1980s increased four times as rapidly as for education, and twice as rapidly as for health and hospitals. Over the decade the number of adults behind bars doubled. Nearly one in four black men aged 20 to 29 now is behind bars, on probation or parole on any given day. The U.S. has the highest rates of imprisonment in the industrialized world—except, significantly, for the [former] Soviet Union and

> ***"Community-based organizations* can *create effective strategies to reduce crime and drug abuse in inner cities."***

South Africa.

Nonetheless, massive and costly ($75,000 per cell) prison building in the 1980s did not result in less crime in the United States. . . .

The Eisenhower Foundation was created on the idea that the "reconstructive" tradition represented by the Kerner and Eisenhower Commissions was even more relevant in the 1980s than in the 1960s. Surely the nation needed a strong and efficient criminal justice system; certainly tactics to reduce opportunities for crime had a place in an overall strategy against crime in the cities. But we had begun to stray too far from the understanding that crime reflected deeper pathologies of urban life in America. A truly effective strategy against violence and crime in the cities would need to address those pathologies as well—particularly the blocked opportunities and multiple disadvantages of low-income youth, the disruption and stress of family life in the city, the erosion of community institutions and a sense of purpose.

In fact, it was apparent that, over the last twenty years, effective solutions had begun to emerge that actually prevented crime and drugs in the first place—and that cost the American taxpayer far less than concrete and hardware.

> ***"Preschool programs, like Head Start, are among the most cost-effective inner-city crime and drug prevention strategies."***

Preschool programs, like Head Start, are among the most cost-effective inner-city crime and drug prevention strategies ever developed. In 1985, the Committee for Economic Development, composed of American corporate executives, concluded, "It would be hard to imagine that society could find a higher yield for a dollar of investment than that found in preschool programs for its at-risk children. Every $1.00 spent on early prevention and intervention can save $4.75 in the cost of remedial education, welfare, and crime further down the road."

In addition to early intervention, one secret to preschool seems to be what might be called "multiple solutions for multiple problems." Disadvantaged children have many needs at the same time—including cognitive stimulation, better nutrition, improved health care and more social support. Preschool supplies them.

Effective Programs

Over the 1980s, the Eisenhower Foundation identified or evaluated programs for disadvantaged junior and senior high school age youth which also suggested such comprehensive solutions.

Illustrative programs which have been evaluated with sufficient scientific rigor as successful include the Job Corps nationally (less crime, drugs and welfare dependency through intensive, supportive job training in what is perhaps the most effective federal prevention program ever created for high-risk youth), the Argus Community in the South Bronx (less welfare dependency, drug use and crime among kids already in trouble), the Fairview Homes public housing crime prevention program in Charlotte, North Carolina (less crime through tenant empowerment, resident management and employment of high-risk youth), the national JobStart program (high school completion among disadvantaged dropouts aged 17-21), and Project Redirection in several locations (employment gains and less welfare dependency among disadvantaged teen mothers 17 or younger lacking high school diplomas).

"The [crime prevention] programs appear to reduce recidivism considerably more than prison."

Although more scientific evaluation is needed, other promising illustrative programs include Centro Sister Isolina Ferre in Ponce, Puerto Rico (less crime among high-risk youth combined with communitywide development), the House of Umoja in Philadelphia (less recidivism among adjudicated black youth in a supportive, homelike setting), City Lights in Washington, D.C. (improved school attendance among delinquent youth aged 12 to 22), the Phoenix Program in Akron (improved school attendance and reduced recidivism among high-risk teens) and the Eugene Lang "I Have A Dream" Program (reduced high school dropouts and increased college attendance among Harlem teenagers).

Though different, these public and private successes often share common, underlying elements. Like preschool, all provide multiple solutions to multiple problems. They often tailor both social support *and* discipline to individual youth—via mentors, counselors, big brothers, big sisters and peers. But, to varying degrees, they link that support and discipline to the development of real opportunities for education, school-to-work transitions, employment training and employment placement. Many work with young people in the context of a supportive, nurturing and disciplined physical setting—an "extended family" sanctuary off the street—which they regard as both a precondition for healthy individual development and a major lack in the lives of the young people served.

Prevention Programs

These are genuinely prevention programs—and so promise to be both more enduring and more cost-effective than the superficial, reactive responses to violence and drugs that characterized too much of our public policy in the 1970s and 1980s. The programs appear to reduce recidivism considerably more than prison. Yet the cost per youth served typically is only half that of prison for residential programs and even less for nonresidential programs.

These multiple solutions usually result in multiple outcomes—increasing self-esteem, staying in school, parenting at a later age, improving life management skills, becoming more independent and less welfare reliant, being more employable and getting less involved with drugs and crime. Sometimes positive change among high-risk youth is part of positive change for the community. Not all of these good outcomes happen in all of these programs—and sometimes evaluators are frustrated by lack of consistency—but the broad pattern is for considerable simultaneous change.

Over the 1980s, in its national neighborhood demonstration program in inner-city communities in Baltimore, Boston, the Bronx, Brooklyn, Cleveland, Miami, Minneapolis, Newark, Philadelphia and Washington, D.C., the Foundation found that some of these underlying principles could be replicated in other locations. In Washington, D.C., the Around the Corner to the World community organization capitalized a housing rehabilitation business which employs at-risk youth who support one another in extended family sessions and who have become role models for minority children who otherwise might become involved with drugs. In Boston, Massachusetts, the Dorchester Youth Collaborative channeled at-risk youth into Prevention Clubs of the youth's own design—leading, among other achievements, to effective anti-crack break dancing videos with national distribution. . . .

"Head Start should be expanded to the four out of five eligible disadvantaged children who presently are left out."

Youth Investment and Community Reconstruction

Over the 1980s, the drug problem escalated relentlessly, destroying individuals and families, besieging communities and massively straining the resources of public and nonprofit institutions in the inner cities. Beneath such horrific symptoms lie deeper changes, less explosive and visible but no less devastating:

- *Half* of the black children under 6 were below the poverty line in 1988.
- The poverty rate among Hispanic children rose by 36 percent between 1979 and 1988.
- The average poor person in the cities is much *farther* below the official poverty line than twenty years ago.
- The urban poor are far less likely to *escape* from poverty than they were in the late 1960s.
- Forty percent of black children are raised in fatherless homes.
- Since the 1960s, the percentage of white high school graduates enrolled in college has gone up, to almost 60 percent, while the percentage of blacks

has gone down, to about 35 percent.

These tragic facts—and we could easily list many more—tell us clearly that, in terms of national impact, the human resource and urban policy we have followed for the past decade has been a failure. We believe that it is past time to return the Kerner and Violence Commissions' vision of "massive, compassionate, and sustained" action to the forefront of the public agenda.

"The [Youth Investment] Corporation will create or enhance local programs that are evaluated to yield less crime."

Private sector intermediaries, like the Eisenhower Foundation, must innovate, evaluate and highlight success. But only at the federal level can enough dollars be earmarked to make a national impact on the inner city.

With sufficient resources and flexible federal-local delivery vehicles, a carefully conceived and comprehensive strategy can reach a wide enough segment of the inner-city disadvantaged to create a kind of "critical mass" that will launch deteriorating communities into an upward spiral of increasing organization and achievement and their disinvested youth into a cycle of increasing self-esteem, education and employability.

That cycle can be facilitated through the following federal and local policy initiatives, based on our experience.

Early Intervention and Urban School Reform

Head Start should be expanded to the four out of five eligible disadvantaged children who presently are left out because of insufficient funds. A good model for how a federally financed Head Start program might be further improved via local funding matches is Project Beethoven on the South Side of Chicago, created by businessman-philanthropist Irving Harris. Working with families in Robert Taylor Homes public housing who send their children to Beethoven Elementary School, Mr. Harris has combined prenatal care, home visits, help with nutrition and counseling to enable teen mothers to complete school and obtain job training. Their infants are prepared nutritionally, psychologically and socially for school entry. All services are integrated and available right on the premises of Taylor Homes.

After the earliest intervention, one promising comprehensive plan which we endorse is for states, localities and the private sector to create variations of the Rhode Island Children's Crusade. The state of Rhode Island is providing state college scholarships for low-income pupils, combined with academic and remedial help from third grade through high school. The only requirements are that parents allow state monitoring of report cards and that students obey the law, shun drugs, avoid early pregnancy and do not drop out. Pupils will be tutored and paired with mentors throughout primary and secondary school. When old enough, top performers will secure summer jobs, where they will serve as role models to others.

To complement such state initiatives, we need more federal leadership and funding for urban school systems and middle school youth, based on well-thought-out reform plans recently proposed by the Carnegie Foundation for the Advancement of Teaching and the Carnegie Council on Adolescent Development. These reforms range from replacement of rigid class schedules with cooperative learning in small groups to creation of new governance procedures that allow a school system to intervene if a specific urban school does not meet agreed upon objectives.

The Youth Investment Corporation

Even as we continue to build understanding with careful evaluations, a new, dynamic, implementing entity is needed to act on what we already know about how to solve the interrelated problems of high-risk inner-city junior and senior high school age youth.

We propose legislation for a national Youth Investment Corporation, operating in the private sector but seed funded by the public sector.

The Youth Investment Corporation will leverage public against private sector monies, fund replications of existing youth successes, expand the number of community organizations which can implement such programs, and improve the programs' executive functioning through a new Youth Management Training Institute—a sort of Harvard Business School or Wharton School for social development and youth empowerment organizations at the local level.

> ***"There is clearly no shortage of public needs to be met through local community enterprise."***

The Corporation is designed to encourage inner-city nonprofits to create or strengthen for-profit entities. Over time, the for-profits will generate income streams which can at least partially finance the operations of the parent nonprofit social development and youth empowerment activity.

The Corporation will create or enhance local programs that are evaluated to yield less crime, less drug abuse, less welfare dependency, fewer adolescent pregnancies, higher self-esteem, more school completion, more successful school-to-work transitions, more employability, and more economic and psychological self-sufficiency among targeted high-risk youth. Other objectives will be success in the for-profit activity (a source of employment for the high-risk youth), management and financial progress by the implementing inner-city organization, and social and economic progress in the surrounding neighborhood.

The Youth Investment Corporation will provide a new, focused operating vehicle that expands the capacity of inner-city nonprofits to train and place high-risk youth.

The exact formula for that training and placement already has been established—through the private sector JobStart demonstration program funded by the Ford Foundation and other institutions. The program provides basic education, occupational training, support services such as child care and transportation, and real job placement assistance to disadvantaged school dropouts. The vehicles for implementation are community-based organizations, Job Corps centers, vocational schools and community colleges.

We recommend that the Job Training Partnership Act (JTPA), the existing system for youth job training, be reformed so that local sites operate more like JobStart.

If there are significant cuts in the size of American armed forces in the 1990s, then the need is even greater for more civilian job training and placement among high-risk youth.

Training must be linked more effectively to private sector placement. There now is a demographic opportunity. The number of 18 year olds in the population will not again reach 1989 levels until 2003. Consequently, companies will need to extend their reach for new workers. If federal training can be better linked to this corporate need, our future work force and our international competitiveness can be strengthened at the same time we invest in disadvantaged youth.

To better manage the training-placement linkage and to ensure that street-level implementation resembles JobStart, a federal office responsible for overall policy and programmatic direction of the government's youth employment efforts should be re-established, along the lines of the short-lived Office of Youth Programs in the late 1970s.

A "Community Enterprise" Development Strategy

Key to a new human resource and urban agenda must be a concerted plan to develop the "whole community" through providing long-term, stable, public sector employment opportunities that address genuine local needs.

> ***"The time has never been more propitious to take up the challenge of the Kerner and Eisenhower Commissions."***

There is clearly no shortage of public needs to be met through local community enterprise. The mile-long collapse of Interstate 880 during the San Francisco earthquake of 1989 was only one of the more tragic illustrations of decrepit urban infrastructure across the nation that urgently needs reconstruction—and that could supply tens of thousands of new economic development jobs to properly trained youth who presently are high risk.

At the same time, we need a renewed federal commitment to the construction and rehabilitation of low-income housing—with budget authority returned to the levels of the late 1970s. The current private sector for-profit system in effect "bribes" developers to build and rehabilitate low-cost housing. A new system should be based on private sector nonprofit corporations that construct and rehabilitate low-income housing. Many of the jobs generated should be for high-risk youth.

The result should be a national policy that treats low-income housing not as an economic commodity but as a human right.

In public housing, there currently is much talk about empowering tenants. We endorse tenant self-determination. But unless tenant management and ownership are expanded from a few exemplary programs to most public housing projects around the nation, unless tenants are adequately trained to manage, unless job training and opportunity for project youth are realized, and unless funds are provided for coordinated social and economic development, our experience predicts little national impact. . . .

> ***"People need to be as concerned by the internal dangers to our free society as by any probable combination of external threats."***

The Challenges from Within

In the late 1960s, the Eisenhower Violence Commission declared its conviction that "this nation is entering a period in which our people need to be as concerned by the internal dangers to our free society as by any probable combination of external threats." Over twenty years later, some of the external threats have diminished. Solidarity leader Lech Walesa and Czech President Vaclav Havel have addressed Congress, the Berlin Wall has come down, and there is Constitutional change in the Soviet Union. But the internal threats—what the Violence Commission called "challenges from within"—have become even greater, fulfilling the prediction made by the Kerner Commission of two societies more separate and less equal. With our symptomatic drug crisis, the time has never been more propitious to take up the challenge of the Kerner and Eisenhower Commissions and to affirm, once again, that "there can be no higher priority for national action and no higher claim on the nation's conscience."

Institute Job Programs to Rehabilitate Violent Youth

by Falcon Baker

About the author: *Falcon Baker has served as director of Juvenile Studies for the Kentucky Crime Commission and as director of Delinquency Prevention Programs in the Louisville public schools. He has developed many experimental and successful youth delinquency rehabilitation programs that have been used as models for programs throughout the country. He is also the author of* Delinquency in Kentucky *and has written numerous magazine articles on juvenile delinquency.*

A popular song in the era following World War I concerned the behavior and morals of many of the returning doughboys. The song succinctly asked: "How ya gonna keep 'em down on the farm after they've seen Paree?"

A very similar question could be asked of thirteen- and fourteen- and fifteen-year-old juveniles who, with no allowance from home and unable to find a job, have engaged in mugging and purse snatching, in burglary and con games, in prostitution and drug dealing. How ya gonna interest them in a dull, low-pay job after they've seen the big money to be had on the seamy side of the law?

Faulty Conclusion

I recall the dismay of a Louisville high school principal some years back when he was trying to persuade an intelligent, personable young dropout to sign up for a new vocational training project. "How much you make a month?" the dropout challenged. When the principal explained that (even back then) it was better than three thousand dollars a month, the youth replied: "Look, man, I made more than that last week. Why should I go through all the hassle just to become a grease monkey?" Then he really rubbed it in. "But thanks. You're an all-right guy. I like you. If you get pushed for bread, man, let me know. Maybe I can help."

Most delinquents fail to achieve the income of that young drug dealer, but it is estimated that more than 25 percent of teenage income in many inner-city areas comes from crime. In American society a teenager must have spending money, and he's going to get it. Many discover it's really not too difficult to obtain—illegally. Later they may have little interest in eight hours of legitimate work at poverty wages.

They've already seen Paree.

When in the spring of 1989 the unemployment rate dropped below 5 percent and for teenagers below 14 percent, many people concluded that teenage unemployment was no longer a critical issue. They pointed to the "help wanted" signs that prior to the Christmas season had become standard window decorations of small shops and fast-food establishments. But it was a faulty conclusion.

Unemployment is allocated unevenly among the various layers and hues of our society and is highly concentrated among racial minorities and children of welfare recipients. The uneducated, the untrained, the undisciplined, are the last to be hired, the first to be let go. Overall unemployment among black teenagers is still above 30 percent. And the figure runs as high as 60 and 75 percent in some blighted areas—areas where future criminals are being bred and nurtured. Here by age twenty-five unemployment has become a way of life. Many have never held a job. Drugs, alcohol, and crime have become quick fixes for their problems.

Society's Loss

The obstacles these teenagers face are many: the small demand for youths who are functionally illiterate, the rapidly evaporating pool of even semiskilled jobs, racial discrimination, union hall efforts to limit the competitive supply of additional laborers, the exodus of industry from the inner cities, the unwillingness of many employers to offer entry-level jobs that include a training feature for disadvantaged applicants. When these are all added together along with the youth's total ignorance of the work ethic, the results spell disaster.

> ***"It is estimated that more than 25 percent of teenage income in many inner-city areas comes from crime."***

Unfortunately, unemployed youths can't sit around idly for years waiting for a paying job. Survival is a basic drive. They can exist for a while, finding an odd job now and then, occasionally begging a few dollars from some relative. Eventually they give up. The Labor Department estimates that nearly a million are in this category, so discouraged they no longer are looking for jobs and are uncounted in unemployment statistics.

But worthy or unworthy, these young people still have to eat, and they have to have pocket money. They'll get it—one way or another.

It is easy for society to say, "Go to work or starve." But if no one will hire these uneducated, untrained, undisciplined youths, it is society that in the end is the real loser.

There is a cliché among youth advocates: find jobs for teenagers and most of the problems of delinquency and drug trafficking will disappear. But it's not that simple. Many soundly conceived demonstration projects have laid eggs. All too often the delinquent has soon quit or is fired—or stays on the job and keeps right on getting into trouble with the law. Those youngsters for whom jobs have been found seem to pop up in court with about the same frequency as control groups for whom the program did not provide jobs.

"To be effective in preventing a youth from turning to crime, the proposed job must offer some hope of advancement."

The success of the few favorably evaluated programs can usually be explained by one of two factors, one good, one bad. In the latter case, project directors, anxious about their own jobs and intent on making a good showing, carefully skimmed the cream of the applicants, selecting only educated and highly disciplined youths who probably would have succeeded anyhow. They excluded those less likely to find work whose failure would put a black mark on the program's record. Consequently, despite the program's "success," it failed to reach those for whom it was designed.

Offering Hope

In the case of the positive factor, the successful program could have been one of the few able to provide jobs in which the participants could see some future, a future worth *working* for. Unlike jobs usually found for delinquents, these were not low-prestige dead-end jobs that generated neither hope nor pride.

So consistent have been the research findings that it should now be considered axiomatic: *To be effective in preventing a youth from turning to crime, the proposed job must offer some hope of advancement, must give the youth some hope of eventually being able to join the mainstream of affluent America.*

A number of these successful programs do exist, proving that runaways, dropouts, and untrained ghetto youths can be trained. IBM, for example, has invested heavily in its Job Training for the Disadvantaged Program. In nine urban-area centers, job training is offered to largely Hispanic youths unable to afford commercial training programs. Many are on public assistance when they start. IBM records show that graduates have a job placement record of 86 percent at an average salary of over twelve thousand dollars. This is training for jobs with a future.

The Vocational Foundation Inc., a nonprofit institution in midtown Manhattan, has been working with troubled youths for fifty-three years. It was created by a visionary industrialist, Walter N. Thayer, who over the years was able to coax money from corporate leaders. Training a teenager for a job has cost around ten thousand dollars including a hundred-dollar-a-week stipend while training—considerably less than the forty thousand a year it costs to keep one in a reform school. Around 70 percent of those enrolled have been placed in building trades, clerical offices, and the food and apparel industries—again, jobs with a future. Unfortunately, the $1.5 million the foundation has been able to raise each year hardly touches the need. And the approach would not be effective with all youths.

For many disadvantaged youths the federal student-loan program permitting them to go to college and trade schools has been a godsend, even though frequently proprietary schools have been scams, ripping off enrollees and giving them false hopes. But again, this program fails to reach the really hard-core unemployables. To provide enough jobs and training to be effective, a coordinated effort of the federal and state governments, local communities, and the public school system will be required. . . .

Creating Job Programs

School Training Programs. The first tier of a comprehensive job-training effort should be within the public school system. School-based vocational and/or career programs need to be radically upgraded for the two-thirds of America's high school graduates who don't go on to college—who now leave with no salable skill by which they can earn a living. . . . New areas of public education to prepare youths for work in modern society were proposed for the Career High, and training for less demanding vocations was scheduled for the alternative schools.

Community Service Corps. Projects under this program would employ youths aged twelve through sixteen in part-time public service jobs. Participants would be selected from schools in high-delinquency areas on the basis of family need. . . .

> ***"New York City's Department for the Aging has a successful program designed to keep potential dropouts in school."***

The Community Service Corps would strive to accomplish a number of goals. It would (1) prevent many from becoming delinquent because of having no spending money, (2) teach welfare children that money is something that can be obtained by working, not just something that comes in the mail each month, (3) give early training in good, responsible work habits, and (4) permit many economically disadvantaged teenagers to remain in school. This is a pretty healthy group of goals—goals that have become increasingly important in view of the rapidly growing number of America's children who are living in poverty.

The program would operate year-round, but would be stepped up in the summer months. Features of both Franklin Delano Roosevelt's National Youth Administration (NYA) and Lyndon Baines Johnson's Neighborhood Youth Corps (NYC) would be incorporated. . . .

While activities would be limited only by the imagination of community leaders (and approval of the state agency), emphasis would be on improvement of the environment and on services to the elderly and disabled, particularly relieving the loneliness many must endure. In Pittsburgh the housing authority has instituted a "read-aloud partners" program which employs students to read to small children of parents who don't know how to read.

"For an effective program, tax credits should be given to the employer."

New York City's Department for the Aging has a successful program designed to keep potential dropouts in school. High-risk students are given training and work experience at senior citizen centers and nursing homes and with the homebound elderly. Four half-days of work a week are provided, with the youth going to school the rest of the time. A strict "no school, no work" policy is maintained. Begun in 1989, the project now employs more than two hundred students from fifteen high schools; some sixty senior citizen programs benefit. The project has brought a bridge of understanding across the generation gap, and early indications are that students are being kept in school—and out of trouble with the law.

Performing Meaningful Service

In my files are dozens of accounts of successful projects which give some indication of the range to be considered for the Community Service Corps. Among them:

- Making life easier for totally or partially incapacitated individuals by doing marketing or laundry, running errands to the post office and bank, walking dogs, or helping clean house
- Reading to blind, elderly, or disabled persons
- Maintenance and other work at senior citizens centers, hospitals, and nursing homes
- Group performances—choral, dance, or drama—at nursing homes and homes for the aged or disabled
- Repair and painting of deteriorating homes belonging to needy, elderly individuals
- Supervision of recreational activities for handicapped children, including taking retarded children on camping trips

- Reading to children at the public library
- Individual tutoring of slow learners in elementary schools
- Restoring neglected cemeteries and other historic spots around the community
- Creating new city parks and improving existing ones
- Development of nearby wilderness areas by constructing hiking trails and paths, clearing away brush and undergrowth, and building picnic tables and bridges
- Painting colorful murals, under supervision of a professional artist, on unsightly city walls and fences and on dismal cafeteria and activity rooms in schools and nursing homes

These jobs are made work—deliberately so. They provide a teenager with a job without taking one away from another individual. They are jobs that perform a meaningful service—a service our affluent society can well afford to provide to its less fortunate citizens. And they are jobs in which a youth can take pride for having reached out and contributed to another human being. . . .

Training Programs by Industry

Private industry could be extremely effective in training disadvantaged youngsters. The current shortage of qualified youths (qualified by educational attainment, social skills, and attitude toward the work ethic) makes this a propitious time to prod industry into establishing training programs for those who are only marginally qualified. The problem is finding the proper carrot to entice industry.

The National Commission on Youth, a think tank created by the Charles F. Kettering Foundation, has urged the use of tax credits as an incentive for employers to set up apprenticeship, internship, and training programs. This would not be entirely new. The 1986 tax overhaul bill revived (over the administration's objections) the Targeted Jobs Tax Credit program which had expired in 1985. This program promotes jobs for various handicapped and economically disadvantaged groups. Unfortunately, the modest funds were reduced. The program allows tax credit for hiring "certified" youths aged sixteen through nineteen who are participating in a qualified cooperative educational project. It fails, however, to encourage industry to set up its own internal training programs designed for its specific needs.

> ***"A residential Youth Conservation Corps would be particularly advantageous to the thousands who are homeless."***

For an effective program, tax credits should be given to the employer for up to 75 percent of the wage of a youth in strictly nonproductive training, then 50 percent for six months of apprenticeship training, and finally, if needed, up to

25 percent of the wages during the next six months. Original approval of a company's training program design would be obtained from the official state youth employment agency, which would then monitor the operations and periodically grant continuation status. Approval would not be given to companies that offered only dead-end jobs, thus preventing industries that required no real training from benefiting from the tax subsidy.

The same state agency would also have the important task of certifying potential trainees as being members of targeted groups. Companies could be encouraged to develop innovative approaches. For example, an older worker could be assigned as an "industry brother" to counsel and encourage the underprivileged neophyte. Such a training program could open up jobs to presently unemployable youths—jobs with a future.

Youth Conservation Corps

Perhaps no New Deal program met with such universal favor among liberals and conservatives alike during its heyday as did the Civilian Conservation Corps, the federal agency that put depression-era youths to work. Many business and community leaders of the past few decades look back in gratitude to the financial and emotional boost the program gave them. . . .

> ***"No time has been more propitious for expanding the Job Corps (and for inaugurating the Youth Conservation Corps) as the present."***

As teenage unemployment among certain groups continues to mount in a nation now far more financially able to offer this helping hand than in the 1930s the time has come to reinstate such a program on a major scale. It need not necessarily be residential, as was the old CCC, but could employ teenagers living at home or in subsidized housing. Regardless of whether the Corps was nonresidential or utilized camp-style living, it would be an opportunity to hand out a check for hard work instead of a welfare check, an opportunity for the nation to receive material benefits for the money paid out to the unemployed—and an opportunity to salvage thousands of our problem teenagers.

A dozen or so states and at least fifteen communities have grown weary waiting for Congress to act. As they have watched penniless youths turn to crime they have in desperation begun small programs on their own. The Human Environment Center, a Washington, D.C., clearinghouse, reports that in 1985 these programs were serving 7,000 jobless youths. The largest is California's Conservation Corps, which employees 2,200. Their activities range from renovating parks to weatherproofing homes of the needy. It is claimed that for every $1.00 spent, their work returns $1.77 in benefits to the state. . . .

A residential Youth Conservation Corps would be particularly advantageous to the thousands who are homeless—a wholesome alternative to prostitution and living on the streets. A healthy camp environment, away from the crime and drugs of the inner city, could be the life jacket needed by many who have been kicked out of, or are running away from, their homes.

Job Corps

It is difficult to name a federal social program of recent years that has received more accolades than the Job Corps, the surviving showpiece of Lyndon Johnson's Great Society. The typical youth in the Job Corps is an eighteen-year-old school dropout, frequently black, reading on the sixth-grade level, and from a socially and financially impoverished family of the inner city. He has never held a legitimate job, has no skills or know-how to obtain one. Only crime and/or welfare loom in his future.

Trainees are enrolled in Job Corps centers across the nation, many located hundreds of miles away from the squalor and deprivation of their homes. For four to six months they are paid to learn marketable skills such as welding, auto mechanics, carpentry, electrical repair, nursing, cooking, secretarial and clerical skills, landscaping and yard maintenance. . . .

To obtain a clearer picture of just how good or bad the program is, Mathematica Policy Research, Inc., was engaged for an independent, long-range evaluation. The report, released in 1982, included follow-up interviews with hundreds of 1977 Job Corps members and with a comparative group who did not receive the training. It declared that the program had been a resounding success in putting disadvantaged youths to work and in keeping them out of jail and off welfare rolls. In addition to the humanitarian values, the report stated, great economic benefits to society had been achieved.

For fiscal year 1984 Job Corps director Peter E. Rell claimed an incredible success of 75.6 percent. Of those who could be contacted, 60.6 percent had found jobs or entered the army, while 15 percent went on for further education. Some centers have at times shown close to 90 percent post-training employment. . . .

No time has been more propitious for expanding the Job Corps (and for inaugurating the Youth Conservation Corps) as the present. The military bases that are to be deactivated would provide already owned, instant campuses. Without extensive capital expenditure, there would be all the dormitories, training areas, and service facilities needed. For Congress to ignore this opportunity to expand a program that has demonstrated its ability to reach many of the "unreachables" would be an American tragedy.

It would compound the present tragedy: that the greatest nation in the world fails to see to it that every youth is trained for and has the opportunity to hold a dignified job that can provide for the basic needs of life.

Expel Violent Youths from School

by Jackson Toby

About the author: *Jackson Toby is a professor of sociology and director of the Institute of Criminological Research at Rutgers University in New Brunswick, New Jersey.*

When two students at Thomas Jefferson High School in Brooklyn, N.Y., were fatally shot by an angry classmate everyone started asking, "Why is there so much more violence now than when I went to school?"

One answer is that schools have been too successful in preventing dropouts among students uninterested in schoolwork. While some stay because they know that they need education to get a good job, others come for more immediate economic reasons—welfare benefits for children over 16 are paid only for those who are enrolled in school, for example. Thus the schools contain students two or three years behind grade level and making no academic progress toward graduation.

No Incentive for Control

Students who experience classroom instruction not as an opportunity but as imprisonment—partly because their families may not value education highly—become truant. They pay little attention when they do go to classes, don't do homework, and undermine teacher authority by defiant behavior. Most of the violent kids come from this group of youngsters.

Does staying in school longer account for school violence? No, not by itself. It takes an aggressive personality to set out to shoot one's schoolmates, and guns have to be available. However, when a significant proportion of kids in a school are trapped for a long time, believing that they are learning nothing worth learning, a climate develops in which arguments escalate beyond fistfights. An angry kid doesn't have an incentive to control himself—or herself.

Jackson Toby, "To Get Rid of Guns in School, Get Rid of Some Students," *The Wall Street Journal*, March 3, 1992. Reprinted with permission of The Wall Street Journal,

Lethal fights between female students occur too.

None of the three youths involved in the Jefferson incident was a model student. Fifteen-year-old Khalil Sumpter, arrested for the crimes after being chased and captured by security guards, was on probation for a street robbery two years earlier to which he had pleaded guilty. That same year Khalil, one of the victims, 16-year-old Tyrone Sinkler, and a third boy had demanded a schoolmate's lunch money; he had none, so they beat him up and took his baseball cap. Tyrone, who had a prior arrest in 1989 for pickpocketing, was convicted of assault and, after violating probation, served six months in a juvenile center. Seventeen-year-old Ian Moore, the second victim, was a close friend of Tyrone's; he had been arrested in February 1991 for assault and in April 1991 for robbery.

Grieving Rooms

Principal Carol Beck came to Jefferson in 1987, instituted a new curriculum, recruited young, energetic teachers, and dealt with the delicate problem of uninterested and undisciplined students, some of them over age 21 and legally no longer entitled to a high school education. Those had to leave, but younger disciplinary problems cannot be expelled in New York, only transferred. *Reader's Digest* named Mrs. Beck an American Hero in Education for the improvement she achieved.

Since Mrs. Beck took over Jefferson High, 50 of her students have died, most in the violent streets surrounding the school. In November, a student was killed in the building by a fusillade of shots that also critically wounded a teacher. Despite that murder, dedicated teachers continue to teach conscientious students at Jefferson. But they have to lock themselves into their classrooms to keep the bedlam in the hallways out. Mrs. Beck has set aside "grieving rooms" where students can come to mourn friends who have died and to talk with counselors. She also plans to create a memorial garden.

Grieving rooms bring some comfort to survivors. The enhanced metal detector program Schools Chancellor Joseph Fernandez announced after the murders, financed by an added $28 million that Mayor David Dinkins promised to find, will reduce somewhat the number of weapons in New York's public schools. But these measures do nothing about the involuntary students who present major disciplinary problems. They used to be transferred to special schools, but the few schools that have survived the effort to mainstream everybody are filled to capacity.

> ***"Students who experience classroom instruction not as an opportunity but as imprisonment . . . become truant."***

On any given day one-fourth of the enrolled students at Thomas Jefferson are absent. Included in this statistic are chronic truants, who may be roaming the streets on more than half of school days. Chronic truants come to school, but not for education. They come when it is raining or cold, when they want to see a girlfriend, to attack an enemy, to buy or sell drugs, or to play basketball in the gym. They cut most of their classes and wander the halls in pursuit of such entertainment as throwing firecrackers or rotten fruit at passing teachers. This behavior intimidates teachers and makes them afraid to attempt to control students more amenable to school discipline.

"They have to lock themselves into their classrooms to keep the bedlam in the hallways out."

In short, the indirect cause of student violence at inner-city schools like Thomas Jefferson is that schools enrolling marginal students are afraid to require daily homework, regular attendance and mannerly behavior. They are afraid the Khalils, Tyrones, and Ians might drop out. On the other hand, such students might shape up if held to high enough standards.

One step needed to make inner-city schools like Thomas Jefferson safer is to use the security guards in the building to keep intruders out. (Although the recent murders were allegedly committed by an enrolled student, suspended students and other intruders contribute disproportionately to school violence.) But schools cannot be made completely safe by security guards or metal detectors. Given fire regulations that mandate many doors capable of being opened from the inside in emergencies, a student who wishes to bring a knife or a gun into the building finds it not too hard to persuade a friend to open a door and let him enter with his weapon.

No safety measure beats requiring all enrolled students to be studious. What makes a school safe is youngsters coming to school because they want to learn what the teachers want to teach them. Two hundred fewer students at Thomas Jefferson would make a world of difference.

Youth Clubs Will Prevent Youth Violence

by Office of Juvenile Justice and Delinquency Prevention

About the author: *The Office of Juvenile Justice and Delinquency Prevention (OJJDP) was established by Congress through the Juvenile Justice and Delinquency Prevention Act of 1974. The OJJDP is a division of the Department of Justice and is the primary federal agency charged with addressing the needs of the juvenile justice system.*

For more than 130 years, the Boys Clubs of America has been working to prevent juvenile delinquency and develop productive citizens and leaders among our Nation's most vulnerable youth. Recently the Boys Clubs of America and the Girls Clubs of America combined and were renamed the Boys and Girls Clubs of America (BGCA). The Clubs provide youth with alternatives to the streets that include activities that develop their sense of belonging, competence, usefulness, and influence. More than 1,100 local Clubs provide activities for 1.4 million boys and girls nationwide. Typically, Club members live in large or medium-sized cities; have three or more siblings; are from minority populations; and have families whose annual income is less than $12,000.

Laying a Foundation

A 1986 Louis Harris and Associates survey—projectable to 3,500,000 alumni—showed that BGCA experiences help youth develop leadership skills and lay the foundation for the successes achieved by Club alumni in later life. Results indicate that Clubs have a positive impact on the lives of young people, especially those from disadvantaged families.

The survey also reported that three out of four Club alumni believe their Club experiences helped them to avoid difficulty with the law, and Clubs were viewed by alumni as a support system against drug abuse.

Activities available at Clubs, such as sports, exercise, and other group activi-

From the Office of Juvenile Justice and Delinquency Prevention, "OJJDP and Boys and Girls Clubs of America: Public Housing and High-Risk Youth," *Juvenile Justice Bulletin*, July 1991.

ties, provide the staff with excellent vehicles to teach members teamwork, responsibility, and leadership.

BGCA's proven record of helping at-risk youth stay out of trouble and preparing them to make worthwhile contributions to their communities as adults earned the organization an Award of Excellence from the Administrator of the Office of Juvenile Justice and Delinquency Prevention (OJJDP) in 1985. However, OJJDP's partnership with BGCA began long before.

"The Clubs provide youth with alternatives to the streets that include activities that develop their sense of belonging, competence, [and] usefulness."

In 1977, OJJDP awarded BGCA a 3-year grant to the then Boys Clubs of America for their Delinquency Prevention Demonstration Project, which tested more than 20 delinquency prevention approaches in 9 Clubs. Examples of the 20 approaches include developing youth employment opportunities, counseling and remedial programs, wilderness challenges, programs for families, and neighborhood reclamation. Ten delinquency prevention program principles resulted from this project and are the foundation of BGCA's Targeted Outreach program.

BGCA's involvement in public housing communities began more than 37 years ago. Many of the original Clubs have expanded considerably as a direct result of identifying and meeting the special needs of communities. The Clubs that operate cooperatively with local public housing authorities have played a critical role in reducing vandalism, curbing gang violence and drug activity, and giving youth a sense of belonging and purpose.

Targeted Outreach

The BGCA Task Force on Inappropriate Detention was created in 1981 with technical assistance provided by OJJDP. The Task Force's work resulted in the unanimous adoption of the program statement Inappropriate Detention of Juveniles by the BGCA National Board of Directors. From this philosophy evolved an emergency response system called Targeting Programs for Delinquency Intervention—or Targeted Outreach—a comprehensive program of effective techniques and strategies that point young people in alternative, positive directions through Boys and Girls Club programs.

The philosophy and purpose of BGCA is enhanced by Targeted Outreach's ability to reach out to adolescents who may never have been inclined to become Club members. After an adolescent has been recruited, methods to mainstream and keep the youth active in the Club are employed, based on past Club experiences and successes. Eighty Clubs in 10 metropolitan areas undertook BGCA's first Targeted Outreach program. They recruited 4,525 at-risk youth and established formal linkages with 335 community-based youth-serving agencies and organizations.

A special Targeted Outreach Case Management System has been developed that tracks the youths' progress and participation, and guides the Clubs in designing individual programs to curb delinquency.

This is a tool by which accurate records are kept on Targeted Outreach participants. It helps in determining, meeting, and evaluating the needs and interests of the Boys and Girls Clubs as they seek to serve youth in their Targeted Outreach programs. The following information on the youth is included in the Case Management System:

- Demographic information.
- Source of referral.
- Attendance record.
- Involvement with the juvenile justice system.
- At-risk status.
- School and Club status.
- Achievements.
- Targeted Outreach goals and objectives for each individual.
- Other pertinent information.

"Statistics show that 39 percent of Targeted Outreach participants demonstrated a positive change in academic performance."

The following are five major reasons for maintaining a Case Management System: Program Accountability, Staff Evaluation, Youth Evaluation, Troubleshooting Problems, and Accountability to Funding Sources. The Case Management System of recordkeeping is conducted in a confidential, nonstigmatizing manner since most of the Targeted Outreach youth do not know they are involved in a special Club program.

As of March 1, 1989, BGCA's national statistics show that 39 percent of Targeted Outreach participants demonstrated a positive change in academic performance; 68 percent remained active in the Club after 2 years in the program; and 93 percent did not have further contact with the juvenile justice system 2 years after joining the Club.

Expansion of Youth Clubs

To date, more than 10,000 at-risk youth, ages 12 to 18, have been recruited and mainstreamed into the programs of the Boys and Girls Clubs. Locally, Clubs have raised over $3 million to continue, expand, and enhance their delinquency intervention programs. The Clubs have built a collaborative relationship of over 1,200 formalized linkages with local juvenile courts, police departments, schools, and other youth-serving agencies and organizations that refer youth in danger of becoming delinquent to programs such as Targeted Outreach.

A particularly successful Club is located at the Wilkinson Terrace Apartments in Shreveport, Louisiana. There the public housing authority, Salvation Army, Boys and Girls Clubs, and the criminal justice department of Louisiana State University (LSU) have joined to design and implement a service program for 379 at-risk youth. The public housing authority provides the facilities for the Club; the Salvation Army and Boys and Girls Clubs provide the program structure, train staff, and purchase equipment and program supplies.

"By interacting and talking with peers, adults, and the older Club members, youth improve skills that will help them cope with stress."

Students from LSU's criminal justice department provide aid in daily programming, community research, and statistical analyses, and they develop outside resources to support the program. Through Targeted Outreach, youth participate in a job search program that teaches them skills in securing employment. They receive information from the Shreveport Police Department about illegal drugs and alcohol. Club members participate in a nutrition class sponsored by the Shreveport Nutrition Program. The members learn how to provide a meal for themselves and others when they are alone. This is beneficial to many that have the responsibility of feeding younger siblings when parents and guardians are not available.

The Shreveport Housing Authority reports that since Targeted Outreach was inaugurated at the Wilkinson Terrace Apartments, there have been markedly fewer incidents of vandalism, burglaries, and muggings—not only in the complex but also in the surrounding neighborhood.

A New Initiative

The Targeted Outreach Youth Gang Prevention and Intervention Program, a new OJJDP and Health and Human Services Interagency Agreement initiative, is being built in its early stages on BGCA's Targeted Outreach Program. It is designed to develop, field test, and replicate effective Club youth gang intervention and prevention techniques aimed at reaching at-risk youth. This 3-year project will serve more than 1,900 youth through a minimum of 200 linkages with community agencies.

Thirty Clubs have been selected as gang prevention sites. The primary goal of these sites will be to deter youth from becoming involved in gangs, with a primary focus aimed at 7 to 11 year olds. Each of the 30 Boys and Girls Clubs will implement its own unique program model—based upon the community, the needs of their members, and the severity of the youth gang problem locally. BGCA will provide training, materials, and technical assistance to all sites. Clubs selected for the program will receive a three-part manual that includes a *Gang Intervention and Prevention Manual* and a *Targeted Outreach In-service*

Training Manual.

Three Clubs have been selected as intervention sites: Crime Prevention Association in Philadelphia, Pennsylvania; Salvation Army Boys and Girls Club in Winston-Salem, North Carolina; and Boys and Girls Club of San Gabriel Valley in El Monte, California. These three clubs will develop and field test intensive youth gang intervention methods. At present, these intervention methods are in the developmental stages. The intervention sites will develop and document model gang intervention programs focusing on activities for youth 12 to 16 years old. Intervention sites will also use the three-part training manuals being used at the prevention sites.

"Parental involvement is an important part of the delinquency prevention strategy."

The first phases of intervention training began in July 1990. Results are not available at this time. An evaluation team will submit an in-depth progress report to the Office of Juvenile Justice and Delinquency Prevention.

Based on a set of program principles and recommendations, the sites will develop programs tailored to the youth they serve and the needs of the community. Training, program manuals and other materials developed as a result of an extensive review of the literature, telephone surveys, training needs assessment, and onsite assessment visits by the program's national staff will be utilized at all sites. A summary assessment report is scheduled.

SMART Moves

To enhance Targeted Outreach's delinquency prevention efforts, OJJDP awarded BGCA a grant, in October 1987, to train staff in SMART Moves, a drug, alcohol, and teen pregnancy prevention program for youth.

SMART Moves is a community-based program helping adolescents learn to say "no" to drug use and early sexual activity. Prevention teams—consisting of Club members and staff, community members and parents—lead small groups to help the participants develop skills necessary to identify and resist negative peer and social pressures. By interacting and talking with peers, adults, and the older Club members, youth improve skills that will help them cope with stress and solve problems. The program increases their self-esteem, and encourages effective communication with their parents, friends, Club staff, and neighbors.

For more than 4 years, the SMART Moves program at the Hillside Community Center in Milwaukee, Wisconsin, has relied on parents to augment its daily operations. Parental involvement has enabled the Center to provide an afterschool hot meal program, with breakfast and lunch programs in the summer. Club staff report that parent volunteers enable the Club to provide a variety of special activities, including celebrations and holiday festivities for Club members.

As one of the original demonstration sites to receive SMART Moves training, Hillside has incorporated all the SMART Moves components in its Club, including these two small group programs: (1) Start SMART for youth ages 10-12, and (2) Stay SMART for youth ages 13-15.

SMART Programs

The Center's parent program, Keep SMART, began in an unusual way. A prevention team took the participants—primarily single parents—to a weekend camp where they learned listening skills, parenting skills, and networking strategies. This became the Keep SMART program. Participants report that they are now better able to communicate with their children as a result of Keep SMART training.

Be SMART provides inservice training for Club staff, prevention teams, and volunteers. It supports the activities and messages of the small group programs. The entire Hillside staff has been trained in this curriculum.

Due to Club participation in Targeted Outreach/SMART Moves, 14,349 youth have received information dealing with drug and alcohol abuse and pregnancy prevention. This information has enabled the youth to make informed decisions on day-to-day issues. Community education, increased communication skills, and the identification of socially appropriate behavior have resulted from participation in Targeted Outreach and SMART Moves.

Boys and Girls Clubs in Public Housing

The successes of Targeted Outreach and SMART Moves helped OJJDP recognize the vital role that youth-serving agencies play in reaching high-risk youth and reducing juvenile crime. In 1988, OJJDP launched the initiative Reaching At-Risk Youth in Public Housing. Working through Boys and Girls Clubs of America, OJJDP provides youth development and substance use prevention programs for our Nation's most at-risk, hard-to-reach youth. This demonstration project is a key element in BGCA's strategy to reach thousands of at-risk youth who reside in public housing. Through OJJDP's initiative Reaching At-Risk Youth in Public Housing, BGCA is:

> ***"Columbia University researchers found that Boys and Girls Clubs exert a positive and consistent influence on youth."***

• Studying existing Clubs in public housing to determine how they were established and how they operate.

• Developing a manual that documents the procedures to establish and operate a Club in a public housing complex.

• Designing and publishing training and technical assistance curriculums and materials so that BGCA Regional Service Directors can assist local organizations in establishing Clubs in public housing.

• Designating four public housing developments as demonstration sites to work closely with the BGCA to form an advisory board, hire and train staff, develop an operating budget, and establish a fully functioning Club.

• Providing materials, training, and technical assistance to enable each local BGCA unit to implement Targeted Outreach or SMART Moves.

The Alice Griffith Branch of the Boys and Girls Clubs in San Francisco received one of OJJDP's initial two grants to support Clubs in public housing developments. Linkages with community agencies, such as the Bayview Hunter's Point Drug Treatment Foundation, C.A.P.E. Job Training, and San Francisco County Social Services, allow the Club to provide facilities and enhance programming and referrals for its 171 members. The San Francisco Police Department operates Safety Awareness for Everyone (S.A.F.E.) to mobilize and coordinate security services. The Parks and Recreation Department has made a city gym and sports field available for S.A.F.E. programs, and six teachers from the San Francisco Educational Service offer Club members remedial education and tutoring twice a week.

Parental involvement is an important part of the delinquency prevention strategy at the Alice Griffith Club. Educational activities, swimming lessons, field trips, and other special events such as weekend minicamps allow parents to interact with Club youth. Staff will be receiving training and technical assistance to help them conduct the Targeted Outreach and SMART Moves programs. . . .

Drug Demand Reduction Program

In April 1988, the FBI established the Drug Demand Reduction Program (DDRP) to augment its enforcement efforts in a long-term solution to the problem of illegal drug use. The DDRP strategy focuses on schools, communities, and the workplace. FBI agents help existing Boys and Girls Clubs implement or enhance drug prevention efforts, and they work to establish new Boys and Girls Clubs that will encourage high-risk youth to participate in positive after-school drug prevention activities.

> ***"FBI agents help existing Boys and Girls Clubs implement or enhance drug prevention efforts."***

The FBI appointed a Drug Demand Reduction Coordinator in each of its 57 field offices across the Nation. The coordinators are responsible for creating and assisting drug prevention and education initiatives. Coordinators and Boys and Girls Clubs are involved in implementing and enhancing drug prevention and youth development programs, recruiting high-risk youth for participation in Club programs, recruiting volunteers, and assisting in community-wide public relations.

Boys and Girls Clubs of America (BGCA) will continue to serve at-risk youth by providing services and support and helping to develop productive citizens and leaders.

BGCA will establish 100 Clubs in public housing developments through Outreach '91, a 5-year plan to expand services for an additional 700,000 youth. This ambitious goal reflects BGCA's commitment to sustaining its record of reducing substance abuse problems in public housing—a record documented in July 1989 by a Columbia University study, and verified by staff who attribute residents' community involvement and increased self-esteem to the presence of the Clubs.

Findings of Columbia Study

Researchers at the School of Social Work at Columbia University compared measures of drug-related problems, such as arrest records, paraphernalia, and drug use (e.g., police records, observational data, etc.), with the activities associated with substance abuse prevention and alternatives to illegal drug use (e.g., SMART Moves community developments) in 15 public housing developments with newly established Clubs, established Clubs, or no Clubs.

Columbia University researchers found that Boys and Girls Clubs exert a positive and consistent influence on youth living in public housing. Children and adolescents living in public housing developments where Clubs have been established are much less involved in dangerous activities than their counterparts who do not have access to a Club.

Adult residents of public housing with Boys and Girls Clubs benefited as well. Compared to parents in housing developments without Clubs, they were more involved in school programs, youth-oriented activities, and resident activities. The study also revealed a reduction in illegal drug use, drug trafficking, and other drug-related activities.

The work done in establishing Clubs in public housing and introducing SMART Moves in these Clubs earned BGCA the 1990 Exemplary Prevention Program Award given by the Office of Substance Abuse Prevention.

OJJDP's partnership with BGCA has provided continuity, direction, and vision to the Targeted Outreach, SMART Moves, and Boys and Girls Clubs in public housing programs. In the future, the partnership will perpetuate these successful delinquency prevention approaches by endorsing their replication and disseminating information about the programs.

The success of OJJDP and BGCA's partnership, combined with other efforts such as the FBI Demand Reduction Program, will benefit communities, individuals, and society as a whole. This continued cooperation will enable the development of new prevention strategies, enhancement of current programs, and strengthening of Boys and Girls Clubs of America.

Reducing Neighborhood Violence Will Reduce School Violence

by Julius Menacker, Ward Weldon, and Emanuel Hurwitz

About the authors: *Julius Menacker is a professor, Ward Weldon is an assistant professor, and Emanuel Hurwitz is an associate professor in the College of Education at the University of Illinois, Chicago.*

Lawlessness, danger, and lack of discipline are perceived to be rampant in inner-city public schools that serve low-income minority children. However, after more than two years of studying four public inner-city elementary schools in one of the poorest and most crime-ridden sections of Chicago, we have concluded that the public school is an island of relative safety in an ocean of danger that surrounds the school. Our findings suggest that communitywide—not just school-based—approaches are needed to solve the problems of lawlessness and fear in inner-city schools.

The Office of Juvenile Justice and Delinquency Prevention of the U.S. Department of Justice funded the study, which aimed at developing rules and enforcement procedures for schools experiencing problems of order and safety. Our purpose here is to describe and support our conclusion that public schools in crime-ridden areas are islands of safety and to suggest ways of providing an adequate education for students in such schools.

Research Results

The motivation for the Justice Department initiative came primarily from the 1978 study, *Safe Schools—Violent Schools*, sponsored by the Department of Health, Education, and Welfare. From a survey of 4,000 elementary and secondary schools, the authors of that study unearthed some alarming facts about the level of danger and disorder in public schools:

Julius Menacker, Ward Weldon, and Emanuel Hurwitz, "School Order and Safety as Community Issues," *Phi Delta Kappan*, September 1989. Reprinted with permission.

• 40% of the robberies and 36% of the assaults on urban youth took place in schools;

• approximately 8% of schools had serious problems of crime, violence, and disruption;

• in a typical month, more than 2.4 million students (11%) reported something worth more than $1 stolen, and about 282,000 (1.3%) reported being attacked, with 4% of that group requiring medical attention;

• in a typical month, 128,000 teachers (12%) had something worth more than $1 stolen, and 5,200 (2%) were physically attacked, with 19% of that group requiring medical attention;

• about three million secondary students (16%) avoided certain places in their schools out of fear, and about half a million students (3%) were afraid at school most of the time; and

• 125,000 high school teachers (12%) were threatened with physical harm each month and reported being reluctant to confront misbehaving students, and half of all the teacher respondents said that they experienced verbal abuse in a typical month.

Discipline and Safety

We repeated many of the questions contained in the *Safe Schools* survey for our study of teachers and sixth- and eighth-grade students in four inner-city Chicago schools. Our findings were similar to those of the national study, and they support the results of the annual Gallup Poll of the Public's Attitudes Toward the Public Schools. For more than two decades that poll has shown one of the major public concerns to be discipline and safety in the schools. In our survey:

• more than 50% of students reported that money, clothing, or personal property was stolen from them at least once during the school year, and 35% indicated that thefts occurred more than once;

• 8% of students reported being threatened by someone with a gun or knife who wanted money or drugs, and 3% reported that they had been threatened more than once;

> ***"Communitywide—not just school-based—approaches are needed to solve the problems of lawlessness and fear in inner-city schools."***

• 4% of students reported being beaten so badly during the school year that they required medical attention;

• 7% of students reported coming to school high on drugs or alcohol at least once during the year;

• 32% of students reported that they had carried a weapon to school at least once, and 14% said that they had done so more than once;

• 10% of students reported using a weapon at least once during the year to steal something, and 5% said that they had done so more than once;

• 15% of students reported hitting a teacher at least once during the year, and 5% reported that they had done so more than once;

• 3% of teachers reported being physically attacked, and 1% reported being threatened by a student with a weapon;

• 42% of teachers reported that they had hesitated at least once to confront misbehaving students out of fear for their own safety; and

• 39% of teachers reported damage to or theft of personal property during the school year in which our study was conducted.

Outside the School

Our data have little meaning to those who do not understand how conditions inside a given school relate to the environment in which that school is located. The *Safe Schools* study indicated that more robberies and assaults on urban youth took place *outside* of school than *in* it, but the *extent* and *seriousness* of out-of-school crime and violence were not discussed. We believe that an understanding of conditions in the broader community is central to understanding and treating school crime, violence, and disorder. Our survey of students and teachers yielded the following information on conditions in the community at large:

> ***"More than 50 percent of students reported that money, clothing, or personal property was stolen from them at least once."***

• 19% of students reported that they avoided the shortest route to school out of fear for their personal safety;

• 20% of students said that they avoided the school parking lot for safety reasons, and 19.6% said that they avoided "other places on school grounds";

• 98% of teachers reported that the neighborhoods surrounding their schools posed threats of vandalism, personal attack, and theft, and 48% said that these problems were very serious; and

• 18% of teachers felt "very unsafe" in the parking lot, and 22.9% felt "very unsafe" elsewhere outside of school grounds.

These findings led us to investigate other sources of information related to order and safety in the neighborhoods immediately surrounding the four schools. We were able to obtain police department records for an area of approximately two square miles that included two of our four schools. The data are for 1987, the same year in which we conducted our study of the schools.

Police records showed that the area surrounding two of those schools had been the scene of five murders, one manslaughter, 17 aggravated assaults, five criminal sexual assaults, 48 simple assaults, 116 armed robberies, 108 strong-arm robberies, 103 batteries with a weapon, 115 batteries with no weapon, 121 burglaries, 58 thefts of more than $300, 193 thefts of less than $300, 11 cases of arson, 67 cases of property damage, and 23 cases of unlawful possession of a handgun.

A third school in our study is located directly across the street from a public housing project, a fact that merits some discussion. In 1968 children from the project raided the school, breaking windows, overturning desks, scattering books, and causing other damage to the building. A 12-year-old student was arrested. By 1984 gang-motivated shootings at the project were increasingly common; five people were killed there in that year. By 1987 the project ranked first in police department statistics for percentage of violent crimes per capita in a Chicago housing project. The rate was nearly eight violent crimes for every 100 residents. Then, in September 1988, gang members attacked a group attending the funeral of a member of a rival gang, shooting at guests and stomping on the corpse. A week later a teenager was shot and killed in retaliation. An all-out war ensued, during which a nearby apartment building was damaged by a bomb. This incident led to a police raid on the worst of the project buildings.

"Schools should be viewed as microcosms of the broader society."

During the same period of gang warfare in the project, the daughter of an active PTA member was injured when she was caught in a gang shootout. The mother had already boarded up the front windows of her apartment to prevent stray bullets from entering, and she would not allow her sons to wear hats in winter for fear that the hats might suggest gang membership and incite rival gangs to violence. The publicity occasioned by the shooting of her daughter enabled the mother to demand and be granted relocation to a safer public housing facility. Her departure was a severe blow to the school's efforts to gain parental support for the newly developed disciplinary code—a project that she had enthusiastically supported.

Policy Responses

The public response to the serious problem of school order and safety has been to pressure authorities to make schools safer and more orderly by establishing tougher rules, hiring security guards, and requiring all faculty members and students to wear or carry identification cards. All schools contact the local police periodically to insure that efficient communication patterns are in place in the event of an emergency.

The state legal system has also been mobilized to deal with the issue of school order and safety. Recent Illinois statutes require that all incidents of intimidation in schools be reported to the principals, that teachers be given the right to remove disruptive students from their classrooms, and that every district form a discipline council that includes representatives from the community.

Federal and state courts have tried to help, as well. Decisions have required the Chicago schools to formulate a district-wide disciplinary code, have forbidden the wearing of earrings in school by male students (since earrings may be gang symbols), and have allowed minors who use weapons unlawfully on school grounds to be tried as adult criminals.

This "get tough" attitude may help to improve school order and safety. But the reforms to date bring to mind King Canute, who tried to hold back the sea with his bucket. The most urgent and important issue—the social pathology of the communities in which these schools are located—has yet to be addressed. The schools are already safer than the surrounding neighborhoods. Further substantial improvement can only be realized by interventions that address conditions within both the schools *and* their communities. Children and their parents must feel safe walking to school, which means controlling gang warfare and recruitment. The flourishing traffic in drugs must be stopped so that youngsters no longer see the drug dealer as the most prominent model of success and power. In short, statutes, court decisions, public and private programs aimed at school improvement, and other attempts to reform public education must address both the community and the school in a comprehensive manner.

Community Order and Safety

Policies and programs that focus on the improvement of *school* discipline, order, and safety must be replaced with policies and programs that focus on the improvement of *community* order and safety. The school should be viewed as just one component—albeit, a very important component—of the total milieu. A comprehensive approach to school order and safety requires coordinated policy making, program planning, and implementation, carried out by a council representing the police department, educators, public housing officials, private businesses, public and private social agencies, and representatives of the local, state, and national governments. This council must have adequate funding and authority to insure that its plans can be effectively implemented over a long enough period to offer reasonable hope of success.

> ***"Programs must be designed to provide immediate results in personal improvement."***

We recommend that the council concentrate on breaking the vicious cycle of inadequate education, jobs, and housing. Schools are one place to begin. However, without simultaneous efforts to improve housing and jobs for both students and their parents, education will continue to fail. Moreover, unless community safety is improved, improvement in jobs, housing, and education will be seriously impeded.

This view is not new. More than 50 years ago John Dewey taught us that schools should be viewed as microcosms of the broader society and that the broader society must play a role in school programs and policies. Dewey recognized the futility of separating school and society into discrete components. He saw that each inescapably affects the other. Dewey's concepts have long been revered, but they have been neglected because they are difficult to implement. However, we are fast approaching the time when attention to the links between school and community is an absolute necessity in many locales.

> ***"Members of the community must be consulted and involved in proposed improvement plans."***

This view has already received serious recognition in some quarters. Private business has begun to play an increasingly prominent role in public school affairs by offering scholarship programs, by adopting individual schools, and by taking over the operation of individual schools and even entire school districts. For example, plans are underway in Chicago for a consortium of private business interests to assume the management of a new public school that will be built, staffed, and operated under its auspices. In Massachusetts, Boston University is preparing to assume control of the Chelsea public schools.

Immediate Feedback

The federal courts are slowly shifting to the view that schools cannot be held solely responsible for the problems that beset them. The most prominent example is the decision on segregated housing in Yonkers, New York, which was handed down by a federal court, affirmed by the appellate court, and allowed to stand by the U.S. Supreme Court. The decision held that the city had contributed to the racial segregation of its public schools through its support of segregated public housing and thus must share responsibility for correcting the problem. The court recognized that school authorities did not have the power to correct unconstitutional segregation without the active participation and help of the city government, whose actions had powerful consequences for the racial configuration of the Yonkers public schools.

These developments auger well for a comprehensive school/community program to improve order and safety. The findings of our research suggest that members of the community must be consulted and involved in proposed improvement plans. The process must allow them to develop psychological ownership of the plans and activities that are formulated and undertaken. They must also be given responsible roles adapted to their interests and abilities. For example, we formulated an effective disciplinary code for two schools because parents, faculty, and students were involved in the process. As a result, the code addressed issues that would otherwise have been left unattended. Moreover, involvement produced a high level of enthusiasm and commitment on the part of those affected by the new rules and regulations. This enthusiasm is best exemplified by the decision of faculty members to accept one extra student in each of their classes in order to free a teacher to conduct an in-school suspension program. Such a voluntary decision by teachers would not have been possible had the teachers not been involved in the formulation of the plan.

Our findings also suggest a need to insure that plans and activities provide immediate benefits and concrete improvements. Community residents, including parents and students, see little likelihood that their lives will improve. Therefore, heavy reliance on deferred gratification is not wise. Programs must be designed to provide immediate results in personal improvement, whether in the form of income for accepting program responsibilities or in the form of improvements in personal status.

To a lesser extent, the same principle applies to educators working in the schools, who labor under difficult conditions and whose efforts are more often criticized than praised. Together, residents and educators who have lived and labored in dangerous surroundings must be given some immediate sign that they have seen the worst and that conditions are now improving. Such a sign would also mean new hope for children in the schools.

Physicians Can Help Curb Youth Violence

by Deborah Prothrow-Stith

About the author: *Deborah Prothrow-Stith was the Massachusetts commissioner of public health from 1987-89. She is now assistant dean for government and community programs at Harvard School of Public Health. Prothrow-Stith is the author of* Deadly Consequences: How Violence Is Destroying Our Teenage Population.

Adolescent violence has reached epidemic proportions in the United States. Homicide is the second leading cause of death for all young males; for African-American men aged 18 to 24, it is the leading cause. Epidemiologic analyses indicate that our recorded homicide rate is among the highest in the world. It is customary to regard adolescent violence strictly as a criminal justice problem, requiring judicial solutions. Yet our court system has not succeeded in stemming the lethal tide. Although our jail cells are overflowing, the assaults and murders continue. Clearly, new perspectives and new sources of energy are needed.

Homicide Prevention

As physicians, we are accustomed to intervening in young people's lives to safeguard health. We inoculate them against preventable diseases, urge them to use condoms with new sex partners, and caution them not to drink and drive. In similar fashion, could we not help them learn to handle their anger and control their aggressive impulses? Could tactics that have proved effective in addressing other public health issues be applied to the violence in our schools and on our streets?

My interest in adolescent violence as a public health problem began when, as a third-year medical student, I did a six-week surgical rotation at Brigham and Women's Hospital in Boston. During one 12-hour emergency room shift, a

Deborah Prothrow-Stith, "Can Physicians Help Curb Adolescent Violence?" *Hospital Practice* 27 (6): 193-207. Reprinted with permission.

young man was admitted with a knife wound over one eye—the result of a drunken argument. As I nervously stitched him up, he described the circumstances leading up to the attack. "Don't go to sleep," he warned me, "because the guy who did this to me is going to be in here in about an hour, and you'll get all the practice stitching you need!"

> ***"As physicians, we are accustomed to intervening in young people's lives to safeguard health."***

Although I did not take his advice—sleep being the most important thing on my mind at the time—his words stayed with me. Had he been a potential suicide who had taken an overdose of barbiturates, my job would have extended well beyond the lavage of his stomach. Certainly, had he announced that he was about to make a second suicide attempt, I would have been medically and legally obligated to consult a mental health professional to assess the situation further and perhaps order a hospital stay for psychiatric observation. This case seemed to have aspects remarkably similar to those of a suicide—the patient was threatening to harm another and might well be harmed himself in the process—yet I had no obligation to intervene.

The Physician's Role

It seemed to me then, as it does now, that there is an essential contradiction here. Physicians spend a great deal of time educating patients about the potential consequences of cigarette smoking, eating disorders, and other behavioral problems. We do this because there is good evidence that such activities place patients at higher risk for illness and premature death. Yet violence—although it results in more than 20,000 homicides a year in this country—is not presented in the medical curriculum as the physician's concern. We just "stitch them up and send them out," knowing that they are at risk for subsequent violence.

Let us theorize for a moment that the pent-up anger that has become epidemic in our society—especially among young men of color growing up in poverty—is at least in part a behavioral disorder with public health implications. What might physicians do to combat it? . . .

Avenues for Intervention

Physicians wishing to combat adolescent violence can start by identifying contact points for intervention within their own practices. One obvious contact point is the emergency room, where the casualties of street battles usually end up. Studies of intentional injury support the observation that emergency room workers actually have far greater interaction with the perpetrators and victims of violence than do the police.

In the Northeast Ohio Trauma Study, investigators found that for every recorded homicide, 25 nonfatal assaults were reported to the police, whereas four times that number were seen at local emergency rooms. Instead of merely stitching up the victims and discharging them—which only leads to retaliation and additional bloodshed—hospital emergency departments should attempt to evaluate the circumstances leading up to the injury-related incident. Diagnostic and service intervention protocols should automatically be instituted for victims of street and family violence, just as they are for victims of other forms of intentional injury such as child abuse, sexual assault, or attempted suicide.

The assessment of a patient who has been intentionally injured should include, at a minimum: 1) circumstances of the injury event, 2) relationship of the victim to the assailant, 3) drug or alcohol use, 4) presence of family violence or other underlying emotional or psychosocial risk factors, 5) history of intentional injuries or violent behavior, 6) predisposing biologic risk factors, and 7) intent to seek revenge. Patients emerging from such an assessment with a high-risk profile may then be referred for behavior modification therapy (one-on-one counseling or group therapy). Simultaneously, community support services can be brought in to assist the family.

"Physicians wishing to combat adolescent violence can start by identifying contact points for intervention within their own practices."

The goal of the hospital-based interventions described is to prevent further escalation of violence after an initial nonfatal event has occurred. Such tactics have not been widely taught in medical schools and tend to be unfamiliar to clinicians, who expect the problem to be dealt with in the context of the criminal justice system. By the time a young man commits a crime, however, the aggressive behavior may be so deeply rooted that it is more resistant to any attempt at redirection.

Preventing Violence

Emergency room workers must resort to secondary intervention strategies because they are faced with a person at considerable risk for future morbidity or mortality resulting from violence. Unhappily, more often than not, this is the only point of contact with medical care. However, pediatricians and family physicians have the opportunity to practice primary prevention (e.g., in a well-baby clinic) and refer older siblings for appropriate help. When behavior modification strategies are applied at such early contact points, the likelihood of success is considerably greater and the cost to society dramatically less.

Peter Stringham of the East Boston Neighborhood Health Center has developed concrete protocols to assist clinicians in identifying potentially volatile situations and providing "anticipatory guidance" to families with young children. Topics for discussion with parents include parental arguing behavior, disciplinary practices, plans for future disciplinary measures, attitudes toward violence in the media, and conflict resolution between siblings.

Because violence is a learned behavior, parents are role models. With encouragement from health care providers, they can begin to reexamine their own attitudes and behavior and become an active force in teaching verbal rather than physical methods of resolving disagreements. Physicians and other care providers can also use their influence to steer parents away from movies and television programs that glamorize weapon carrying and bloodshed. Although the effect of media violence on children has been hotly debated for many years, most recent studies suggest that violent programs do not provide healthy catharsis but rather promote negative behaviors in young viewers. Parents are also caught in a dilemma as to what advice to give a child regarding an escalating conflict. Often because they do not want their children to be wimps, they effectively encourage fighting. Children of such parents appear to be at the greatest risk for participating in violence.

As the child matures, the clinician can approach the subject of anger and violence more directly by asking questions about how conflicts are handled in and out of school. If a youngster brags that he has a reputation for toughness, or if he has already been suspended from school for carrying a weapon, it is obvious that attention must be paid. Unless an effort is made to reach that youngster and teach him alternative means of conflict resolution, he is likely to be labeled a problem by teachers and school administrators, to fall behind in his classroom work, perhaps to drop out of school altogether. Once on the street, his aggressive impulses may be channeled into criminal behavior, and he risks winding up behind bars or becoming a homicide statistic.

Weapons at School

Unfortunately, the situation in our schools is such that many youngsters have begun carrying weapons out of fear of assault. Data from the 1990 national school-based Youth Risk Behavior Survey indicate that approximately one out of every five high school students carried a firearm, knife, or club at least once during the month preceding the survey. Among black male students who carried a weapon, firearms—usually handguns—accounted for 54.2%. Among white and Hispanic male students who carried a weapon, knives and razors were the most frequently carried (54.7% and 46.9%, respectively).

> ***"Open discussion with the pediatrician or family physician can help the youngster explore ways of avoiding dangerous situations."***

Often, parents are aware of the dangers but feel helpless to interfere. Some are even supportive; if Johnny goes to a high school where knives or guns are commonplace, a parent may think Johnny is safer if he carries a weapon to defend himself. In such situations, open discussion with the pediatrician or family physician can help the youngster explore ways of avoiding dangerous situations, rather than running headlong into them. Families living in high-crime areas may need to be reminded that weapons intended only for self-defense have a nasty habit of being used in altercations with family and friends.

> ***"The question posed to students is not how to stifle their anger but rather how to channel it into constructive action."***

Reducing access to handguns would almost certainly make a sizable dent in the incidence of adolescent homicides. Across most of the United States, it is easier for a teenager to obtain a handgun than a driver's license. A recent study compared the homicide statistics of Seattle with those of Vancouver, B.C., a city with similar demographics located only 140 miles away. The number of handgun homicides in the U.S. city was more than five times that of its Canadian counterpart, whereas the rates for homicides with knives and other weapons were not too dissimilar. The investigators concluded that Vancouver's restrictive handgun laws accounted for most of the difference in overall homicides. Some have suggested that people will find other ways to kill if handguns are not available—the "guns don't kill people, people kill people" argument. Yet this two-city comparison directly challenges that contention.

A Coordinated Approach

Routine screening of children and teenagers for a history of family or peer violence, substance abuse, depression, low self-esteem, and other factors predisposing to intentional injury can permit early identification of those at highest risk. But identification alone is not enough; responsive mental health services are also needed, along with school-based preventive education programs and active community support. The vicious circle of adolescent violence can be broken only by interweaving the public health and criminal justice approaches and obtaining the cooperation of all parties concerned: social agencies, police departments, health care providers, educators, teenagers, parents.

Disturbed by the epidemic of violence that was sweeping our country in the late 1970s, the then Surgeon General Julius Richmond included the reduction of interpersonal violence among the health care priorities in the first national agenda for health promotion and disease prevention, which appeared in 1979. Subsequently, the CDC [Centers for Disease Control] established a violence epidemiology branch to track the national incidence of interpersonal violence, including assault, homicide, child abuse, spouse abuse, and rape. When these intentional injuries were examined as a group rather than independently, the data emerged confirming the tendency of violent acts to occur between close acquaintances or family members.

In 1980, the first symposium exploring homicide among black males was organized by the federal Alcohol, Drug Abuse, and Mental Health Administration. Five years later, Surgeon General C. Everett Koop convened the Surgeon General's Conference on Violence as a Public Health Problem, a multidisciplinary forum designed to encourage the application of public health techniques of investigation and preventive intervention to the issue of violence in our society. Participants in the conference drew encouragement from the recent success of similar interventions designed to discourage young people from smoking. Within a single generation, perceptions about smoking have shifted from viewing it as a glamorous pastime linked to movie stars and high-fashion models to viewing smoking as a stupid and unhealthy addiction.

National Health Objective

In 1991, the Public Health Service cited reduction of physical fighting among adolescents aged 14 to 17 as one of the national health objectives for the year 2000. Strategies recommended for achieving this objective include 1) counteracting the cultural acceptance of violence, 2) decreasing aggressive behavior among parents and their children, 3) reducing the exposure of children and adolescents to violence in the media, and 4) improving the recognition, management, and treatment of adolescent victims and those at high risk for assaults.

> ***"The proposed public health approach to the prevention of adolescent violence complements the existing criminal justice approach."***

Educational interventions that stress nonviolent conflict resolution skills have been strongly advocated as a means of reducing the need for more extensive rehabilitative efforts later on. One such educational intervention is the Violence Prevention Project of the Health Promotion Program for Urban Youth, a service of the Boston Department of Health and Hospitals. At the core of the intervention is a 10-session course for high school students that provides descriptive information on the risks of intentional injury, teaches alternative techniques of conflict resolution, and creates a classroom ethos that values nonviolent responses to anger.

Channeling the Anger

The Violence Prevention Curriculum acknowledges that anger is a normal and even essential emotion and that institutional sources of anger, such as classism, racism, and sexism, are prevalent in U.S. society. The question posed to students is not how to stifle their anger but rather how to channel it into constructive action. Role-playing and videotaping are extensively used to enable students to analyze the dynamics of physical fighting (the initial argument and its escalation, the role of principal participants, the behavior of friends or the observing crowd) and come up with less dangerous alternatives. The curriculum is also suitable for use outside the classroom: for example, in alternative schools, recreational programs, public housing developments, Sunday schools, and neighborhood health centers or YMCAs.

When we consider how to address the problem of adolescent violence from a public health perspective, the influence of concerned parents should not be overlooked. The organization Mothers Against Drunk Driving (MADD) has been an effective catalyst in focusing public attention on the problem of alcohol-related automobile fatalities among teenagers. Similar grassroots organizations are springing up across the country to tackle adolescent violence and its consequences. Save Our Sons and Daughters (SOSAD), a national organization founded in Detroit, Atlanta's Mothers of Murdered Sons (MOMS), New York City's Mothers Against Violence, and Parents of Murdered Children are examples of parent groups that promote nonviolent conflict resolution and provide community support for the families of murdered youths.

Gradually, local mental health centers are beginning to recognize this need as well; an example in the Boston area is the Roxbury Community Health Center's Living After Murder Program, which was specifically designed to provide psychological support to bereaved families. As the problem of adolescent violence receives broader attention, the number and scope of such programs will undoubtedly increase.

Changing Perceptions

The proposed public health approach to the prevention of adolescent violence complements the existing criminal justice approach. Whereas the latter concentrates on incarceration or other punishment for crimes already committed against society, the former seeks to avert those crimes by changing the perception of violence as glamorous and successful and by applying behavior modification techniques to children and teenagers exhibiting high-risk behavior.

Chapter 4

How Can Gang Violence Be Reduced?

CURRENT CONTROVERSIES

Reducing Gang Violence: An Overview

by Irving A. Spergel and G. David Curry

About the authors: *Irving A. Spergel served as the principal investigator for the National Youth Gang Suppression and Intervention Program, a federal research program. Spergel is a professor at the University of Chicago School of Social Service Administration. G. David Curry is an associate professor of criminal justice at West Virginia University in Morgantown.*

A major objective of the National Youth Gang Suppression and Intervention Research and Development project in cooperation with the Office of Juvenile Justice and Delinquency Prevention is to identify promising approaches to dealing with the youth gang problem. . . .

Focusing on Violent Youth Gangs

Our interest in youth gangs was defined primarily in law enforcement terms. Therefore, our study deals mainly with high-profile youth gangs who have come to police attention usually for violent, but sometimes for various other kinds of criminal behavior, including drug use and trafficking. Youth gangs tend to be better organized than delinquent groups, with established traditions in some of the larger cities where the problem is chronic. Youth gangs also tend to have a communal and more complex functional character probably serving a greater variety of interests and need than ad hoc delinquent groups. The two concepts, youth gangs and delinquent groups, are overlapping and distinctive rather than categorically different. Moreover, the definition of the youth gang also varies within cities by different kinds of agencies and especially across cities, and probably by sizes of cities. The term *youth gang* refers often (but not always) to youths, mainly males between the ages of 12 and 25, in various organizational forms. Race/ethnicity, region or city, economic opportunities, and traditions appear to influence organizational forms and behavioral patterns.

The data were obtained from 254 respondents in 45 cities and six institutional agencies (mainly correctional sites) selected through a process that began with the screening of approximately 100 cities. . . .

Social problems wax and wane, but our responding organizations have to sustain themselves whether a youth gang problem is present or not. The relationship between gang problem and program strategy, however, must be made sooner or later for the sake of logic or common sense (as well as public relations) and more often to justify requests for additional funds for gang program initiatives. In order to understand and evaluate the organization's or community's response to gangs, we believe it is important to describe and analyze the nature of the specific strategy or set of strategies developed within and across agencies and communities and to assess the effectiveness of these strategies in reducing the problem. . . .

Gang Strategies

The strategies are conceptualized as *community organization, social intervention, opportunities provision, suppression,* and *organizational development.* The strategies are defined and their indicators or statements or program activities are classified as follows.

Community organization: local community organization or neighborhood mobilization. Irving Spergel's literature review lists community organization as one of four major strategies that have been employed historically in dealing with the youth gang problem: "Community organization is the term used to describe efforts to bring about adjustment, development, or change [in or] among groups and organizations in regard to community problems or social needs." The term *interorganizing*, a key dimension of community organization or community organizing, also is used to refer to "efforts at enhancing, modification, or change in intergroup or interorganizational relationships to cope with a community problem."

Key words and phrases were employed by the respondents that at times could be included clearly in this community organization category, and at other times not. Much depended on the context and intent of the key words used. Decisions for placement of items in a category had to be made based on some appropriate rationale. For example, the contemporary term *networking* was classified under the strategy of community organization, unless it referred to networking among law enforcement agencies. (When networking involved only law enforcement agencies, it was classified under suppression; see below.) References to prevention, when they implied (and they usually did)

> ***"Our study deals mainly with high-profile youth gangs who have come to police attention usually for violent . . . criminal behavior."***

intervention efforts across agencies, were coded as community organization. When prevention referred primarily to a service activity such as counseling by a specific agency focused on at-risk youth prior to full-fledged gang membership, the reference was placed in the category of social intervention. All references to attendance at meetings of community organizations or with community leaders were regarded as pursuing a community organization strategy. After much consideration, we included advocacy for victims under the general strategy of suppression rather than community organization, because it can be viewed as part of a more basic strategy of crime control and justice system processing. Additional goals or activities encompassed by the community organization strategy included the following:

"Street work is . . . the systematic effort of an agency worker . . . to help a group of young people who are described as delinquent."

cleaning up graffiti in the community
involving the schools
mobilizing the community
building community trust
involving parent groups in community programs
educating the community
changing the community

Social intervention: youth outreach and street work counseling. Spergel lists youth outreach and street work as a second major gang program strategy. Street work [according to Spergel] is

> the practice variously labeled detached work, street club, gang work, area work, extension youth work, corner work, etc. It is the systematic effort of an agency worker, through social work or treatment techniques within the neighborhood context, to help a group of young people who are described as delinquent or potentially delinquent to achieve a conventional adaptation. This requires the agent to work with or manipulate the people or other agency representatives who interact critically with members of the delinquent group.

The traditional notion of street work may be somewhat outdated or limited and can be regarded as part of a larger, more contemporary strategy of social intervention that focuses on individual behavioral value change or transformation. Therefore, we place street work under the more general category of social intervention. Recreational and sports activities also are encompassed by this strategy. Social intervention includes mainly counseling or direct attempts—informational or guidance—to change the values of youths in such a way as to make gang involvement less likely. References to knowledge improvement or general education, however, especially for certain groups or populations of youth, are included under opportunities provision, below. Social advocacy for individual gang members is classified as a social intervention goal. The following key words or indicators fall into the social intervention category:

crisis intervention
service activities
diversion
outreach
providing role models
leadership development
intergang mediation
group counseling
temporary shelter
referrals for services
religious conversion
counseling of gang members
drug use prevention/treatment
all psychological approaches
all social work approaches
postsentencing social services
work with the gang structure
helping members leave the gang
tattoo removal

Opportunities: jobs, job training, and education. Spergel lists opportunities provision as a third major gang strategy. This approach emphasizes "large scale resource infusions and efforts to change institutional structures, including schools, job opportunities, political participation, and the development of a new relationship between the federal government and local neighborhoods in the solution not only of delinquency but of poverty itself." Here are included efforts to stimulate the development of new and improved school, special training, and job programs, and business and industry involvement in the social and economic advancement of people, including and targeting gang youth. Key words or phrases under opportunities provision include the following:

job preparation
job training
job placement
job development
school tutoring
education of gang youth

Suppression: arrest, incarceration, and supervision. Spergel lists suppression as the fourth major gang program strategy. Under this approach gang members may be "arrested, prosecuted, and removed for long prison sentences," although the strategy may be employed in less drastic form by non-justice system personnel, as well. Tactical patrols by police gang units, vertical prosecution, intensive supervision and vertical case management by probation departments, legislation targeted at gang members, and interagency task forces involving criminal justice actors are placed in this category. Also included are the development and implementation of information systems (i.e., gathering/collecting and maintaining information), as well as information sharing or publishing of information on gangs that facilitates law enforcement. Other key words or phrases included are the following:

enforcement
neutralization
investigation
adjudication
apprehension
monitoring
restraint
arrest
discipline
intelligence
identification of suspects
legal consequences
removal from community
correctional placement
law enforcement liaison

Organizational development and change: institutional and policy adaptations and mechanisms. A fifth category has been added that has a modifying or limited organizational development quality. This strategy refers to organizational adaptations and changes that mainly facilitate the achievement of the other strategies. Especially characteristic is organizational structure and process specialization in order to deal with the gang problem—for example, forming a special gang unit in the police department for gang information, investigation, and enforcement purposes. . . .

The most common first or primary strategy of agencies in our survey is suppression (44%), followed by social intervention (31.5%). Organizational change (10.9%) and community organization (8.9%) are comparably less common as first or primary strategies. Provision of opportunities as a primary strategy is most infrequent (4.8%). Over the total listing of strategies regardless of rank, suppression was still the most often chosen, and opportunities and organizational change or development the least frequently selected. Because the majority of respondents are from criminal justice agencies, this distribution is not surprising.

"Under [suppression] gang members may be 'arrested, prosecuted, and removed for long prison sentences.'"

Society Must Address Social Issues to Reduce Gang Violence

by Greg Boyle

About the author: *Greg Boyle served as pastor of Dolores Mission Church in east Los Angeles from 1986 to 1992, and helped many gang members to reform.*

I caught the phone on its third ring. "Rusty's been shot. Can you come quick to Popeye's house?"

I didn't recognize the young, breathless voice. I said I'd be on my way. It was 1:30 a.m.

Images of Rusty

While driving up 4th Street, I repeated the words over again in my head. Rusty had been "shot," he hadn't been killed. I conjured up quick images of Rusty. He was *bien jugueton*, always very playful and wildly funny. His humor was just a little bit crazed.

Once, when I was driving Rusty and a carload of his "homies" (which is short for "homeboys" and means buddies from his neighborhood), Rusty completely changed the lyrics of the song "Just Because," as it blared from my oldies tape, to "bag" on my large forehead. "Just because your forehead is so immense," he sang, and it went on like that for the remainder of the song. He substituted "Frenton" and "Bumper" to vary his kidding of my receding hairline. He had often told me that I didn't have a "forehead" but rather a "tenhead."

Rusty was also a "chillon"—meaning he'd cry at any vulnerable or difficult time. Whenever I'd visit him in Central Juvenile Hall, he'd tear-up on me. The times we spoke in my office alone would almost certainly end with him losing the battle against his tears.

One such time was after he and about 30 of his homies had finished watching

Greg Boyle, "Deadly Despair," *Sojourners*, October 1990. Reprinted with permission from *Sojourners*, P.O. Box 29272, Washington, DC 20017.

a local news show in our rectory that had done a piece on the gang problem in Los Angeles. This particular evening's installment was the last in a continuing series meant to drum up support from the citizenry to "wipe out gangs." The correspondent would end each segment with a 900 number urging people to call and donate money so these gangs could be "wiped out."

This last report featured Dolores Mission and juxtaposed our strategy with gangs with that of the local police precinct. Many of Rusty's homeboys were covered in this piece. When it ended, Rusty asked to speak with me. He was uncharacteristically somber. I sat him down in my office after evicting the six or so homies who were gathered there.

"What's up, homes?" I asked him, unfamiliar with this grave expression on his face.

"They Want to Wipe Us Out"

"That TV thing got to me," he began. He was staring off beyond me and his gaze locked vacantly on my bookshelf. He cradled a pair of "locs" (sunglasses) on his knee. "They want to wipe us out, G. They even have a number you can call if you want to wipe us out. They are even asking for money so they can wipe us out. What d'ya think they want to do, G?"

"I guess they want to wipe ya out," I answered with a laugh, but Rusty was unmoving and grim. "I wish they'd help you out. I wish they'd give you better schools and jobs and things to do. But I guess they just want to wipe you out."

"And they were talkin' s--- about you, too, G. How come?" The local police commander had made a few disparaging remarks about my preferred strategy with these "street terrorists."

"I don't really know, Rusty. I suppose it's because I refuse to hate you guys and that's what they want me to do." I paused. "Do you think I should hate you?"

Rusty shook his head and barely pronounced "no." Then nothing prepared me for what he did next. He silently grabbed his sunglasses and put them on, and then leaned his head way back and began to sob. We sat in silence. He cried for some time. I told him that I loved him and would always be there for him. All he said to me was, "I know, G, I know." He soon composed himself and joined his homies gathered in the parking lot of the church.

> ***"I wish they'd help you out. I wish they'd give you better schools and jobs and things to do. But I guess they just want to wipe you out."***

It was this image of the chillon, of this super-sensitive kid, that dominated my thoughts as I pulled up to Mott and Eagle Streets and saw the yellow police tape draped from side to side. The ambulance pulled away too slowly. Not a good sign, I thought. I reached the yellow tape and saw a body wrapped in a white sheet.

Rusty had been killed instantly with one bullet to the head. He and his homies had been "kickin' it" in front of Popeye's house when a car with rival gang members came by. They all engaged in the ritual dance of "gang-bangers," meaning they "mad-dogged" each other (stared each other down), "hit up" each other (asked "Where you from?"), and finally "dissed" each other's neighborhood (said "F--- the Locos").

"He knew that life was not meant to be nor to end like this. He cried because he knew that gang-banging was killing us all."

They drove away but all knew they would be back. Within minutes they returned with guns, and Rusty had just been too slow in diving to the sidewalk.

Since I had offered to inform his parents, the police at the scene allowed me to cross the line to identify Rusty. When the officer pulled back the sheet, Rusty had the same empty and sad stare on his face that had preceded his crying jag in my office that day after the TV program.

I hugged and tried to console the homies as they arrived, and then I left to tell Rusty's parents that their eldest son was dead. As I had experienced many times before, the words "*Lo mataron a Mando*"— "They've killed Mando" (Rusty's real name)—cut through the stillness of the early morning and the yelps of grief that began from his mother pierced the silence and our hearts with it.

Rusty's death was the fourth such murder in two weeks in our community. As I had been called upon to do just a week before, I preached to a church full of homeboys who were enraged by yet another loss from their neighborhood.

What Life Was Meant to Be

I spoke of Rusty's humor, and I shared the story of his tears in my office. I told his gathered friends that Rusty felt things deeply. That he laughed and cried readily and with ease, for he was a young man and great of heart. I insisted that this was what life was meant to be.

I said that we are meant to grow old together and watch our children grow and their children as well. And that all the while we are meant to have a great appetite for what life does to us—making us laugh and cry and wonder. We are meant to feel things deeply. I went on like this in the church.

Then I told them that it was "gang-banging" that had killed Rusty. It was gang-banging that had killed Trigger, Cricket, Flaco, Chopper, and the others. It wasn't some particular gang but rather gang-banging itself. And to the extent that we have ever engaged in gang-banging—ever maddogged, hit-up, or dissed someone else; packed a gun, pulled a trigger, or "gone on a mission"—then we are responsible for this death.

I didn't know how to end the homily. Then it came to me. That is why Rusty cried that day in my office, I said to them. He knew that life was not meant to be nor to end like this. He cried because he knew that gang-banging was killing us all.

At the end of the Mass, the coffin was rotated and opened for viewing. As is customary, I was the first to see Rusty and give him my blessing. I noticed when the casket was opened that a drop of liquid rested on Rusty's heavily made-up face, probably a result of the intense heat of the evening and the terrible job done by the morticians. It looked like Rusty had one solitary tear streaking down his face. It remained there for the duration of the viewing—a testimony to this lovable chillon, and a challenge to the madness that had caused his death.

Symptoms of Greater Problems

Gang activity and gang-related crime and death are not problems in our community, they are symptoms. They point beyond themselves to even greater problems of education, joblessness, boredom, dysfunctional families, intense poverty, and despair.

> ***"Our energies of opposition must be directed toward the poverty, unemployment, and failures of the school system that keep gang-banging alive."***

In the city of Los Angeles, our analysis of this "problem" has been consistently shallow. Tax dollars and public sentiment have been invested in campaigns to wipe out gangs, rather than address the source of such behavior. Many Christian communities and church organizations have cast their lot with the prevailing cultural response to gangs, and so "the jailer and the cop" keep receiving a blank check to do what they will.

But it is precisely because we are unwilling to hunker down and deal with the root causes of gang activity and violence that there is a marked increase in gang membership and gang-related deaths. We should not be surprised.

In areas of the city of Los Angeles where gang activity is most dominant, police officers have a secret code among themselves. If they receive a call that two gang members are fighting or that rival gangs are having a "rumble," especially if there is shooting between them, the police characterize the call as an "NHI" meaning No Human Involved. An NHI gives the police permission to have a lighter touch on the gas pedal and to arrive just in time to be too late; in time to mop up afterward. After all, NHI.

Our born-again vigilance loses sight of the fact that there are human beings involved here. The cry of the urban poor is partly expressed in the madness and despair of gang violence. In fact, many humans involved. The "hate 'em and hurt 'em" strategy of local law enforcement officials and the "take no prisoners" approach of the city's leadership never even get in the vicinity of a solution to this problem. Our churches have blessed campaigns to "take back our streets" and have forgotten that kids are involved. We have allowed them to be called the enemy.

What Christians Must Do

People of faith must pose a countersign to society's prevailing analysis of the "gang problem." Christian communities must stand in hopeful defiance of tactics that seek to frame these youth as "enemies of the people." The gospel insists that we make connections between increased gang violence and the lack of job opportunities in the inner city; between ever-growing gang allegiance and the gap between the rich and the poor (the widest in 40 years); between gang-related deaths and soaring drop-out rates. If our churches adopt campaigns based on an attitude of "We're mad as hell and we're not going to take it anymore," we'll succeed only in further alienating youth already paralyzed by despair.

Rusty was a 17-year-old Latino gang member. He was no "street terrorist," but rather a kid who dressed a certain way, drank on the weekends, was estranged from his parents, and could not see his way clear to imagine a future for himself. Perhaps it was this last fact that made his timing so deadly that night. Perhaps it was his deep sense of hopelessness that compelled him to stand defiantly while the others dove for protection.

Rusty and 80,000 young people like him in Los Angeles challenge Christian communities to redouble our efforts to become instruments of hope to youth unfamiliar with hope. The gospel leaves us the task to imagine a future, bright with possibility, for kids stuck in a despondent pattern of violence and self-destruction.

> ***"The gospel insists that we make connections between increased gang violence and the lack of job opportunities."***

"Gangsters" are not the enemy. Adults don't declare war on kids. Our energies of opposition must be directed toward the poverty, unemployment, and failures of the school system that keep gang-banging alive. The teardrop frozen on Rusty's cheek that hot, summer evening of his funeral Mass calls us all to a compassionate love, soaked with the sure hope of the risen Lord.

Police Gang Units Can Reduce Gang Violence

by Richard F. Kensic

About the author: *Richard F. Kensic is a detective in the Los Angeles Police Department's Criminal Conspiracy Section.*

A particular street gang operating in Los Angeles was responsible for 168 gang-related crimes in 1987, including two homicides, three attempted homicides and 86 assaults with deadly weapons. This violent activity, coupled with involvement in narcotics sales and trafficking, made the gang one of the most criminally active in the city.

In order to affect the gang's criminal activity and determine whether or not an organizational structure existed, a closer look at the gang was undertaken. A plan was developed with the goal of eliminating or reducing the crime activity of this gang. Traditionally, the Los Angeles Police Department (LAPD) has concentrated its efforts on either crime area or crime specialty (i.e., burglary, narcotics, robbery). This approach has proven effective and successful, reducing the crime problem significantly.

Effectively Sharing Information

The department's traditional model of gang targeting involved specialized units individually directing their efforts to a specific gang, and putting the gang out of business through enforcement. However, the traditional structure did not facilitate easy exchange of information among the various units, and the past few years have seen marked escalation of the gang problem—especially in terms of violent deaths resulting from gang activity. Obviously, the situation called for the implementation of new strategies, both short- and long-term.

A new approach was undertaken to gather all the specialized units working on a specific gang and have them work in concert under one command. Rather than form a new entity, this concept was implemented within an existing department organization using the existing resources. Officers working on the targeted gang from different directions would then have the benefit of sharing information and insights regarding the full spectrum of the gang's activity. This would bring various pieces of the puzzle together to form a clear picture of the gang's dynamics and structure.

> ***"The past few years have seen marked escalation of the gang problem—especially in terms of violent deaths resulting from gang activity."***

In order to realize the benefit of this exchange of information and insight, there had to be regular face-to-face contact among specialized unit officers. Additionally, it was determined that a group of selected uniformed officers would be assigned to patrol the geographic territory of the targeted gang. The information gained through this traditional enforcement method would be used by detectives when debriefing recently arrested gang members.

The implementation of this concept required

- the assembly under one command of the appropriate investigative personnel from each of the units;
- the ability to request additional sworn or civilian personnel from other entities as needed;
- arrangements for these officers to interact with one another for the purpose of exchanging information and coordinating their efforts on a regular basis; and
- the development of a system for collecting, collating, analyzing and displaying the information gathered by these various units.

As expected, the analytical portion of this process proved to be the most time consuming. However, this was critical to the determination as to whether the gang in question was a "criminal enterprise" under the law, if it had an organizational structure, and to what degree it was involved in the city's total crime picture.

Accumulating Gang Member Data

In order to establish complete and relevant individual profiles, each of the 703 names associated with the targeted gang in the department's Gang Tracking System was processed through automated information systems, including the Los Angeles County Warrant System and the California Department of Justice Criminal Identification and Information System. A total of 22 computerized systems were accessed regarding each of the 703 individuals.

Additionally, the Los Angeles County Probation Department, the California

Youth Authority and the California Department of Corrections were queried to determine the status and conditions of probation or parole of each gang member.

Once this was accomplished, an Assessment Unit comprised of investigative personnel conducted an exacting evaluation of the gang members. Based upon the accumulated data, each individual profiled was classified as either a hardcore, secondary or associate gang member. He was then categorized according to his criminal history, i.e., narcotics trafficker, warrant suspect, parole violator, etc.

A system for recordation called Criminal Activity Tracking System (CATS) was developed to collate and display this collected information. The CATS report is comprised of six separate files:

1. Personal history file—a record of the personal history of the individual under investigation, including arrest history, significant criminal activity, current status (i.e., arrest, trial, probation) and information regarding the individual's involvement with any criminal organization.

2. Event synopsis file—a record of the individual's criminal history, with each entry containing a brief synopsis of his contact with law enforcement.

3. Associate file—a record of any identified individual who had been arrested, interviewed or identified as an associate of the individual under investigation, along with the nature of their criminal relationship.

4. Address file—a record of all known addresses of the individual under investigation.

"The total reduction of targeted gang crime in the gang territory for the time periods examined was 53 percent; citywide, it was reduced by 40 percent."

5. Phone file—a record of all known telephone numbers connected to the individual under investigation.

6. Vehicle file—a listing of all vehicles, descriptions and license numbers used by the individual during any law enforcement contact or crime.

The targeted individual was then assigned to the appropriate department entity (i.e., narcotics, gangs, robbery, burglary) for investigation. A contingent of uniform personnel was also assigned to directed patrol duties in the specific geographic territory identified as that of the targeted gang.

Targeted Gang Crimes Drop

There were three primary methods employed in evaluating the success of the target gang operation:

1. The comparison between previous crime statistics and current criminal activity attributed to the targeted gang.

2. The department's ability to coordinate and interact daily in this project.

3. The use of link analysis to determine organizational structure, if any,

within the targeted gang.

A statistical review was made of repressible crime and gang crimes committed by the targeted gang in its territory. Citywide, crimes committed by the targeted gang were examined for three specific time periods:

1. January-June 1988, immediately prior to the implementation of the target gang project.

2. July-December 1988, after the project had been implemented and the guidelines set.

3. January-June 1989, when the project was totally operational.

During period 1, repressible crimes (burglary, robbery, grand theft auto, burglary from motor vehicle) within the targeted gang's known territory totaled 1,665. Repressible crimes known to have been committed by the targeted gang totaled 82 citywide, and 47 within the territory.

During period 2, when the project was implemented, repressible crime in the territory was reduced by 2 percent. Repressible crimes known to have been committed by the targeted gang decreased 22 percent citywide, and 29 percent within the territory.

During period 3, repressible crime in the gang's known territory increased 11.5 percent. However, repressible crimes known to have been committed by the targeted gang citywide were reduced 23 percent, and in the gang's known territory decreased 29 percent.

The total reduction of targeted gang crime in the gang territory for the time periods examined was 53 percent; citywide, it was reduced by 40 percent. During the period the project was implemented (June 1988-June 1989), a significant crime reduction occurred involving targeted gang members.

No Organized Gang Structure

The Assessment Unit, through review of available documents in conjunction with link analysis, found no evidence of a formal organized structure within the targeted gang. Although there were indications that organized criminal activity did exist within two smaller subgroups, it did not appear that these two subgroups operate under a combined leadership. Additionally, the Assessment Unit identified several groups of individuals who occasionally operated together, engaging in criminal enterprise on an opportunistic basis. These groups appeared to be void of any apparent leadership, acting without the direction of any particular individual.

> ***"At the conclusion of the project, 172 of the original 214 targeted gang members were arrested or determined no longer to be workable targets."***

Of the 703 individuals assessed, 481 were identified as gang members of the targeted gang and were classified as follows:

- Assigned for follow-up investigation—214.
- In prison or jail awaiting trial or sentencing (at the time of assessment)—123.
- Insufficient level of activity to warrant targeting—124.
- Deceased—10.

"The information formulated during this project provided significant insight into the makeup of a street gang."

At the conclusion of the project, 172 of the original 214 targeted gang members were arrested or determined no longer to be workable targets. In 52 cases, follow-up investigation ascertained that the subject's gang/criminal activity had diminished and was no longer a viable target. In those cases where a subject had relocated outside of Los Angeles or was a fugitive, the appropriate law enforcement entity was contacted and provided with the individual's gang activity and warrant information.

Success of the Police Operation

As a result of the target gang operation, the following objectives were achieved:

1. Gang crime committed by the targeted gang was reduced.
2. The assessment of the gang was completed without an organizational restructuring of the department.
3. The absence of an organizational structure within the targeted gang was clearly established.
4. The total number of gang-related crimes—both citywide and in the targeted area—dropped during the target gang operation. This was accomplished by using the uniformed element and support units within the department's current structure.

The criminal analysis technique and link analysis developed during the project offered a means of providing individual criminal profiles, along with a system of targeting future criminal conduct.

Except for the two subgroups identified as leaning towards organized criminal activity, the individuals targeted during this operation were committing crimes either on their own, or with gang and non-gang members for their own personal gain. They held no allegiance to any organization and did not act at the direction of a recognized leader.

Benefits of this unified target approach included attacking the gang from different angles and sharing information and insight about accomplishments and setbacks during the process. The information formulated during this project provided significant insight into the makeup of a street gang.

Prisons Can Reduce Gang Violence

by Thomas Regulus

About the author: *Thomas Regulus is a criminal justice professor at Loyola University in Chicago, Illinois.*

Youth gangs and the problems associated with them have proliferated in correctional institutions over the past two decades. They have increased in juvenile detention centers, jails, correctional institutions, and prisons. Gang youth often maintain close ties with their gangs of origin in their communities. Compared to traditional correctional populations, some young gangs are more organized, manifest greater solidarity, and present greater problems to correctional management. Other youth gangs are less organized, possess less internal solidarity, and present equally challenging problems to management because of their violence and criminal behavior. In some correctional settings today, youth gangs are responsible for high levels of contraband activity including drug distribution, a large proportion of prison violence against staff and inmates, and in some instances the coordination of crime between the correction setting and the community.

Differences in Youth Gangs

Problems of controlling youth gangs in correctional settings differ from those of controlling youth gangs in the community. One reason is that their confinement in the limited space of the correctional setting sometimes contributes to an intensification of collective solidarity and resistance to authority. Another is that gang youth in the institution are in a sense members of the correctional organization itself, albeit as involuntary members. Ordinarily they are not members of larger sanctioned organizations in the community. Gangs in correctional institutions tend to have extensive knowledge of operations and can make stronger claims on the resources of the correctional facility. The correctional or-

From Thomas Regulus, "Corrections Model," in *National Youth Gang Suppression and Intervention Program*, published by the National Youth Gang Information Center, Arlington, Virginia, 1992.

ganization is consequently more vulnerable to internal disruption and subversion by gangs than are community-based organizations. Furthermore, these problems are more serious or chronic in those institutions with a history of gang problems, usually when the proportion of gang offenders to total inmates is high. In the emerging gang problem institutional context, fewer gangs and gang members are usually present, and their gang behaviors are less problematic.

> ***"Problems are more serious or chronic in those institutions with a history of gang problems."***

The community, the correctional institution, and the gang problem are closely interconnected. Youth gangs in correctional institutions are, by and large, outgrowths of street-based gangs. In some situations, gangs first developed in the correctional setting and later transferred their organization to the community. It is important to recognize that members of youth gangs, despite often receiving enhanced sentences, do not remain in correctional institutions for long. These youth return fairly quickly to their community and often to their prior criminal gang patterns. It is imperative therefore that the correctional institution and the ways it deals with its gang problem be viewed as part of a community-institutional continuum since the basis for the gang problem is still largely in the community.

Mission, Goals, and Strategies

Corrections provides restrictions on the freedom of offenders. By legal mandate, it incapacitates them and reduces their offending in the community while they are in the facility. Hopefully it also contributes to a reduction in their criminal activity upon reentry into the community. Four broad, often conflicting, goals are associated with the correctional mission:

1) stable control of the operations of the correctional facility and its programs;
2) community safety through the separation of offenders from the community;
3) care and development of the physical, social, and mental well being of inmates during their stay in the institution; and
4) preparation of inmates for noncriminal behavior on their reentry into the community.

Stable control of operations of the correctional institution and its programs is the most important of these goals. It is the prerequisite for, or the means of, community protection, provision for inmate well being, and preparation of inmates for reentry into the community. Achievement of stable control of operations and the other correctional goals is contingent on the organization's ability to meet two interrelated challenges. One is the translation of these goals into a set of specific objectives and program designs. The second is that youth gang inmate interests and goals are often in conflict with those of the correctional facility. Strategies to induce or force inmate compliance with organizational goals are necessary to meet these challenges and overcome gang youths' interests. Four specific gang-related goals for suppression and intervention should therefore be included in the correctional management agenda:

1) prevent and control youth gang violence, other youth gang crimes, and covert gang disruption of facility operations;
2) weaken youth gang organization and solidarity and substitute conventional alternatives;
3) reduce the ability of youth gangs to participate in crimes which transcend the boundaries of the institution into the community; and
4) provide assistance to gang members in learning social values and behaviors and developing skills that contribute to the adoption of conventional lifestyles upon their return to the community.

To achieve these specific goals, corrections management should develop a gang suppression and intervention program. Such a program relies on five general strategies: Organizational Development and Change, Community Mobilization, Opportunities Provision, Social Intervention, and Suppression. This document outlines a model for a general gang suppression and intervention program for a correctional facility. . . .

Networking with Communities

Community Mobilization. This strategy signifies that a network of organizational and program relationships and resources should be established with outside organizations and groups to both support and reinforce the work of the institution as well as that of community agencies and groups in control and rehabilitation of gang youth. The correctional institution and the community should be viewed as a contiguous social environment.

> ***"Parole and community agencies and organizations have vital roles to play in the supervision and rehabilitation of gang youth."***

Systematic contact and networking with community agencies contribute to the correctional facility's efforts to: a) protect the community from crime while youth are incarcerated and after their reentry into the community and b) enhance the likelihood that youth will make successful adjustments when they return to the community through positive involvement with representatives of community groups. Parole and community agencies and organizations have vital roles to play in the supervision and rehabilitation of gang youth. Contacts in regard to community education, job training, and placement services should be initiated by parole and community agencies while the youth is still in the institution, and prior to release.

A key function of community networking, especially with the police, should be shared intelligence on a continuing basis about related gang problems both in the correctional facility and the community. This could include collaborative case assessment and planning for individual gang members upon entry as well as prior to release from the correctional facility. Such networking could provide timely prevention and control of gang problems. For example, gang problems in the community can spill over into the correctional facility and vice versa.

Finally, both community organization and organizational development suggest a role for inmates in the development of a legitimate and productive corrections environment. To the extent feasible, and within the limits of a stable and orderly correctional environment, attention should be given to participation by youths and/or their representatives, preferably on an advisory basis, in decisions affecting rules and regulations, development of services, and opportunity programs as well as facility improvements. A system of communication between inmates, staff, and administration is also required so that consideration is given to inmate grievances and to insure due process for youths. The youths as a principal component of the correctional community must be given appropriate recognition in, and some responsibility for, the legitimate and productive development of that community.

Opportunities for Gang Members

Opportunities Provision. This strategy emphasizes the development of programs and services of remedial education, training, and jobs, both during the gang member's incarceration and during his transition back into the community. Youth gangs may be viewed as an alternative means for status and success that legitimate opportunities in the community did not provide. The provision of legitimate opportunities is therefore essential to correct lost and missed conventional opportunities experienced by gang youth. For younger gang members, 16 and under, opportunities provision should emphasize remedial educational and work awareness programs; for older youth, remedial education or GED, job training, apprenticeship, job referrals, and career development would be essential.

"Youth gangs may be viewed as an alternative means for status and success that legitimate opportunities in the community did not provide."

Although these programs should have immediate relevance for the youth upon release from the correctional institution into the community, they should be designed and managed with long term utility for inmates in mind. Younger youth returning to academic settings should be assisted with placements in school or vocational programs which best serve their needs. Mainstream placement of gang youth with regular student populations is the ideal. However, when local schools cannot accommodate gang youth who have special needs, alternative schools, community agency GED programs, and special work study programs would be the logical alternatives.

Preparation of older gang youth for reentry may be more complex and difficult. Major academic deficiencies have to be overcome. Ingrained gang attitudes have to be changed. Many of these deficiencies and work attitude problems should be targeted even before the youth leaves the institution. Satisfactory job adjustments in the community will be delayed if a suitable program of training and work experiences are not provided in the institution before inmates leave. . . .

"An early distinction should be made as to whether violence and other disruptive activities are due to gang activity."

Our survey of 45 cities and jurisdictions found that community mobilization and opportunities provision were the strategies of intervention cited as significantly associated with reported (and actual) reduction of gang problems. The strategies of community mobilization and organizational development and change may be considered equivalent in the institutional setting which is itself a kind of community context.

Strategies of organizational development and opportunities provision should have some priority in correctional settings. Exclusive focus on suppression or controlling behavior can aggravate problem behavior. Organizational development and opportunities provision approaches should be used to improve gang youths' institutional adjustment and to facilitate noncriminal adjustments in the community. They serve better than suppression to: a) address the goals and objectives of the institution in relation to the legitimate interests and expressed needs of inmates; b) reduce deprivations associated with involuntary incarceration; and c) result in the provision of program alternatives to gang membership.

Issues and Contexts of Gang Control

In this final section, we identify four sets of issues that influence the mix and priority of program strategies and programs, particularly in chronic and emerging gang problem contexts.

1) Gang- and nongang-related problem activities of gang members. An early distinction should be made as to whether violence and other disruptive activities are due to gang activity or problems unrelated to gang function, even when youth involved are gang members. In the first instance gang-specific control activities are clearly appropriate. In the second, gang control activities may not be justified. Nongang-motivated problems created by gang youth should be generally addressed as though the youth involved were nongang members. This is not to deny that distinctions between gang and nongang-motivated are at times difficult to make. Nevertheless, we are more concerned with the consequences of exaggeration than denial or narrow perception of the gang problem in the correctional setting. Otherwise, the expectation of gang problems might stimulate such activity. It could contribute to a widening of the net of activities indirectly regarded as gang-related. It could increase stigmatization of certain inmates. Furthermore, time and resources invested in designing and implementing gang-specific interventions would probably be wasted.

Gang Problems at Different Stages

2) Chronic and emergent gang problems. Gang problems may be at different stages of development. In some the problems are emerging and less serious while in others they are chronic and more serious. Obviously there are correctional settings where the state of the gang problem lies somewhere in between. Some indicators of emergent versus chronic gang problem contexts include differences in inmate organization and influence, the number and size of gangs, the intensity and seriousness of intergang conflict, and the extent of inmate participation in illegal gang criminal activities. Youth gangs are more likely to have established a base of power, influence, and inmate control in chronic gang problem settings. Programs and tactics to reduce gang influence and power are likely to encounter more resistance in chronic compared to emergent gang problem situations. While a simple strategy of exclusive suppression may not be the answer in either case over the long term, it is likely to be more effective in the short term in the emerging gang context. In both settings a more complex set of strategies should be tried sooner rather than later.

"Youth gangs are more likely to have established a base of power, influence, and inmate control in chronic gang problem settings."

3) Imported and indigenous characteristics of gang problems. Imported characteristics refer to the attributes which gangs and their members bring with them into the correctional setting from their gang experience or history out in the community or from another correctional institution. Indigenous characteristics refer to attributes of gangs which develop because of factors unique to the particular correctional setting. Whether gang problems originate inside or outside of the correctional facility similar strategies of control are required. However, additional collaborative interventions with community agencies and other correctional facilities may be necessary when gang problems originate or are influenced by problems outside the particular institution.

In the case of the indigenous development of youth gangs, greater efforts should be directed to understanding and modifying the internal causes of these problematic behaviors and particular organizational characteristics associated with them, e.g., authority which is too lax or too strict, poorly trained staff, or too few activities to occupy inmate time and energy. Imported and indigenous sources of gang problems may also be interactive and further complicate and entrench the facility's gang problem.

4) Age of youth gang members. Finally, corrections policies and programs must be designed to address differences in ages or levels of maturity of gang members. Young adult gang members (ages 17 and above) are more likely (but not always) than younger gang members (ages 16 and below) to: 1) have longer and possibly more serious histories of violence; 2) use gang organization for predatory and exploitative criminal activity; and 3) be more sophisticated in their gang crime behavior. Young adult gang members consequently may present a greater challenge to correctional management. More sophisticated suppression, opportunities provision, and organizational development strategies may be required for this population.

"Young adult gang members (ages 17 and above) are more likely . . . to . . . be more sophisticated in their gang crime behavior."

Nevertheless, correctional authorities should be especially alert to the receptiveness of some older youth to rehabilitative interventions and attentive to requests for assistance in leaving the gang. These older youth may be prepared to mature out of the gang, particularly if they have responsibilities toward wives, girl friends, and children. Younger gang members may still be in the process of developing their gang "rep."

The mix of opportunities provision, social intervention, and community organization strategies ought to be different for older and younger gang members. Again, as suggested earlier, there should be greater emphasis on job training and job placement in addition to remedial and GED educational services for older youth and relatively greater emphasis on remedial education and job orientation experiences for younger youth. Different types of counseling or values training may also be necessary. To a large extent these emphases can grow naturally out of the general separation of juveniles and adults in correctional institutions. Most states have laws requiring such separation.

Programs for Chronic and Emerging Gang Situations

In chronic gang problem contexts, gangs will have existed for a long time, have a sizeable membership, and through use of violence and intimidation will have developed considerable power and influence over the inmate population and operations of the institution. Central administration objectives should be 1) the reduction of the gang's control over institutional operations and 2) the reduction of gang violence. Each of these objectives should be defined in measurable terms in regard to specific housing or institutional areas to be cleared of gang members and gang influence. A key intelligence activity should be identification of gang leadership, core and fringe members, and their principal methods, locations, and patterns of activity.

A set of meaningful channels of communication with principal gang influentials should be established in conjunction with high levels of suppression. Strong, clear, and fair disciplinary procedures should be implemented and the institution's anti-gang posture communicated through appropriate policies. It is possible that these initial efforts by the institution will be resisted and an escalation of negative gang activity will occur. A related reduction of access to institutional resources should occur. It is likely that some of the more overt forms of criminal or egregious gang activity will be reduced as this occurs, particularly if a strong steady suppressive posture is maintained. A variety of organizational development and suppressive measures will have to interact. The parent correctional agency should be supportive by permitting transfers of selected gang members out of the facility, if necessary. Certain key gang members should be swiftly prosecuted for their criminal gang activity in the institution. Staff must be prepared to effectively manage the problems they will confront through additional orientation and training, if not staff reorganization or redeployment.

Integrating Gang Strategies

Although suppression plays a central role in initial institutional efforts to deal with chronic gang situations, strategies and programs for opportunity provision, social intervention, and community organization should be integrated with them. Special activities and services should be offered as inmates respond favorably to these new arrangements. Inmates should come to view the changing policies and practices of the institution as fair and benefitting them in the long term, particularly as they permit inmates to pursue conventional and satisfying lifestyles whether in or outside the institution. The restoration of stability and social order in the institution and the reduction of the influence of gangs are contingent on the availability of adequate resources of staff and program as well as intelligent, benign, and strong institutional leadership.

"Certain key gang members should be swiftly prosecuted for their criminal gang activity in the institution."

In emerging gang problem contexts, gang problems are relatively recent with little tradition of serious gang crime, complex organization, and solidarity. Youth are just learning to be gang members and only moderate degrees of suppression should be used. While gang leaders or influentials should be targeted for sanctions, emphasis should be placed on the development of special program activities, such as extra educational classes, constructive recreational activities, counseling, and the introduction of outside agencies into the lives of inmates. Positive alternative activities should be emphasized without treating the gang situation as extremely serious and requiring major institutional change and extreme measures of suppression.

Extensive research is required into the nature of the gang problem in correctional institutions. Special attention should be directed to different organizational responses to similar gang problems that produce different effects. We also need to know more clearly whether certain approaches work better in chronic or emerging gang problem contexts with certain types of gangs and under what conditions of correctional housing, staffing, and programming.

More immediately required is a set of definitions of terms such as gangs, gang members, and gang incidents as used across correctional institutions in different states and the different procedures used by these institutions in dealing with gang youth and gang problems. Description of specific behaviors which indicate a rise or fall of the gang problem should be standardized. Changes in the incidence of gang and nongang-motivated offenses within the institution should be carefully assessed. Finally, the effectiveness of certain institutions should also be measured based on long-term recidivism rates associated with different institutional policies and programs. It would be important to determine whether similar gang inmates recidivate less after experience in a particular kind of institutional environment than in another.

Local Law Enforcement Agencies Can Cooperate to Reduce Gang Violence

by Office of the District Attorney of the County of Los Angeles

About the author: *The Office of the District Attorney is responsible for prosecuting suspected lawbreakers within Los Angeles County.*

Crisis conditions evoke extraordinary responses. At the peak of the previous gang crisis, in 1980, a series of measures were taken to attack gang violence. The Interagency Gang Task Force [IAGTF]; the D.A.'s Hardcore Division; the Probation Department's SGSP [Specialized Gang Supervision Program]; Community Youth Gang Services [CYGS], and a number of law enforcement partnerships originated at that time.

A Decline in Violence

Something appears to have worked in 1980. Gang violence fell sharply over the next four years: There are those who believe that the decline in violence was not due to all the new programs. In support of that conclusion, they note that the programs were mostly created in late 1980 and 1981, after the homicide rate had already begun to drop. By this line of reasoning, that particular cycle of gang violence had simply run its course. The decrease in crime and the increase in government attention were related but not causally. They were different—and, perhaps, mutually reinforcing—responses to the same social crisis; the result of a kind of social bio-feedback loop. Violence had gotten so bad that gang members began to hold back out of fear, communities began to react out of desperation and government—trailing the curve—bestirred itself out of necessity. Thus did the cycle pass its peak and turn downward. The new programs, to the extent that they had any effect at all, served only to accelerate the trend.

From "Gangs, Crime, and Violence in Los Angeles," a proposal by the Office of the District Attorney of the County of Los Angeles, May 1992.

The cyclical analysis is unproductive for policy purposes. If correct, it leads nowhere except to an anxious wait for the next statistical downturn. Those who believe that Los Angeles can affect its fate through public and private action would do better to examine the 1980 responses for clues to our current crisis. If something worked, what was it? And will it work again?

Specialization and inter-agency cooperation were the key elements of the response in 1980: Then as now, there was a perceived need for substantial additional resources. Then as now, the fiscal situation did not permit massive expenditures. Quite the contrary; this was the era of the first cutbacks in social services in the aftermath of Proposition 13. As a result, the new resources allocated to fight gang violence were modest at best. They were used primarily to create specialized gang units in Probation and the D.A.'s Office; to strengthen anti-gang efforts in L.A.P.D. and L.A.S.D. [Los Angeles Police Department and Sheriff's Department]; to build some links between intervention activities and law enforcement (including CYGS); and to establish regular communication and cooperation between agencies. In essence, the goal was to see the gang problem as a whole and to address it in a coherent way that made the best use of existing resources.

Communication and Cooperation

Those who participated in that effort believe it was the new emphasis on communication and cooperation between agencies that made things work. A degree of trust and understanding developed between the gang experts in different agencies which made it possible to try things that would have been doomed to failure a few years earlier. Indeed, their response to the critique outlined above—that the downturn in gang violence started before the new programs did—is that the determination to address the gang problem as a whole through cooperative efforts preceded the new programs and made them work. It was this change in attitude and approach which began to turn things around on the streets. A key question: If all this worked so well a decade ago, why doesn't it continue to work today?

> ***"A degree of trust and understanding developed between the gang experts in different agencies."***

The specialized gang enforcement units of a decade ago have been overwhelmed by burgeoning caseloads: Programs like Hardcore and SGSP were never lavishly funded. They were barely adequate to cope with a gang violence caseload roughly half that which L.A. is experiencing today—and trending downward. As violence declined throughout the early '80's, and funding remained tight, there was little incentive for government to spend more on a problem that seemed to be more or less under control. By 1986-7, when it became clear that a new surge of gang activity was underway, crack cocaine had created an emergency on the streets. The fight against drugs had first claim on new law enforcement dollars. Anti-gang spending began to rise again, but not at a rate that kept pace with the problem.

Revitalize Anti-Gang Programs

The result, as has been described elsewhere, is a series of specialized gang enforcement programs that are no longer able to function as intended—police gang units that have remained static while gang membership has soared; a Hardcore Division that can handle nothing but murder cases, and not all of those; an SGSP that can accommodate only a small fraction of gang members on probation. Restoring anti-gang programs to at least the levels of strength—vis-a-vis the gang population—of a decade ago would be one of the most cost efficient steps that policy makers could take to address the current crisis.

L.A. County and City should clearly define the missions of the specialized gang units and fund them at levels that permit those missions to be performed: Redefined missions for prosecutors and probation have been proposed. But they cannot be implemented unless police gang units also take on expanded missions.

> ***"L.A. . . . should clearly define the missions of the specialized gang units and fund them at levels that permit those missions to be performed."***

• *Targeting:* The proposals presented here depend, in large part, on carefully targeting a relatively small group of hardcore gang members—and an even smaller "core of the hardcore." Computerized targeting is the key to sensible and limited expansion—achieving results at an affordable cost. It is essential, therefore, that the gang units within L.A.P.D. and L.A.S.D. receive additional resources—some short-term, some permanent—to implement and maintain effective targeting.

• *Inter-agency cooperation:* If Los Angeles expects to reap the benefits of expanded law enforcement cooperation based on a collaborative targeting process, police gang units must also be staffed at levels which permit them to invest in effective cooperation. It is not easy, automatic or free.

Hardcore Gang Members

• *Focusing on hardcore gang members:* In addition to doing the targeting, and cooperating with other agencies in making it effective, L.A.P.D. and L.A.S.D. must make better use of their personnel by re-orienting their own enforcement efforts toward investigating and arresting hardcore gang members. For gang units, this will not be a major change since current practice sets the same goal. It is simply a matter of using the database to target less subjectively. However, the new focus would require an important change for regular deputies: It is important that *all* potential gang cases be checked against GREAT/GTS [Gang Reporting Evaluation and Tracking System/Gang Tracking System] to determine whether hardcore gang members are involved. Without this step, prosecutors and probation will not be able to prioritize effectively.

• *Expanded street-level gang enforcement:* New missions for police gang units must not be permitted to interfere with the basic work of street-level intelligence gathering and gang enforcement. That work has suffered in recent years because gang units have not kept pace with gang growth. Both L.A.P.D. and L.A.S.D. should bring their gang units up to levels of strength that are commensurate with today's problem instead of maintaining the staffing levels of seven or eight years ago when gang violence was at a modern low.

"New missions for police gang units must not be permitted to interfere with the basic work of street-level intelligence gathering and gang enforcement."

• *Regular, independent evaluation:* Solid information on what works and what doesn't is at a premium. Law enforcement efforts should not be exempt from requirements for regular evaluation. Because gang activities are only a tiny piece of each agency's responsibility, such evaluations are unlikely to come from inside. They must be conducted by outsiders with a strong focus on gangs and gang activity. Ideally, the [County] Board of Supervisors and the CAO [Chief Administrative Officer] (or the City Council and the Mayor) should do this as part of a regular evaluation of anti-gang efforts, including prevention. Failing that, the task of contracting for evaluations could be delegated to the Interagency Gang Task Force, or to its parent body, the County Criminal Justice Coordinating Committee.

Although L.A. gang enforcement officials continue to have strong and cordial working relationships, some of the old spirit of cooperation has dissipated: The history of GREAT is a metaphor for the change that has taken place. As the product of an earlier era of easier cooperation, GREAT was envisioned as a unified effort. But as the idea moved to fruition, the goal of unity never quite materialized. Now we have a good system that is far less than it could be: L.A.P.D. and L.A.S.D. have separate-but-not-quite-equal systems and probation is not a meaningful part of either system.

Problems with Gang Programs

Other worthy efforts have similar stories that differ only in detail. The reasons are both simple and complex. On one level, it is as simple as the loss of some key individuals. People move on and the inter-agency relationships they built are not quite the same without them. On another level, the relative success of anti-gang efforts a decade ago permitted top policy makers to turn their attention elsewhere. Shifting priorities at the top lessened the pressure for cooperation in the middle ranks. Natural institutional rivalries reasserted themselves to some degree.

Such changes are inevitable with the passage of time. If things are better on the cooperation front today than they were in the late 70's—and they *are* better—it is because of the work of the Interagency Gang Task Force.

The Interagency Gang Task Force continues to do valuable work but its focus is no longer primarily on law enforcement and suppression: The Interagency Gang Task Force is a permanent subcommittee of the Countywide Criminal Justice Coordinating Committee. Created by Los Angeles County in 1980 to facilitate and institutionalize inter-agency cooperation in gang enforcement, the IAGTF has been a much-imitated success. In its early days, it was a forum for collaboration on projects like GREAT. It continues in that role today, especially for key projects that involve joint law enforcement and prevention efforts. Through its regular monthly meetings, and through its widely disseminated newsletter, the Task Force functions as a network for all agencies working on the gang problem in L.A. County. It also acts as an advisory body to the County Board of Supervisors (and, informally, to the City of Los Angeles), compiling data and making policy recommendations.

A Broader Focus on Prevention

The IAGTF was originally focused on communication between law enforcement and gang suppression workers. Over time, the membership of the Task Force and its mission have shifted to include a much broader focus on prevention. Indeed, the current Task Force structure includes sub-committees for education and community mobilization, but none for suppression or law enforcement.

Comments on the IAGTF during interviews were mildly schizophrenic. On the one hand, there is strong support for the Task Force's ongoing work, and a real emotional investment by many people in the institution and its past. On the other hand, there is frustration and a sense of wasted time and effort. To some degree, this is probably displaced anger over what many members regard as inadequate county and city funding—and the seeming inability of the Task Force to change that reality. . . .

> ***"If things are better on the cooperation front today . . . it is because of the work of the Interagency Gang Task Force."***

The IAGTF may want to consider organizing along sub-regional lines: Reorganization along more local lines was suggested independently by several sources. Though logical, the proposal may envision a more activist role than the Task Force has played heretofore. Much of the Task Force's current work already deals with encouraging community mobilization in targeted geographic areas. Apart from issues of authorization and funding, such projects fail or succeed based on cooperation between local players. Pulling them together into sub-regional task forces might be sensible—especially if the target areas are defined by law enforcement jurisdictional boundaries.

The Importance of Gang Suppression

The IAGTF should seek to sharpen the focus on its original goals of suppression without damaging the new emphasis on prevention: In addition to exploring possibilities for sub-regional organization, the Task Force should re-examine its balance between suppression and prevention. In talking with members and observers of the Task Force, it is clear that little in the way of law enforcement initiative moves through that channel—except as it relates to joint community mobilization efforts. Yet there is a need for dialogue on the professional agenda for law-enforcement cooperation in gang suppression. The IAGTF could perform a valuable service by providing a forum for regular law enforcement consultation—perhaps by establishing a suppression sub-committee that would include federal representatives.

> ***"The IAGTF could perform a valuable service by providing a forum for regular law enforcement consultation."***

Some such forum, with an agenda limited to improving gang suppression, and membership limited to law enforcement, will be necessary if proposals like targeting hardcore gang members via the GREAT system are to be implemented across agency lines. If the IAGTF is not an appropriate or workable forum, one should be developed through other channels.

A key goal of county gang enforcement should be to develop a basic coordinated strategy for gang suppression in target areas: As detailed above, law enforcement has developed a number of tools that can clearly have major short-term impacts on gang activity in any given area. The STEP [Street Terrorism and Enforcement Program] process (and Civil Abatement); vertical prosecution; gang sweeps (or other forms of temporarily stepped up levels of gang enforcement); all these strategies work. They all produce immediate drops in gang activity. They all leave a lingering "aftertaste" that keeps gang activity artificially low for a while after the programs end. Unfortunately, they are all labor-intensive as well, which renders them ill-suited for use county-wide. They are, by nature, confined to use within one or more limited target areas at a time. A key goal of county gang enforcement should be to transform this limitation into a virtue.

The exciting questions for law enforcement are these: What would happen if all these strategies were applied simultaneously in the same target area? How far down could gang violence be driven? How long would it stay down? What "booster" efforts would suffice to extend the period of inoculation? Could such a program be used to permanently lower total violence by breaking a cycle of gang warfare?

"Law enforcement has developed a number of tools that can clearly have major short-term impacts on gang activity in any given area."

The District Attorney's Office, the Sheriff's Department and the Probation Department are currently engaged in an experiment to attempt to find some answers to those questions. . . .

The target area suppression strategy should be used only in coordination with (and as an incentive for developing) an effective local prevention strategy: Even the most optimistic goals for a target area suppression strategy do not envision permanent eradication of gang violence. Perhaps, with luck and several months of intensive effort, an area could be given substantial relief for a year or so. While that kind of breathing space has value, it is not an end in itself. It is better seen as a tool for achieving a higher goal.

Suppression Along with Prevention

Since the ability to provide all-out suppression in a target area is a limited resource, it should be deployed in a way that provides maximum benefit. Law enforcement should commit to such an effort only when a community has developed, and is prepared to implement, an effective local prevention strategy. The goal of the suppression effort should be to provide a "window of opportunity" for the community efforts to take hold. In a perfect world, the improved prevention programs would then enable the regular contingent of local law enforcement personnel to sustain the lower levels of gang activity more or less indefinitely—perhaps with occasional "boosts" from outside. . . .

Over time, using a limited set of resources, Los Angeles City and County could have a system of rolling suppression efforts moving around the region on a cyclical basis. A short burst of coordinated suppression activity would be repeated in gang-infested areas at regular intervals (perhaps every four or five years, if needed—sufficient time for generational turnover among the local gang population). These bursts would be conducted in support of a regular, planned evaluation and renewal of local prevention efforts. If left in place and nurtured, this system could prove to be a flexible, coordinated and effective long-term answer to Los Angeles' endemic gang problems. Repetition and evaluation would doubtless bring refinements and improvements. Combined with the cooperative, targeted gang enforcement efforts, it could develop into the strategy that allows us to repeat, and improve on, the successes of the early 1980's.

Gang Truces Can Reduce Gang Violence

by Andy Furillo

About the author: *Andy Furillo is a senior writer for the* Sacramento Bee *daily California newspaper and a former newspaper reporter for the* San Francisco Examiner.

Back in April 1989, when gun-toting youths were shooting each other in Hunters Point, Sunnydale and the Western Addition, a deep depression fell over longtime San Francisco social worker Leonard C. "Lefty" Gordon.

This was the worst kind of black-on-black crime. The shootings were not borne of economic necessity or driven by uncontrollable inner demons. Instead, it was hard, raw gang violence, the likes of which had already torn apart black communities in cities like Los Angeles and Oakland.

Gordon, 49, had spent 30 years—his entire adult life—working with underprivileged kids in The City. But with each blast from a youthful drive-by gunman, Gordon, executive director of Ella Hill-Hutch Community Center in the Western Addition, saw his work unraveling around him.

"It was probably the low point of my professional career," he said, reflecting on the unprecedented gang-style activity that swept San Francisco's black neighborhoods.

Forging a Truce

But out of the despair came opportunity, and it has been seized by Gordon. Working in conjunction with city recreation officials and the mayor's office, Gordon and others have hand-picked gang leaders from some of the toughest neighborhoods in San Francisco to forge a truce that by police accounts has shown dramatic success.

"I think it has been very successful," said San Francisco Police Capt. Jim Arnold, commanding officer of the Potrero Station. "It's been a question of the

Andy Furillo, "Social Workers Broker Street Truce," *San Francisco Examiner*, January 22, 1990.

community coming together."

A 70 percent decrease over the last half of 1989 in drive-by "incidents"—the major indicator of gang violence in San Francisco—demonstrates the truce's effectiveness.

In the first six months of 1989, there were 51 such drive-bys, according to police. Over the final six months of the year, there were only 15, police said.

A major law-enforcement effort toward tracking down and arresting leading gang suspects in 1989's drive-by shootings has greatly assisted the truce. Without the crackdown, some police officials say, there would be no truce.

"A 70 percent decrease over the last half of 1989 in drive-by 'incidents'. . . demonstrates the truce's effectiveness."

"Once we took off the titular heads of some of these gangs and put them in jail, then the other programs could work," said Capt. Timothy Hettrich, formerly in charge of the department's Special Operations Bureau task force, which has focused on street gang activity.

But there is no denying that the truce—orchestrated by Gordon, city recreation superintendent Joel Robinson, Hunters Point Gymnasium supervisor Tom Mayfield and Sunnydale housing project recreation specialist Shirletha Holmes-Boxx—has played at least as vital a role in laying the groundwork for a lasting peace.

"There are some traditionalists out there who say, 'You're taking too light a hand with these thugs,'" Robinson said. "But it's the (get-tough law enforcement) approach that I feel has not worked. Others have taken that approach, and we can see what's happening, like right across the Bay in Oakland.

A Difference in Philosophy

"They're going to break homicide records over there, and for just those few miles between cities, you have to point to some difference in philosophy to justify the dramatic difference in this type of activity."

Choosing an unconventional approach, the recreational and social workers scoured the streets to open a line of communication with neighborhood youths who had solid gang connections, established criminal records and the ability to influence their younger peers.

Once they made contact, Gordon & Co. transformed their proteges from troublemakers into peacemakers. They got them to talk to each other, molding the four representatives from each neighborhood into a 12-member executive council.

"We felt something had to be done," Gordon said. "Specifically, we felt it was time to bring the warring gangs together, around what we call, 'It's Truce Time.' And, from our discussions with some of the youths, we found this is something they really wanted, too.

"They realized that going to funerals was very depressing."

The truce idea began after an April 3, 1989, drive-by shooting in Hunters Point that left two people dead and nine injured, including one of the first innocent victims of gang violence in The City's history.

Mayfield got his prospects together from Hunters Point. Holmes-Boxx found hers in Sunnydale. Gordon came up with a team from the Western Addition. The three groups sat down together for their first meeting in Lincoln Park.

Negotiations: No Hidden Agenda

By design, the council sessions have been conducted in near secrecy, with the adults acting to shield the gang council members from virtually any contact with the press and blocking them from being interviewed for this story.

"We had to commit to them early on that this was not for publicity, or for somebody's political motivations," said Robinson. "They then developed a sense of trust with us."

The meetings were later moved to the City Hall offices of Mayor Art Agnos, whose support and approval of the truce has been crucial to its early success.

Agnos himself spoke personally with the youths from Hunters Point in the days after the April 3 shooting. Occasionally, he has participated in the monthly meetings at City Hall.

In addition to the peace meetings, the mayor's office put together a summer jobs program that employed 150 young people from the three neighborhoods and held a black-tie dinner for the council participants last November.

"We kind of mediated the dialogue, let them talk and air some things out," Deputy Mayor Gayle Orr-Smith said. "We challenged them and explored options with them. We worked to deepen the ties between the neighborhoods. We also encouraged them to police themselves."

"Now, as opposed to kids saying, 'Let's go spray 'em up' when something happens, the word is 'One on one.'"

The impact of Agnos' presence has not been lost on the truce participants.

"The youth are starting to see that people in powerful positions do care about them," said Melvin Smith, executive director of Operation Contact, a social service center that is not involved in the truce. "It gives them a different type of outlook. They see somebody who knows who they are, who knows what their needs are."

With the dialogue established, people from Hunters Point who might be angry at somebody from Sunnydale can bring the issue to their neighborhood's representative on the executive council, who can then bring the matter up for a full hearing.

The result has been that individual differences are kept from exploding into group confrontations and gunplay, allowing an unusual calm for the most part to settle over the rival neighborhoods.

"Now, as opposed to kids saying, 'Let's go spray 'em up' when something happens, the word is 'One on one,'" said Holmes-Boxx. "And now it is not unusual to see Sunnydale kids in Hunters Point and Hunters Point kids in Sunnydale. Now, you even see Hunters Point boys over there dating Sunnydale girls. It used to be they couldn't drive through there.". . .

But tension still permeates the streets of Hunters Point, Sunnydale and the Western Addition. A couple of drive-by shootings ripped up the Tenderloin and Hunters Point in January 1990, pushing the tension level up a few notches.

"It was distressing," Orr-Smith said. "It is a setback, but I am impressed with the way our kids are working with us. They immediately got on the phone with Tom."

The shootings served to underscore what all of the experts know to be true, that plenty of work remains to be done.

Gordon sees the truce as only "the first step of a long journey." He said society must attack the root causes of gang membership and drug dealing, such as the high unemployment rate among young blacks, if there is to be a long-term solution to the problem.

Chapter 5

Should Violent Youths Receive Harsh Punishment?

Chapter Preface

In the United States, each state determines the type of punishment violent youths receive. This results in a wild disparity between harsh and lenient punishment, even when youths commit similar crimes. For example, in 1986 the state of Texas tried as an adult and later executed Jay Pinkerton, who at age seventeen had raped and murdered a thirty-seven-year-old woman. In Massachusetts, however, fourteen-year-old Matthew Rosenberg, who had raped and drowned a five-year-old boy, was tried in the juvenile court system and sentenced to undergo sex-offender therapy. Such disparity raises questions of when juveniles should be tried as adults and how severely they should be punished.

As the map below illustrates, state laws differ for juveniles charged with felonies. At the discretion of juvenile court judges, many states can try adolescents in adult criminal courts if they are at least sixteen years of age. In Vermont and South Dakota, children as young as ten can be waived to adult courts. Several states set no minimum at all.

Minimum Age at Which Juveniles May Be Tried as Adults for Felonies

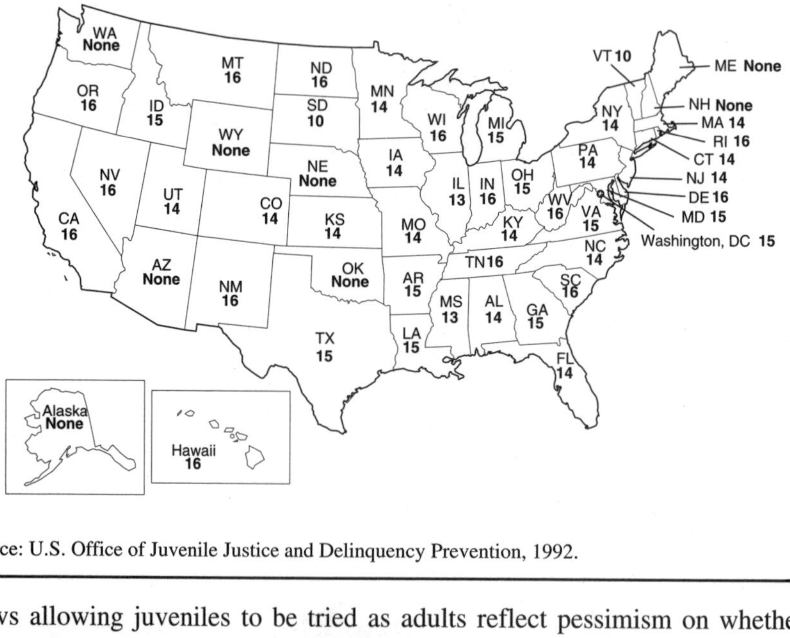

Source: U.S. Office of Juvenile Justice and Delinquency Prevention, 1992.

Laws allowing juveniles to be tried as adults reflect pessimism on whether young violent offenders can be rehabilitated to rejoin society. In the words of former Philadelphia district attorney Ronald Castille, "If a kid shows a nasty, vicious streak, forget the rehabilitation, we're going to go with the punishment."

Yet many experts oppose harsh forms of punishment for youths. Just placing youths in jail, they contend, jeopardizes their lives. According to former Oregon juvenile offender John Trappe, "At least half of the teenagers I've known in [juvenile] institutions claim to have attempted suicide." But suicide is only one peril for imprisoned youths. Critics argue that jailed juveniles face the risk of beatings and rapes by other inmates and even by adult supervisors. Opponents of harsh punishment advocate detention in an environment that stresses rehabilitation over punishment. Programs that promote responsibility and skills through job training and other activities are the only way to treat youthful offenders, these experts contend.

People on both sides of the punishment debate agree that poverty, lack of parental responsibility, and drug use, are the real issues that must be addressed to counter youth violence. Asks former U.S. attorney general Richard Thornburgh, "What chance does a child have under these unhappy conditions to become a law-abiding citizen?"

The Juvenile Justice System Is Too Lenient

by Rita Kramer

About the author: *Rita Kramer is the author of* At a Tender Age: Violent Youth and Juvenile Justice.

Anyone who reads newspapers or watches TV is familiar with scenes of urban violence in which the faces of those who rob and rape, maim and kill get younger and younger. On the streets, in the subways, and even in the schools, juvenile crime has taken on a character unthinkable when the present justice system was set up to deal with it. That system, like so many of the ambitious social programs designed in the '60s, has had unintended results. Instead of solving society's ills, it has added to them.

The juvenile justice system now in place in most parts of the country is not very different from New York's Family Court. Originally conceived to protect children (defined by different states as those under age 16, 17 or 18) who ran afoul of the law, it was designed to function as a kind of wise parent providing rehabilitation.

The 1950s delinquent, who might have been a shoplifter, a truant or a car thief, would not be treated like an adult criminal. He was held to be, in the wording of the New York statute, "not criminally responsible . . . by reason of infancy." He would be given a hearing (not a trial) closed to the press and public and the disposition (not a sentence) would remain sealed, so the juvenile would not be stigmatized by youthful indiscretion. The optimistic belief was that under the guidance of social workers he would undergo a change of character.

A Juvenile Court Nightmare

It was a dream destined to become a nightmare. In the early 1960s, the character of juvenile court proceedings underwent a radical transformation. Due process was interpreted to grant youthful "respondents" (not defendants) not

Rita Kramer, "Juvenile Justice Is Delinquent," *The Wall Street Journal*, May 27, 1992. Reprinted with only the services of a lawyer, but also the protections the criminal justice system affords adults, who are liable to serious penalties if found guilty.

In the hands of Legal Aid Society lawyers (and sometimes sympathetic judges), the juvenile system focuses on the minutiae of procedural technicalities at the expense of fact-finding, in order to achieve the goal of "getting the kid off." The question is not whether a teen-age boy has beaten up a homeless old man, shot a storekeeper or sodomized a little girl. He may even admit the act. The question is whether his admission can be invalidated because a police officer forgot to have him initial his responses to the Miranda warnings in the proper place or whether the arresting officer had probable cause to search him for the loaded gun that was found on him.

It has become the lawyer's job not only to protect his young client from punishment, but from any possibility of rehabilitation in the system's various facilities. The best interests of the child or adolescent have been reinterpreted to mean his legal rights, even when the two are in opposition. He now has the right to continue the behavior that brought him into the juvenile court, which he leaves with the knowledge that his behavior had no real negative consequences to him.

Even when there are consequences, they are mild indeed, a fact not lost on his peers. Eighteen months in a facility that usually has TV, a basketball court, and better food and medical care than at home is the worst that all but the most violent repeat offenders have to fear in New York. The system, based on a person's age and not his crimes, fails either to restrain or retrain him.

The Turn Toward Violence

As juvenile courts were changing, so were juvenile criminals. As recently as the early '70s, the majority of cases before children's and family courts were misdemeanors. In New York City, the most common charge was "jostling," pickpocketing without physical contact. By 1991, robbery—a charge that involves violence against people—had outpaced drug-related offenses as the largest category of crimes by juveniles. Between 1987 and 1991, the fastest-growing crime by juveniles was loaded gun possession, and metal detectors and spot police checks had become routine in some inner-city high schools.

> ***"These are dangerous people. . . . We hardly ever see the non-violent any more."***

Cases of violent group assault—"kids" causing serious physical injury "for fun"—had increased dramatically. Predatory behavior was becoming a form of entertainment for some of the urban young, white as well as black and Hispanic. In 1991, according to Peter Reinharz, chief of New York City's Family Court Division, 85% of the young offenders brought into Family Court were charged with felonies. "These are dangerous people," Mr. Reinharz says. "We hardly ever see the non-violent any more."

Nationwide figures compiled by the FBI's Uniform Crime Reporting Program in 1990 showed the highest number of arrests of youth for violent offenses—homicide, armed robbery, rape, aggravated assault—in the more than 25 years that the statistics have been compiled. Juvenile arrest rates, after rising steadily from the mid-1960s through the 1970s, remained relatively constant until the 1989-90 statistics revealed a 26% increase in the number of youths arrested for murder and non-negligent manslaughter, while arrests for robbery had increased by 16%, and those for aggravated assault by 17%.

"A significant number of boys arrested for violent crimes were out on parole at the time of the arrest."

But the system still defines juveniles as children rather than as criminals, a distinction that makes little sense to their victims or to the rest of the public. Family Court turns the worst juvenile offenders over to the adult system for trial, but they are still sentenced as juveniles.

When anything does happen it's usually so long after the event, so short in duration, and so ineffective that it's no wonder the young men who rob, maim, rape and terrorize don't perceive those actions as having any serious consequences. Eighty percent of chronic juvenile offenders (five or more arrests) go on to adult criminal careers.

Is it possible to change these young criminals? And what should be done to protect the community from them?

Open Court Proceedings

The first necessity is legislation to open juvenile court proceedings to the public and the press. It makes no sense to protect the privacy of those who are a palpable menace to their neighbors or scruple about "stigmatizing" them. A repeat offender should know the authorities will make use of his past record in deciding what to do with him next time. At present, a young habitual criminal is born again with a virgin record when he reaches the age to be dealt with by the adult system.

Opening court records would also make it possible to undertake follow-up studies to find out what works and what doesn't in the various detention facilities and alternative programs designed to rehabilitate. Taxpayers have a right to know what outcomes they are getting for the $85,000 a year it costs to keep a juvenile offender in a secure facility in New York state.

Intervention should occur early, while there is still time to try measures that might make a difference. First offenders should be required to make restitution to their victims or perform community service. A second arrest should be followed by stronger measures. For those who have families who undertake to be responsible for them, there should be intensive supervision by well-trained probation officers with manageable caseloads. For those who require placement out of the home, it should include intensive remedial schoolwork and practical training in some job-related skill. The youth should remain long enough for such efforts to have some hope of proving effective.

Swift and True Punishment

Sanctions should be swift and sure. Once arrested, a court appearance should follow without delay, preferably on the same day, so that there is a clear connection made between behavior and its consequences. Placement in appropriately secure institutions, locked away from the community for definite periods of time, should be the immediate and inevitable response to repeated acts of violence. And incarceration should involve some form of work that helps defray its cost to the community, not just a period of rest and recreation. Young criminals should know that is what they can expect.

"We owe it to the law-abiding citizens who share the streets and schools with the violent few to protect the rights of the community."

A growing cadre of violent teenage boys are growing up with mothers who are children and no resident fathers. What they need most of all is structure and supervision. We may not be able to change attitudes, but we can change behavior. While there is no evidence that any form of therapy can really change a violent repeat offender into someone with empathy for others, it has been demonstrated that the one thing that can result in impulse control is the certainty of punishment.

The present system actually encourages the young to continue their criminal behavior by showing them that they can get away with it. No punishment means a second chance at the same crimes. A significant number of boys arrested for violent crimes were out on parole at the time of the arrest.

They think of the system as a game they can win. "They can't do nothing to me, I ain't 16 yet" is a repeated refrain in a system that breeds contempt for the law and for the other institutions of society. It is time to acknowledge its failure and restructure the system so that "juvenile justice" ceases to be an oxymoron. We owe it to the law-abiding citizens who share the streets and schools with the violent few to protect the rights of the community and not just those of its victimizers.

Violent Youths Should Be Punished as Adults

by William P. Barr

About the author: *William P. Barr is the attorney general of the United States.*

Juvenile justice reform is an essential part of the war on crime. It is no mystery who commits the lion's share of crime in this country. Study after study show that there is a small segment of our population who are repeat violent offenders and who commit much, if not most, of the predatory violent crime in our society.

Unfortunately, these habitual offenders usually embark on a career of crime as juveniles. They begin committing crimes in their mid-, or even early teens, and by the time they reach the age of majority they are experienced, incorrigible criminals. Most kids who get into trouble have only one or two brushes with the law and straighten out as they get more mature.

A Small Segment of Violent Youths

A small group of juvenile offenders, however, become habitual offenders—progressively committing more serious and more violent crimes. Marvin Wolfgang's famous study in Philadelphia showed that 7% of male youths were responsible for about two-thirds of all serious offenses committed by juveniles. Later studies in Philadelphia found that 15% of juveniles accounted for 82% of the serious offenses committed by juveniles. Wolfgang's studies suggest that, by the third arrest, a juvenile delinquent is almost sure to continue in a life of crime.

The juvenile justice system needs to do two things better. First, it has to be more effective at intervening early enough to divert troubled youths away from a career of crime. Second, it has to be more effective at identifying and dealing decisively with the chronic offender who has embarked on a career of crime.

The problem is an urgent one. Today, juveniles are responsible for a large part

From William P. Barr's speech to the Governors Conference on Juvenile Crime, Drugs, and Gangs, Milwaukee, Wisconsin, April 1, 1992.

of the violent crime we see about us. When you look at the *percentage* of total crime that is committed by juveniles, the news is disheartening.

Juveniles under 18 accounted for:

- 33% of all burglary
- 30% of all larceny
- 24% of all robbery
- 15% of all rape.
- And, 14% (or 1 in 7) of all murder and nonnegligent manslaughter.
- And if you add 18-year-olds into the equation, the numbers are even more staggering. For example, in 1990 persons under 19 accounted for over 21% of all arrests for murder.

Worse still, the *rate* of juvenile crime continues to increase, and this increase among juveniles is driving much of the general increase in crime we are seeing today. For example, between 1965 and 1989:

- the arrest rate of juveniles for murder almost *tripled.*
- the rate of aggravated assault *tripled.*
- and the rate of weapons violations increased by *2 and ½ times.*

More Effective Juvenile Justice

With numbers like these, one thing is clear—if we are going to deal effectively with violent crime generally, we are going to have to improve the way we are dealing with juveniles.

Broadly defined, I see the juvenile justice system as comprised of three distinct components:

First, there is the constellation of private and public institutions that socialize the child and shape his or her moral character.

Second, there is the official juvenile delinquency system—including the juvenile courts—that is designed primarily to intercede in the juvenile's life early enough to straighten out the basically good kid who has "strayed" and to prevent the delinquent child from becoming the career criminal offender. The primary goal is to do what is "best for the child."

> ***"If we are going to deal effectively with violent crime generally, we are going to have to improve the way we are dealing with juveniles."***

Finally, there is the regular criminal justice system that must take over when the juvenile delinquency system fails to turn around the youthful offender or when the juvenile's offense is sufficiently serious. At this stage, society's primary goal shifts from serving the best interests of the child to serving the best interest of society.

In my view, we must take a hard look at each of these three stages of the juvenile justice system and apply some common sense to make them work better. . . .

As I said, there is a small group of juveniles who become chronic offenders, responsible for progressively more violent crimes. This hardened group has proven impervious to rehabilitation. Once a juvenile has embarked on a career of crime, the goal of protecting society must become paramount.

Harsher Penalties for Violent Youths

Our objective should be to identify as early as possible the habitual offender and to incapacitate that offender through stiff adult penalties. We must stand ready to prosecute and punish serious violent offenders and repeat offenders as adults. Every experienced law enforcement officer has encountered 16- or 17-year-olds who are as mature and criminally hardened as adult offenders. Public safety demands that these habitual and dangerous criminals be tried and punished as adults.

Unfortunately, many of our criminal justice systems in this country harken back to a more innocent age, and have strong built-in presumptions against treating juveniles as adults. In general, I think we have to provide greater flexibility—and give law enforcement wider latitude to prosecute serious juvenile offenders as adults.

> ***"Every experienced law enforcement officer has encountered 16- or 17-year-olds who are as mature and criminally hardened as adult offenders."***

While the procedure for certifying juveniles into adult courts is available in most states, it can be cumbersome and difficult, and in practice it is rarely used. The resulting unlikelihood and uncertainty of waiver into the adult system reduces or eliminates any deterrent effect that the threat of adult prosecution could have on juveniles. Again, every law enforcement professional knows the stories of juveniles who when arrested laugh in their faces and brag about how quickly they'll be back on the streets.

Moreover, in many states, the records kept of juvenile offenses are wholly inadequate and laws governing the sharing of what little information does exist are unduly restrictive. Without meaningful and accessible information about a juvenile's criminal history, it is virtually impossible to determine whether he has become the sort of habitual offender who should be tried as an adult.

While laws providing for the sealing of juvenile records for purposes of later employment applications may be warranted, there is no justification for not keeping adequate juvenile criminal history records and sharing that information with other parts of the criminal justice system. The theory of sealing these records is to give a clean slate to the juvenile who committed a youthful error but has since mended his ways. That theory simply does not apply where the juvenile continues to commit crimes.

Let me tell you some of the measures we are considering at the federal level to strengthen our ability to deal with juvenile crime.

First, the Department of Justice is now in the process of promulgating a rule that would authorize the FBI to include juvenile records in the FBI criminal history information system. Currently, offenses committed by juvenile offenders cannot be included unless the juvenile was tried as an adult. The purpose of the proposed rule is to make the records of serious crimes committed by juveniles available for law enforcement and judicial use. The rule does not compel the states to provide such information to the FBI, but only provides the FBI with the same authority to receive juvenile records. State law and policy will dictate whether a state forwards juvenile records, and if so, what types of records are forwarded. We have received comments about the proposed rule, including some expressing concerns about blurring the distinctions between the adult and juvenile systems. Overall, I believe that the basic premise of the rule is sound, and that these juvenile records are important to our law enforcement system.

"There is no justification for not keeping adequate juvenile criminal history records and sharing that information with other parts of the criminal justice system."

Second, I am considering amendments to the federal code that would give the federal government more flexibility to try juveniles as adults. Under current law, a juvenile may be tried as an adult in the federal system only for certain violent felonies or serious drug offenses, and only if he meets certain age requirements.

Broader Adult Prosecution

Moreover, under current law, there is a presumption *against* adult prosecution that can be overcome only by finding in the federal court that it is "in the interest of justice" to transfer the juvenile to the adult system. We are considering changing this system in two ways.

First, we may propose to broaden the types of crimes for which adult prosecution is available to other areas of strong federal law enforcement interest. In addition to violent felonies and serious drug crimes, we are considering adding serious firearms offenses and certain other gang-related crimes where there is a strong federal interest.

Second, we may suggest certain adjustments in the current age requirements and in the presumptions and the required court approvals to make it less difficult to try juveniles, especially repeat offenders, as adults in appropriate cases.

Let me make clear what we are *not* considering. We are not suggesting that the prosecution of juvenile crime should be federalized. On the contrary, as is the case with violent crime generally—where 95% of the cases are handled by the states—the primary responsibility for the prosecution of juvenile offenders lies with the states. The ideas that I have discussed relate only to certain uniquely serious federal offenses that the federal government has a strong interest in prosecuting.

On the other hand, I hope that the states will amend their codes where necessary to allow for the adult prosecution and punishment of juveniles who commit serious, violent acts or who are repeat felons. Indeed, I understand that many states have already made substantial progress in amending their laws to allow for the adult prosecution of serious juvenile offenders. I applaud and encourage that trend.

The Death Penalty Should Be Imposed on Juvenile Murderers

by Frederic J. Cowan, Elizabeth Ann Myerscough, and David A. Smith

About the authors: *Former attorney general Frederic J. Cowan, now an attorney in Louisville, represented the state of Kentucky in the 1989 U.S. Supreme Court case* Stanford v. Kentucky, *excerpted here, which upheld the death sentence of Kevin Stanford, a 17-year-old who committed murder. Elizabeth Ann Myerscough and David A. Smith are assistant attorneys general for Kentucky.*

Among the 36 States which endorse capital punishment, there is no consensus of a minimum age at which defendants may be sentenced to death. Seven States, Arizona, Delaware, Florida, Oklahoma, Pennsylvania, South Carolina and Wyoming, have no age limitation. South Dakota specifies a minimum age of 10 years. Montana specifies age 12; Mississippi age 13; Alabama, Idaho, Missouri, North Carolina and Utah age 14. Arkansas, Louisiana and Virginia have a minimum age limitation of 15. Indiana, Kentucky, Nevada and Washington limit execution to individuals age 16 or older. Georgia, New Hampshire and Texas specify a minimum age limitation of 17. California, Colorado, Connecticut, Illinois, Maryland, Nebraska, New Jersey, New Mexico, Ohio, Oregon and Tennessee draw the line at 18 years of age.

Draw No Bright Line

There is no broad agreement among the States at what age capital punishment can be imposed. Since no societal consensus can be discerned from legislative enactments, no bright line should be drawn prohibiting the death penalty for any person under 18 years of age.

Analysis of jury deliberations and verdicts affords no evidence of consensus

From a brief filed January 25, 1989, by Frederic J. Cowan, Elizabeth Ann Myerscough, and David A. Smith in the U.S. Supreme Court case of *Stanford v. Kentucky*.

as to the appropriateness of executing 16 and 17 year old murderers. Petitioners and their *amici* assume that since few 16 and 17 year olds have received the death penalty or been executed, it must mean there is a general abhorrence throughout society of inflicting the death penalty on persons of those ages. Petitioners' proposition fails to account for the realities of the juvenile justice system.

The Office of Juvenile Justice and Delinquency Prevention recently commissioned a research, test and demonstration study (The Juvenile Serious Habitual Offender/Drug Involved Program) which focused on serious, chronic, violent juvenile offenders.

The SHO/DI program found that most juvenile delinquents

> do not even make it into court. Rather, they are diverted out of the juvenile justice system, early in the process, often before they ever get to court. According to Paul Strasburg [author of *Violent Delinquents, A Report to the Ford Foundation*]: Between 80 and 90 percent of arrested children are diverted or dropped from the judicial process with little or no supervision. Half are diverted by the police themselves. And up to two-thirds of the cases left may be withdrawn, dismissed, or adjourned in contemplation of dismissal.

Data analysis obtained during the program revealed that the "serious juvenile population is very, very small. Overall, they represent less than one percent of the entire juvenile population."

No Conclusions from Few Jury Verdicts

The fallacy of Petitioners' reliance on jury verdicts and the conclusions drawn therefrom become apparent when other factors such as the following are considered:

1). The relatively small number of violent juvenile offenders.

2). The disproportionate number of juveniles diverted or never brought into the juvenile justice system, much less the criminal system.

3). The safeguard of waiver hearings by juvenile courts before transfer of offenders to criminal court.

4). The fact that several States have no death penalty at all.

5). The consideration by juries of the mitigating factor of the defendant's youth.

> ***"No bright line should be drawn prohibiting the death penalty for any person under 18 years of age."***

The fact that there are few jury verdicts sentencing 16 and 17 year olds to death does not indicate a consensus against such penalties. All indicators suggest instead that there are few opportunities to even consider them.

The violence of chronic youthful offenders is recognized as the major problem confronting the juvenile justice system. The National Council of Family

Court Judges attempted to address this problem by endorsing 38 recommendations. Among the various recommendations, two are particularly relevant to the issue presented to this Court.

> Recommendation #1: *Serious Juvenile Offenders Should Be Held Accountable By The Courts.* The primary focus of the juvenile court for the disposition of serious chronic or violent juvenile offenders should be accountability. Dispositions of such offenders should be proportionate to the injury done and the culpability of the juvenile and to the prior record of adjudication if any. In conjunction with this recommendation, the Council acknowledges that the principal purpose of the juvenile justice court system is to protect the public.

> Recommendation #13: *Offenders Unamenable To Juvenile Treatment Should Be Transferred.* The judges note that "there are juveniles for whom the resources and processes available to the juvenile court will serve neither to rehabilitate the juvenile nor to protect the public."

Juvenile court judges face the problem of violent youths every day. These recommendations acknowledge actual experience and observation that persons of any age engaging in violence should and must be held accountable for their actions. By their acts, some youths have placed themselves beyond the pale of treatment recognized as appropriate for other individuals of their age group. The remedy left to society at this point is to treat these anomalies of the juvenile justice system as it would any other violent offender. The individual violent youth's culpability and society's expectations of accountability demand nothing less.

> ***"The fact that there are few jury verdicts sentencing 16 and 17 year olds to death does not indicate a consensus against such penalties."***

The Council's recommendations do not include a call for abolition of the death penalty for youths. This non-recommendation becomes conspicuous by its absence. It must be assumed that juvenile court judges are aware that once a juvenile is transferred to stand trial on murder charges as an adult, the State may impose its maximum penalty. In 25 States, this includes the possibility of death for persons less than 18 years of age. The Council's silence on this question lends support to *amici's* position that no national consensus exists condemning the death penalty for persons under 18 years old.

Death Penalty Opponents

In a concerted and well-organized effort to persuade this Court, which they are entitled to do, 34 different organizations have filed or joined *amici curiae* briefs on behalf of the Petitioners. These groups largely oppose capital punishment under any conceivable circumstances. Several of these organizations are already suggesting that the "bright line" should be drawn beyond the age of 18.

E.g., the American Society for Adolescent Psychiatry, the American Orthopsychiatric Association, the National Legal Aid and Defender Association, the National Association of Criminal Defense Lawyers, the Defense for Children International, and the West Virginia Council of Churches.

If this Court were making a legislative judgment as to whether those who commit a capital homicide at age 16 should be eligible for the death penalty, the views of "respected professional organizations" might well be relevant, both as arguments on the merits of the proposed legislation and as an expression on the part of the small segment of society which such groups represent. The views of these individual interest groups, however, are not reliable "objective factors" in judging whether a national consensus exists against the execution of 16 and 17 year old killers. By definition, positions taken on behalf of a particular organization at most represent the opinion of its members, not society as a whole. Since no need exists for those entities which approve an existing practice to formally state that fact, resolutions of this character inevitably represent the voices in opposition. Consequently, Georgia and Missouri do not attempt to inundate this Court with *amici curiae* briefs by the countless victims rights groups which more accurately reflect societal consensus.

No Reflection of Society

As this Court has acknowledged, it is not designed or intended to reflect the views of society, as are legislative or other representative bodies. In paying heed to these groups which have gone to the effort of expressing formal opposition on the present issue, there is a considerable risk of mistaking the clamor of organized protest for a settled national consensus.

A ruling by this Court that juveniles are invariably too immature for capital punishment would establish precedent for exempting them from lesser penalties on the same ground.

At least for the time being, the Petitioners and their *amici* do not challenge the prerogative of State legislatures to establish various age ranges for juvenile court jurisdiction. Neither do they, as yet, argue that the transfer of individual offenders from juvenile court for trial as adults is constitutionally prohibited. And although *Kent v. United States*, (1966) extends minimum Due Process standards to juvenile transfer proceedings, not even the defense bar suggests that the Court should prescribe the criteria for determining whether a particular offender deserves to be treated as an adult.

> ***"The remedy left to society . . . is to treat these anomalies of the juvenile justice system as it would any other violent offender."***

State legislatures set the maximum age for juvenile jurisdiction as high as they do to benefit every arguably immature offender, even at the obvious expense of including many individuals who do not deserve such protection. By using this approach to reach beyond the common denominator of chronological immaturity, the States are justified in examining each juvenile individually to determine whether an exception should be made in his or her particular case. As the Court has emphasized on prior occasions, maturity and sophistication are factors which vary from individual to individual, so chronological age is only one of the various circumstances that should be taken into account.

[According to *Fare v. Michael C.*:]

> Minors who become embroiled with the law range from the very young up to those on the brink of majority. Some of the older minors become fully "street wise", hardened criminals deserving no greater consideration than that properly accorded all persons suspected of crime. Other minors are more of a child than an adult. As the Court indicated in *In Re Gault*, (1967), the facts relevant to the care to be exercised in a particular case vary widely. They include the minor's age, actual maturity, family environment, education, emotional and mental stability, and, of course, any prior record he might have.

All the States recognize the special mitigation of youth in their juvenile transfer proceedings long before they do so, again, in capital sentencing trials. Consequently, there is no more reason for this Court to draw a "bright line" age requirement for capital punishment than there is for it to do so in the context of juvenile jurisdiction waiver proceedings. In both situations that decision is better left to the individual States whose legislative determinations, for the sake of comity, should be accorded deference by the federal judiciary.

Determine Death Sentences Case by Case

[*California v. Brown*, (1987) states:] "It is generally agreed 'that punishment should be directly related to the personal culpability of the criminal defendant.'"

Guided, individualized consideration of the offender's character and the circumstances of his crime is the touchstone of capital sentencing. *Gregg v. Georgia*, (1976) and its progeny are intended to avoid the kind of "rigid," "mechanical" and "wholly arbitrary" determination urged here by the Petitioners. No particular circumstance of a capital offender's crime should automatically require the death penalty or automatically foreclose it. Rather, the sentencer must be "free to consider a myriad of factors to determine whether death is the appropriate punishment," [according to] *California v. Ramos*, (1983). Youthfulness is only one such factor and it is not necessarily the most important.

> ***"A ruling . . . that juveniles are invariably too immature for capital punishment would establish precedent for exempting them from lesser penalties."***

Maturity varies from individual to individual. Some individuals never attain it; some do at an age labeled "child."...

The need for individual consideration of the defendant's character and the circumstances of the crime becomes glaringly apparent now that a question of Jose High's true age has been raised [in Georgia]. Has High suddenly become more deserving of the death penalty as a 19 year old murderer, or less deserving of the death penalty as a 17 year old murderer? Neither the circumstances of the crime nor the defendant's character at the time he committed the crime have changed. There is no reason relating to the crime or the defendant which should preclude the death penalty for High. To draw a bright-line rule prohibiting execution of anyone less than 18 years of age, and thus prohibiting High's execution if Georgia cannot establish his age at 19, undermines the very purpose of individualized sentencing of offenders, which is to fashion a sentence appropriate to the crime.

"Some of the older minors become fully 'street wise', hardened criminals deserving no greater consideration than that . . . accorded all persons suspected of crime."

Juveniles Are Protected by Due Process Rights

No national policy of automatic exemption for 16 and 17 year olds from the death penalty exists. For those 16 and 17 year olds subject to juvenile court jurisdiction, waiver proceedings provide individual consideration of whether the offender can best be served by the juvenile or criminal justice system. *Kent v. United States* requires a hearing, assistance of counsel, and a statement of reasons for the transfer. These minimum Due Process rights provide additional safeguards that offenders with presumptive juvenile status will not be arbitrarily reclassified as adults.

In *all* States where 16 or 17 year olds are eligible for the death penalty, their youth must be presented as a mitigating factor to the sentencer. Twenty-nine States have adopted the holding of *Eddings* through legislation designating the defendant's age as a mitigating factor in capital cases.

In every trial where death is a possible penalty, a 16 or 17 year old will be accorded consideration of his youth in the assessment of punishment. Age alone should not exclude a punishment otherwise deemed appropriate considering the defendant's character and criminal act.

Violent Youths Need Rehabilitation, Not Harsh Punishment

by Robert S. Weaver

About the author: *Robert S. Weaver is the executive vice president of Associated Marine Institutes (AMI), a Tampa, Florida, organization that contracts with several state agencies to provide rehabilitative services for teenage offenders.*

Each morning most of us wake up to a "play by play" account of violent crime. The morning news, radio shows, and the newspapers provide us with the latest updates on assaults, stabbings, murders, and rapes. We tune in to a major television network and get a summary at day's end. When a kid commits one of these crimes it's even bigger news.

The fact that juveniles account for approximately 30 percent of the serious crime is cause for concern. However, the media-fed public perception of rapidly increasing juvenile crime is not accurate. The rates of serious juvenile crime declined between 1979 and 1984. Nationally, we experienced an increase for the first time in six years in 1985. What can be done about serious juvenile crime? This is the story of one successful program designed to serve this small but volatile portion of the delinquent population.

Protecting the Public Safety

Public perception ultimately drives public policy. Protecting the public's safety is the first and most important issue in providing service to violent offenders. For six years the Florida Environmental Institute (FEI) has worked with some of the most serious and violent youthful offenders in Florida. This work has been accomplished without fences, lockdowns, or the restraints normally associated with maximum security programs. There have only been three

From Robert S. Weaver, *Programs for Serious and Violent Juvenile Offenders*. Ann Arbor: University of Michigan Center for the Study of Youth Policy, 1989. Reprinted with permission.

successful escapes in the camp's six years of operation. Political rhetoric about "getting tough" is popular. However, in all but a handful of cases, youthful offenders will return to their respective communities. We propose that humane and effective treatment of tough juveniles is in the best interest of the public on both long and short term. According to the Bureau of Justice Statistics (Criminal Justice Newsletter, 1989) 94 percent of young prisoners with extensive prior records were rearrested within three years. Clearly, it is in the best interest of our society and our economy to look at alternative methods of dealing with serious juvenile offenders.

"Phase I students live in an austere military-type dorm without air conditioning, television, or other amenities."

The FEI was dubbed "The Last Chance Ranch" by the youths served. The program is located in a remote area of the northern reaches of the Florida Everglades. The ranch is surrounded by swamp, sloughs, pine and palmetto forest. The facilities are rustic, wooden structures built by students and staff. FEI has a capacity of 22 youths in residential care and 20 youths in non-residential or aftercare status. The program began in 1982 and has served 173 youths since inception. The catchment area is the southern half of Florida, including the major metropolitan areas of Tampa, Orlando, West Palm Beach, Ft. Lauderdale, and Miami.

Each youth participates in three program phases with a total average length of stay of 18 months. The average length of stay in the non-residential community phase is six months.

When youths are referred, they arrive at a stage site approximately 10 miles from the camp. They then travel to the area of the camp and backpack into a remote, forested area for a three-five day orientation called "0 Camp." At "0 Camp" they work hard each day and learn the basic rules of the camp. Each manager and several senior students participate in the orientation. This process is designed to bond the youths to key staff and student leaders in order to start them off on the right foot. The foundations of a case treatment plan are established and if all goes well, the youth will join the camp for the evening meal on the third day, becoming a part of a large and extended family.

What the Program Entails

The first phase of the program emphasizes work and education. Each youth spends his day completing work projects at or close to the camp and attends education and safety-related classes. Phase I students live in an austere military-type dorm without air conditioning, television, or other amenities. Performance must precede reward as youth earn "points" and privileges towards graduation into Phase II.

Phase II focuses on continuing work in education and expanding work related activities into community and environmental work projects. Wherever possible, youths earn money for restitution and savings. The dorm is air conditioned and has a television and other amenities. The focus is on work, education, and preparing to return home. Towards the end of Phase II, students earn the right to return home with their community coordinator to find work, begin networking and rebuilding family relationships.

Community Challenges

Phase III is an intense, advocacy-based aftercare program. Community coordinators with case loads of approximately 6 to 1 assist youths in findings jobs, dealing with family issues and the myriad of other challenges they face in successfully adapting to their communities. Serving a small but widespread aftercare population poses many logistical problems which FEI community coordinators must overcome. Phase III is the community battleground where the skills and education learned at the camp are put to the test. Weekly parent visitations, an annual Thanksgiving rodeo and regular written and phone communications are focused on keeping parents informed and involved. Community coordinators regularly visit families and get to know the strengths and weaknesses of each family unit. We do not believe it is helpful or effective to force youth into choosing between the value system of the family and that of the program. Our approach is to work with the conditions and problems the family presents in an affirmative way while helping each youth discern alternatives and choices. If we expose youth to a more effective value system without condemning their families, chances are they will make future decisions in their own best interest.

> ***"We believed that a program for violent offenders could be safely operated without the fences, lockdowns, and restraints."***

All key leadership personnel are talented veterans with successful histories of operating AMI programs. Due to the remote nature of the location, executive directors accept a "tour of duty" of approximately two years.

There are 22 direct service employees at the camp. Employees work five 8 hour shifts each week and the actual staff to student ratio in the classroom and on work projects is typically 3 or 4 to 1. One of three managers is responsible for each of the 14 morning and evening shifts. One manager is on call for each night shift.

People create environments which encourage change. Good program design, effective administration, adequate funding and appropriate facilities all fall short without the right people. Serious offenders are typically gang members with a strong desire for affiliation. We believe the staff must offer a powerful alternative peer group to which offenders can relate and become part of.

The cost per day of the residential components of the camp is approximately $102. The cost per day of the non-residential components is approximately $20. The average cost per case is $40,000.

The original program design for FEI drew heavily from AMI's previous work with over 10,000 delinquent youths. We believed that a program for violent offenders could be safely operated without the fences, lockdowns, and restraints characteristic of maximum security facilities. We knew that we needed to prepare participants for successful re-entry into the world of work. In all likelihood they would go to work in blue collar fields. Our own research had demonstrated a close correlation between educational level and recidivism. We knew the youths referred would be functioning at 5th grade level or below. Education would be a key component. We wanted to create an atmosphere that was family-like, stressing discipline, cooperation, and everyone having a job to do. Our plan included stressing a "performance precedes reward" format which would encourage youths to defer gratification and set long range goals. Lastly, we knew that the success of the endeavor would hinge on the effectiveness of the aftercare component.

Less Hardware, More Supervision

These concepts were translated into five key elements of the original program design. A more in-depth look at each is as follows:

1. *Violent Offenders Without Hardware.* A cornerstone of the Associated Marine Institute (the parent organization that FEI is a part of) philosophy is to serve youths in the least restrictive environment possible. Our practical experience has been that unnatural constraints and security encourage unnatural behavior. AMI programs have always protected the public's safety through supervision rather than hardware. We believed this concept could be extended to serious offenders. Our strategy was to find a location so remote that the setting itself would discourage escape attempts and protect the public's safety. There is no fence surrounding this program, nor any hardware except a pair of handcuffs available for restraint of participants in an extreme emergency situation.

> ***"When we use fear to motivate youths, they almost always return to the inappropriate behaviors if the fear of being caught or punished diminishes."***

2. *Hard Work as Therapy.* At AMI we believe that the single greatest weakness in the juvenile and adult systems is the lack of meaningful work for those incarcerated. By failing to provide offenders with a role, we clearly indicate their value to us and to their own communities. A cornerstone of the FEI approach is that every youth would work hard on projects in the camp and com-

munity. Staff and students work side by side on community and environmental projects providing taxpayers with tangible results. FEI students have completed over 75 projects allowing each youth the opportunity to give something back to the community surrounding the camp. Environmental projects often generate income for participants allowing students to pay restitution and save money for community re-entry.

3. *Education Equals Lower Recidivism.* Our research indicates a close correlation between low grade levels and recidivism. Referrals to FEI typically read at a 5th grade level or below. The curriculum and schedule at FEI focuses on improving each youth's reading and math skills and, wherever possible, helping them earn a GED. Since inception, 24 youths have earned GEDs. This focus on education, in itself, is not a distinguishing characteristic. The intensity with which we pursue each youth's improvement is.

Punishment: Cornerstone of Discipline

4. *Punishment and Rewards.* Youth perceive the removal of their freedom and control of activities as a form of punishment. We choose not to gloss over these facts. Punishment for inappropriate behavior is a cornerstone of effective discipline. At FEI, punishment is individualized wherever possible, and never corporal in nature. The continuum begins with removal of privileges at the camp and ends at removal from the camp to a remote location for one-on-one work projects with a staff member. To be effective, punishment must meet three important tests.

> ***"FEI provides a structured learning environment and an intensive education while protecting the public during the high crime period of 15-18 years of age."***

A. Does the punishment fit the crime?

B. Is the time frame one which the offender can relate to?

C. Does the person doing the punishing have the best interest of the offender at heart?

The third test is the most important. The most unfair discipline is that which treats individual youths with a wide range of problems and behaviors the same. Most human beings instinctively know whether our actions are conceived in their best interest. AMI staff training is designed to teach each staff to differentiate between those behaviors which control others and those likely to change the behavior of others. We believe punishment falls into the control category. When we use fear to motivate youths, they almost always return to the inappropriate behaviors if the fear of being caught or punished diminishes. Understanding this important but subtle distinction is what creates an atmosphere which encourages youths to change. Failing to understand this difference results in compliant offenders institutionalized for long periods, interrupted by release, recidivism, and subsequent reincarceration.

5. *It's a Sign of Progress that "Aftercare" Programs are Making Appearances in the Continuum of Programming in Many States.* Our AMI experience and research ten years ago indicated aftercare was the weakest link in residential programming for juvenile offenders. At AMI and in other programs we observed youths committing themselves to more effective behaviors only to regress rapidly upon return to the challenges of their communities and negative peer group back home. We resolved to assist our participants in making the transition back into the communities, with a wide range of services all built upon a bond between a community coordinator advocate and the youth.

"FEI is a proven success in protecting the public safety."

Our approach has been to view violent offenders as youths who shared a commonality of deficits with their delinquent counterparts. Practical experience over six years has taught us that violent offenders have many of the same problems troubling their delinquent counterparts—fragmented families, single parents, greater education deficits, histories of abuse and neglect as children, and significant health and nutritional problems. A larger percentage of these referrals come from inner city minority families living below the poverty level.

The criminal history of the youths included averaging 18 offenses and 11.5 felonies. Sixty-three percent of the referrals were for crimes against person, the remaining were for chronic property and drug offenses. Sixty-seven percent of the referrals were minorities.

There is little evidence indicating specialization by individual youths in violent crime. Rather, serious juvenile crime is likely to be a part of a wider, very active pattern of delinquency. FEI referrals reinforce this pattern and have typically been seen by the juvenile court at a relatively early age, accumulating 20 or more adjudications prior to enrollment in the program.

Sixty-seven percent of the FEI referrals came from the adult system. Under Florida law, a juvenile who has been found guilty as an adult may be returned to the juvenile system for treatment. Typically, these youths will have to complete the program or a prison sentence. The State of Florida provides four separate paths from which a youthful offender may be tried. As an adult if over 16 years of age, the state attorney's office may elect to file criminal charges. If less than 16, the state attorney may file a petition for waiver of the juvenile to adult court. As a result of the state attorney's right to direct file, Florida ranks first in the nation in prosecuting juveniles in adult court.

Both Offenders and the Public Benefit

FEI is a proven success in protecting the public safety. Of the three successful escapes, only one resulted in a serious new law violation and it did not involve injury to the victim. We believe that FEI's remote location has been a significant advantage allowing us to avoid the physical security measures and restraints which provide offenders with powerful negative messages about their self worth. These youths are potentially some of the society's most dangerous and volatile members. FEI provides a structured learning environment and an intensive education while protecting the public during the high crime period of 15-18 years of age.

We have shown that this can be done at a cost per day and per case below that of many large juvenile institutions. The high cost of building prison beds and maximum security units makes programs like FEI a bargain. The average national cost for building a prison bed is over $50,000. An entire FEI type facility can be built for under $300,000. Small intensive programs for violent offenders make sense. They are cost effective in both the short and long run for society.

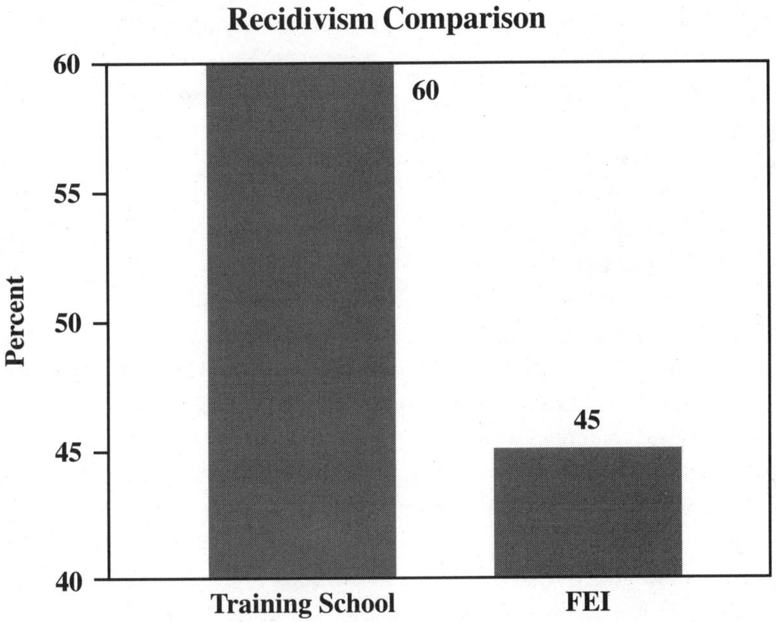

The chart uses Florida Department of Health and Rehabilitative Services Outcome Evaluation Component statistics to compare FEI recidivism to that of the Florida training schools. Forty-five percent of the FEI participants recidivated as compared to 60 percent of the training school population. At the time of the study, 80 percent of the training school population had criminal histories less serious than youths enrolled at FEI. . . .

Putting troubled kids back into the picture is a good investment. Helping our most troubled youth is not a lofty goal, it is an achievable objective. We're working hard to do our part at the "Last Chance Ranch."

Imprisoning Violent Youths Exposes Them to Physical and Sexual Abuse

by Dwight Boyd Roberts

About the author: *Dwight Boyd Roberts is the author of the book* I Cried, You Didn't Listen, *which describes his incarceration within the California Youth Authority. Roberts was serving a ten-year sentence for assault with a deadly weapon at Washington State Penitentiary in Walla Walla when this article was originally published.*

This is my story, how I was introduced to a brutal, warped and perverted world at the age of nine.

Why was I locked inside an institution? I had not committed a crime. My offense was that my parents had both been seriously injured in an automobile accident. I had no relatives or guardians to turn to.

I was placed inside Los Angeles County Juvenile Hall and was told I would be there until my parents "were well." I was put into a dormitory-living situation with other children ranging in age from seven to seventeen. Some kids were confined because of broken homes, but most were there because of their participation in criminal activities: burglary, auto theft, even murder.

For me, a nine-year-old boy who had never been in trouble with the law, juvenile hall was to quickly become a nightmare. Upon my arrival, one of the older black kids severely beat me, while a counselor looked on and made no attempt to stop it. That night, I watched three Mexican kids sexually assault a white child. Their victim was about seven years old. They were about fourteen or fifteen.

An Environment Full of Violence

During the four months I was initially incarcerated in juvenile hall, I experienced another side to life that is known only by the people confined to such an

Dwight Boyd Roberts, "I Cried, You Didn't Listen," *Arete*, December 1988.

environment. I experienced my first physical beating, my first sexual molestation, my first placement in solitary confinement, and I watched, for the first time, an act of rape. I also committed my first act of violence, and my victim nearly died. . . .

Driving past the entrance to the Los Angeles County Juvenile Hall was a terrifying experience. As I got out of the car, I glanced several times at the high wall, while two men led me to a large metal door that was unlocked from the inside. The door opened, and I was nudged through the doorway into a small room.

A counselor appeared and escorted me to another building. Its door was unlocked from the inside, too. I stepped through the doorway. The noise was deafening. There was a fight going on just a few feet from the counselor. He ignored it. Kids were hollering and running all over the place.

There were two rows of beds to my right, about twenty in each row, lined against walls on the opposite side of the room. To my left was an office from which another counselor was just exiting. Across from this office was a door that I later learned led to the shower area.

> ***"I'd never been spanked before, let alone punched or kicked. When I was unable to control my crying, the counselor slapped me hard."***

The counselor who had escorted me inside took me by my arm and led me to his office. There he told me the rules, most of which were being violated when I entered the dorm. He said, among other things, there was no loud noise allowed, no smoking and no fighting.

He then took me to my assigned bed and said, "Make it up before you do anything else."

Seconds later, I made my first mistake. I took the blankets and sheets folded at the foot of my bed and laid them on the bed next to mine. A black kid, twice my size and several years older, picked up the bedding and threw it on the floor.

Beaten by a Bully

"You better watch what you put on my bed," he said, staring at me.

I looked at him, saying nothing. I had never seen a black person before. He scared the hell out of me.

He shoved me, asking, "What do you think you're doing?"

I started to tell him as he took a step forward and hit me hard, right on my mouth.

I had never been hit with a closed fist until then. The punch knocked me to the floor. I laid there with the pain. The bully began kicking me. I did my best to cover my head. The counselor allowed this to go on for a few minutes before he pulled the kid away from me. Crying, I stood up and saw the other kids looking at me. My nose was swollen and bleeding.

"You'll be okay," the counselor said. "You better learn not to mess with anybody. Stop being such a baby."

I was confused. I *was* a baby. I'd never been spanked before, let alone punched or kicked. When I was unable to control my crying, the counselor slapped me hard. I fell down onto my bed, rolled over it and landed on the floor.

He said, "You better fight next time, boy. I'm not here to baby-sit you."

Witness to a Rape

That evening, as was done every night after returning from supper, everybody undressed and stood in front of their beds with a towel wrapped around their bodies and waited for their turn to shower. Five kids showered at a time, while a counselor sat at a table observing us, making sure no one talked during this period. He should've been more concerned about what was going on in the shower room.

When it was my turn to shower, I walked in and saw a couple of older kids holding a white boy of about my age, bent over in front of a black guy. The black kid had his penis inside the little boy's bottom. A Mexican kid held his hand over the child's mouth, but I could still hear him crying. The bigger kids were all about fifteen or sixteen. Each time the boy struggled, one of them hit him on the back of his head.

I didn't understand what was happening, other than the boy was being punished for something he had done. I knew nothing about sex.

I showered quickly and said nothing. I suppose even at my age I instinctively knew it was best to mind my own business. I had already been beaten once that day and did not intend to make anyone mad at me again.

That night, when the lights went out, I cried in my pillow until I fell asleep. I never needed Mom and Dad as badly as I did that night, and the many that followed. More than anything, I wanted to go home.

The next couple of days went the same as the first except I wasn't beaten up. Noise and fighting were continuous. Rape of the younger children was an everyday happening. The older and stronger kids forced themselves onto the younger and weaker ones, those unable to defend against such attacks.

> ***"He pushed my face against the wall, then pulled my underwear down and told me to step out of them. I felt him touching my penis."***

I cannot honestly say all the counselors allowed the fights, nor can I say how many knew of the rapes yet still allowed them. But I do know of a black counselor who would arrange bare-fisted fights between kids. He gave cigarettes to the winner. I also watched him observe, from beginning to end, black children raping white ones.

On my third night there, I was sleeping soundly when one of the counselors woke me.

He whispered, “I want to talk to you in the bathroom.”

I had already learned each kid had best do what a counselor ordered or risk getting hit. I got out of bed and, as I walked to the bathroom, I was hoping the man had good news about my parents. Since my arrival, no one had talked to me about them.

A Victim of Rape

I entered the bathroom, and the counselor closed the door. He took my arm and walked me to the far end of the room. He pushed my face against the wall, then pulled my underwear down and told me to step out of them. I felt him touching my penis. He pulled me around to face him when it became erect. He then placed his mouth on me and orally copulated me for a short time, as I watched in terror and confusion. I felt a finger touching my bottom. I tried to cry out in pain as he jammed his finger inside of me, but his hand covered my mouth and muffled the cry. I had absolutely no idea why he was doing this. I had done nothing wrong. I was very frightened but stopped crying so he wouldn't hit me.

“Lay down on the floor,” he ordered.

> ***“My father was correct that he was no longer looking at the well-behaved, polite and loving son he had raised. He was looking at a walking time bomb.”***

I laid down onto the cold floor as he directed. I felt something cold and wet being rubbed on my rectum. He again put his finger inside of me. I tried to wiggle away from him, and he slapped me, saying, “Don't move.”

I looked over my shoulder and saw he had his pants opened and was putting something from a can he held onto his penis. I started crying. He reached down and squeezed my mouth so hard it hurt my lips. I had trouble breathing and was beginning to panic when I felt him lay his body on top of mine. I cannot describe the pain I felt as he rammed his penis into my bottom, though I seem to be feeling it all over again as I write it here. I had never before experienced pain like this.

It was over very fast. I heard him make strange, moaning sounds, then he pulled himself out of me and stood. He yanked me upright with him, keeping a hand over my mouth until I stopped crying. He handed me my underwear and said, “Put them on.”

I watched him wipe himself with a towel and zip his pants. He took me out of the shower room and to his office, where he sat me in a chair in front of his desk.

"If you say anything to anyone about what just happened, I'll make sure you never go home," he said.

I believed him. This is the first time I've ever mentioned what occurred that night. I returned to my bed and, again, cried myself to sleep. I awoke the next morning and walked to the bathroom. A couple of kids began snickering while they pointed to my bottom. I felt the back of my underwear, and they were damp. Inside a toilet stall, I pulled my underwear down and saw a large spot of blood. I returned to my bed, removed another set of undershorts from the small dresser and put them on. I was terrified that someone would find out what had happened, and then I would not be allowed to go home.

> ***"People I had not yet come in contact with were going to suffer at my hands because I unconsciously sought revenge."***

During the next week, the counselors took us out for recreation. They chose which kids would be on each team, and a softball game began.

When it was my turn to come to bat, I noticed the other team's catcher was the black kid who had beaten me. The first ball was pitched and, setting myself to swing, I felt a hard pinch on my behind. I ignored it. As I waited for the next pitch, the catcher did it again. I turned and looked down at him. He looked at me and winked. When I looked back to the pitcher, I felt him pinch my bottom again.

Then I lost control. I turned around and brought the bat down on the top of his head. The bat was made of a heavy hardwood and weighed several pounds. I put all I had into that swing. I hit him several times, but I clearly remember only the first one. I still feel the blood that spurted from his head onto my bare arms and chest.

Solitary Confinement

After wrestling the bat from my hands, two counselors took me to solitary confinement. Solitary consisted of an almost soundproof room with a bed, a sink and a toilet. Encased in the steel door was a metal flap that could be opened only from the outside, so a counselor could look inside. The only other time it was unlocked was during meals. I thought I would go crazy.

Breakfast always consisted of a bowl of oatmeal, two pieces of cold toast and a plastic cup of warm milk. A half-hour later, the bowls were picked up and I was taken from my cell and given a shower, alone. Before I returned from my shower, my mattress and blanket would be removed and placed on the floor outside my cell. They would be returned at ten o'clock in the evening. I was not allowed any reading material, and the only articles of clothing I wore were jockey shorts and a pair of socks. I had contact with another person only when I was fed, showered and counted. At those times, the counselors refused to talk. At no time did I hear or see anyone else inside the building.

I remained in solitary for three months.

One day, the cell's door was opened and the clothes I'd worn into the dorm were thrown at me. Then, the first human voice I'd heard for months told me my father had come to take me home. I stood there, frightened. I was unwilling and unable to leave the cell where I had sat staring at the walls, seeing no one. I was convinced Mom and Dad had given me away and had forgotten about me.

At nine years of age, I no longer believed what I was told. I felt unwanted, unloved and thought I was being tricked. The counselor shouted at me to move. Then he entered the cell, took me by the arm and guided me from the building. I remember how bright the sun was. I had to cover my eyes with my hands all the way to the juvenile hall's waiting room.

Then, walking into the room, I saw my father. I stood looking at him and watched as a puzzled expression covered his face. Years later, I recalled that look when Dad told me he'd had a strange feeling come over him when he first saw me and looked into my eyes. He said it was as if his eyes told him I was his son, but my eyes told him his son was no longer there.

I regret his ignorance, and I see how tormented he was because of it, burdened with the guilt he felt. It was not his fault. He had no way of knowing. Only those who know and understand what continues to go on behind the walls of the nation's juvenile penal institutions and have made no effort to change the system are at fault.

A Walking Time Bomb

My father was correct that he was no longer looking at the well-behaved, polite and loving son he had raised. He was looking at a walking time bomb that had taken the County of Los Angeles just four months to construct, behind the walls surrounding that gladiator school they call juvenile hall.

> ***"I was loaded down with guilt and shame. I felt as if I had somehow brought it all upon myself. This feeling remained with me far into my adult years."***

My parents were going to suffer by my actions from the first day I returned home until the day they died. People I had not yet come in contact with were going to suffer at my hands because I unconsciously sought revenge; revenge that would cause many to hurt and some to die. In a few short months, a seed had been planted that the system would water and nourish during my incarcerations in other institutions throughout the state and the country.

The system assured that I, an innocent little boy, learned to hate authority of all sorts; that the color of a man's skin decided if he was friend or foe. The color of the man's skin became so important that I grew up to become a high-ranking member of a nationwide white-supremacy group in which the only way to become a member is to kill. The only way out is to die.

> ***"During my youth, I witnessed thousands of other kids suffer the abuses I endured. Today, thousands exist under similar circumstances."***

With both Mom and Dad out of the hospital and all of the kids together again, my feelings began to show themselves. I rebelled against Dad and was unable to get along with the other kids. I disobeyed him and did not do what he asked or ordered me to do. But no one saw my behavior for what it was. Dad felt my rebelling against authority was a phase many children go through.

My grades went from B's and C's to D's and F's. I began skipping classes. When I did go, I'd just sit at my desk, staring out the window or looking at the floor.

It was close to my eleventh birthday when all I had bottled up inside me came to the surface. For the first time, my family saw the anger inside me.

An older kid at school had chosen me to pick on. I was still a runt and a target for the bullies. I had been walking home from school when the bully began to shove me around. He took my spelling book and tore it in half. By the time I got home, I was crying. Dad yelled out for the bully to leave me alone. I ran into my room and stayed there until Dad talked me into eating dinner.

The next morning, I went to the garage and found a piece of wood; a two-by-four about three feet long. I took it outside and leaned it against a bush in front of our house.

As soon as the bully, who lived down the street, spotted me, he began calling me "Momma's Boy" and a few other things I didn't care for. He swaggered over and shoved me. I backed up a step, grabbed the board and began hitting him with it. I really got into that. The more he cried and yelled, the harder I hit him. Some people across the street saw what was happening, and one of the men ran over and took the board away from me.

Abused by a Stepbrother

Later that afternoon, two police officers came to our door. My father spoke with them and, after asking me about the incident, he agreed to pay the bully's medical bills. That was the end of that.

Not long after that I began to steal, beginning with a few dollars I'd taken from a neighbor's unlocked house. My problems were compounded when my stepbrother, David, attempted to sexually molest me. When I refused, he repeatedly beat me with his closed fists. This began a pattern of hatred and mistrust between the two of us, which ended one day when I decided to run away to stop his abuse. I stole his car, drove it in first gear for thirty miles or so, blew the motor, then parked it on the side of the road and continued my journey on foot.

I began breaking into a lot of homes. I found two pistols and stuffed them in my pockets. Later that day, awfully tired and hungry but not able to go back home for fear of David, I walked to a police station, resolved to tell them of all the crimes I had committed. Putting me back in juvenile hall, I felt, was the only way I'd get away from a stepbrother who abused me so much.

Sitting at his desk, a police officer looked up and asked, "May I help you?"

I reached under my shirt and pulled out one of the pistols I had stolen.

Someone shouted, "Look out, he's got a gun!" Four cops grabbed me and threw me to the floor, breaking my arm in the process. Later that evening, after having my arm set in a cast at the hospital, I was taken to juvenile hall, processed through and taken to the same dorm I had been in my first time through.

Although I was frightened, I was determined that this time I was not going to do anything I didn't want to do.

Fighting Back

That first night, an older kid beat me up just to convince me he was in charge. After he finished with me and went to sleep, I got up from my bed and went over to the card table, where I picked up a folding, metal chair. I reached the bed where the bully slept and, before the counselor could run from his office, brought the chair down hard, hitting the bully square on the face.

My greatest satisfaction was in watching the bully lay under his bed, where he had scurried, and cry. The counselors took me to solitary again, but it did not seem to matter. Nothing did.

Two days later, appearing before the juvenile court to face charges for that attack, I saw my parents and watched their grieved reactions when the judge decided I was to be remanded to the care of juvenile hall until my "best interest" was decided. Being led out of the courtroom, too afraid to show my pain, I didn't glance back at my parents. I had already learned that to show emotion in such a world was to show weakness to my peers as well as to my keepers. Weakness invited abuse from everyone.

> ***"Nothing has changed since my first incarceration at Los Angeles County Juvenile Hall."***

That day in the courtroom, and even during my brief return home, I refused to talk to my parents about the abuses I had suffered for the same reasons I didn't discuss any of my experiences at juvenile hall with them. I was loaded down with guilt and shame. I felt as if I had somehow brought it all upon myself. This feeling remained with me far into my adult years. I wanted so badly to be

Daddy's little man that I felt he would be ashamed of me if I told him what had happened.

Little did I know, walking back across the yard that day toward my cell in solitary confinement, that my chance for anything remotely resembling a normal life had already been lost a few years back. I would never be allowed to go back to being just a kid. I would spend the next thirty-six years locked inside penal institutions across the country.

A few years later, I was once again raped by another Los Angeles County Juvenile Hall counselor, inside the solitary-confinement ward. I was molested by the operator of the Optimist Home for Boys in Highland Park, California. Physicians at the Camarillo State Mental Hospital gave me powerful drugs and electroconvulsive therapy. I watched a California Youth Authority counselor stab a young boy to death at the Nellis School for Boys, in Nellis, California. I suffered vicious, physical abuses at the hands of my keepers, counselors and guards at all institutions, including the Paso Robles School for Boys, in Paso Robles, California. It was in Paso Robles that I first stabbed a person. . . .

During my youth, I witnessed thousands of other kids suffer the abuses I endured. Today, thousands exist under similar circumstances inside this country's juvenile penal systems. I have corresponded with incarcerated children in New York, Florida, Texas, Oregon, New Mexico, Kansas, Georgia, Oklahoma, California and Washington. After I shared my story with each of them, they have each shared with me the same kinds of stories of assaults that have happened and are continuing to happen to them. Nothing has changed since my first incarceration at Los Angeles County Juvenile Hall, except children are now abused with more sophisticated methods that are difficult to expose and prove, like solitary confinement for undetermined periods of time, separation from family and deprivation of all rights. . . .

Obviously, I could have written many things about myself as an adult. Instead, I've taken you through my childhood and youth, to show what continues to happen to thousands of our children inside juvenile penal institutions.

I close this in memory of an eleven-year-old boy who, incarcerated several times for different reasons, killed himself a short time ago. We corresponded often. Here is his last letter to me, printed exactly as it was written, except that I changed the names, including that of Mr. Forest. The reason? On a certain day, time and place, the boy's older brother got even with "Mr. Forest."

> Dear Dwight,
>
> Four a long tyme, I want to have sumone I can talk to but I no if I told about Mr. Forest no buddy wood want me no mor. Mr. Forest has been doing things tyme sence I was 6. He made me do nastie things. I hope you will still lyke me becase I luv you a lot. Please dont bee mad at me.
>
> Your pal,
>
> Wess

What else can I say? Wess said it all.

The Death Penalty Should Not Be Imposed on Violent Youths

by Victor L. Streib

About the author: *Victor L. Streib is a law professor at Cleveland State University. As an attorney, Streib has represented juveniles on death row before the U.S. Supreme Court and other courts.*

Paula Cooper, an articulate, attractive college-correspondence student at age twenty, can barely remember the impulsive fifteen-year-old she was when she and three friends committed a brutal murder. Bounced around from school to school, Paula had been repeatedly abused by her parents and was personally adrift in a Gary, Indiana, ghetto. After her unexplainable emotional explosion resulting in the murder, Paula was convicted and sentenced to die in Indiana's electric chair—an adult sentence for an adult crime committed by a child. That sentence was reversed shortly before Paula's twentieth birthday, but the alternative given her was sixty years in prison. Even at her earliest parole date, this blossoming woman-child will be on Social Security before she is released from prison.

Not as Lucky

Dalton Prejean may not be so lucky. He has turned thirty while sitting on Louisiana's death row, awaiting execution for murdering a policeman when he was a drunken seventeen-year-old. Dalton also was abused as a child, is mildly retarded, and has lived a tumultuous life. In 1974, at age fourteen, he killed a taxi driver and was sent to a reform school for three years. Dalton was out of reform school only six months when he murdered the state police officer. Louisiana seems determined to execute Dalton, having come within a few hours of doing so on November 19, 1989. But the U.S. Supreme Court granted yet another stay

Victor L. Streib, "An Unjust Punishment? The Juvenile Death Penalty." This article appeared in the April 1990 issue of, and is reprinted with permission from, *The World & I*, a publication of The Washington Times Corporation, © 1990.

so that the case can be reviewed one more time. Meanwhile, Dalton waits.

Paula and Dalton are just two of the approximately seventy-five offenders sentenced to death in the 1980s for crimes committed while under age eighteen. Such sentences represent less than 3 percent of the total death sentences imposed during that decade. Since earliest colonial days, probably several thousand juveniles have been sentenced to death.

"Some juvenile executions, particularly those early in our history, were for crimes committed by juveniles as young as ten and twelve."

As rare as juvenile death sentences have been, it has been much rarer for actual executions to result from such sentences. In fact, the 1980s saw only three persons executed for juvenile crimes, and only 282 such executions have occurred throughout American history. Compare those numbers to the 117 adults executed in the 1980s and more than 16,000 adults executed in American history. The three actual juvenile executions carried out in the 1980s were

- Charles F. Rumbaugh; executed September 11, 1985, in Texas; seventeen at crime and twenty-eight at execution;
- James Terry Roach; executed January 10, 1986, in South Carolina; seventeen at crime and twenty-five at execution; and
- Jay Kelly Pinkerton; executed May 25, 1986, in Texas; seventeen at crime and twenty-four at execution.

Some juvenile executions, particularly those early in our history, were for crimes committed by juveniles as young as ten and twelve. Apparently the youngest at actual execution was Hannah Ocuish, a twelve-year-old retarded girl hanged in Connecticut in 1786.

Approximately thirty of the more than twenty-two hundred persons now on death row awaiting execution were ages sixteen or seventeen at the time of their crimes. Almost all are in the southern states, most are black, and almost all killed white victims. And most have spent many years on death row, exhausting their legal appeals and getting nearer and nearer to death.

Current Law of the Juvenile Death Penalty

Although executions for juvenile crimes began in Plymouth Colony in 1642, few legal challenges were made dealing directly with the issue of the condemned offender's youthfulness. Finally, in the late 1980s, the U.S. Supreme Court addressed the issue squarely and settled it, at least for the foreseeable future.

In 1988, the Supreme Court decided *Thompson v. Oklahoma*, involving a death sentence imposed on a fifteen-year-old boy who had committed murder. A fragile five-justice majority of the Court agreed that it would be cruel and unusual under the Eighth Amendment to the U.S. Constitution to execute someone for crimes committed at age fifteen, at least under the state laws as they then existed. Barring an unforeseen and major change in these state laws, the *Thompson* case establishes an absolute minimum age of sixteen for the death penalty.

The Supreme Court reaffirmed that conclusion in 1989 in *Stanford v. Kentucky*. In this decision the Court examined the claims of two more convicts under juvenile death sentences and was urged to raise the constitutionally mandated minimum age to eighteen. In another extremely close decision, the Court rejected this argument and left the minimum age at sixteen. The Court did not endorse the wisdom of the death penalty for those who were sixteen or seventeen at the time of their crimes, but it did interpret the Constitution as permitting the states to enact such a limited juvenile death penalty if they wished.

"Although they may have the criminal intent required for a conviction of first-degree murder, they seldom have such intent to the fullest measure."

The thirty-six death penalty states, along with the federal government, must now consider what minimum age to place in their statutes. Most already have chosen age eighteen, but some have yet to designate any age. The early 1990s should see considerable action in the state legislatures as those latter states debate establishing minimum ages of sixteen, seventeen, or eighteen, and as those former states consider raising or lowering their present minimum ages.

As legislators, lobbyists, and the informed general public engage in this debate, they must address at least ten major issues. Each issue is complex, and the facts can too easily be warped by the heat of political rhetoric. No issue can be resolved to the satisfaction of all concerned, but no issue can be ignored if a wise resolution is to be reached.

Assessing Harm and Criminal Intent

First. Under the American legal system, the choice of punishment for any crime is based both upon the harm inflicted and upon the criminal intent of the offender. This is the fundamental legal principle underlying the conflict between the simplistic slogans of "old enough to kill, old enough to die" and "but he is only a boy."

For crimes such as murder, American criminal law has consistently required careful evaluation of the criminal intent of the offender. For all homicidal crimes, the harm inflicted is the death of an innocent person. However, the difference between the less serious level (such as negligent manslaughter) and the capital level of first-degree murder is typically the personal culpability of the offender. Therefore, in deciding the basis for imposition of criminal punishment, one must consider in part the harm inflicted but must concentrate primarily on the criminal intent involved.

It is generally accepted that adolescents typically do not have an adult level of maturity and sophistication in their thought processes. Teenagers can commit very adult acts and certainly can and do know right from wrong, leading many to assume that teenagers should be held fully accountable for their acts. Others believe that this "knowing right from wrong" test ignores the much more complicated thought process the law seeks to ascertain in trying to distinguish between degrees of crime. While sixteen-year-olds can intend behavior, it may be unlikely they have thought about it deeply, with insight and understanding. Although they may have the criminal intent required for a conviction of first-degree murder, they seldom have such intent to the fullest measure.

Since such a very small percentage of murderers are sentenced to death, society presumably reserves that penalty only for the very worst murderers. And by "very worst" the law means those with the most condemnable frame of mind. The issue remains: Can teenagers, due to their inherent immaturity, impulsiveness, and lack of full appreciation of the consequences of their acts, ever be in that "very worst" category and thus be deserving of the death sentence?

Demands for Retribution

Second. The harm inflicted in these murders is tragic and enormous, giving rise to strong emotional feeling in the community. The outrages these youthful offenders have imposed upon innocent citizens lead many toward the conclusion that justice demands the death penalty. However, soaring anger at the misdeeds of children is always blunted somewhat, at least for many persons, by the knowledge that children cannot be expected to behave as adults all of the time.

"If we need retribution, and we do, doesn't ordering a boy or girl to spend life in prison satisfy that need?"

This category of desire to punish criminal offenders, called *retribution* by criminologists, is undeniably human and can be an overwhelming emotional feeling. It tends to overcome us as we read or hear of the grisly details of the crime and the helplessness of the victim. Whether labeled a vengeful need to get even with the murderer or a loftier feeling that we should exact an eye for an eye, it is an emotional, visceral feeling and almost universal within our society.

In striking contrast are our less emotional, more rational reactions to murder. While not denying the societal and personal need for retribution, this side of us weighs the relative retributive merits of the death penalty against the alternative, long-term imprisonment. If we need retribution, and we do, doesn't ordering a boy or girl to spend life in prison satisfy that need?

Third. The most coveted goal of criminal law is deterrence of crimes in the future. Nothing we can do after the murder will bring back the victim, but maybe we can find a way to reduce the number of future victims. Following this universal desire for crime reduction, some argue that the death penalty for juveniles will send a message to other would-be juvenile murderers and reduce the chances of those murders ever occurring. Skeptics note that few juvenile murderers think before they act and thus are unlikely to receive any such message. Moreover, it seems clear that juveniles do not fear or even comprehend death, tending to believe they are immortal and that death is something that happens only to old people.

> ***"It seems clear that the juvenile death penalty is reserved solely for black juveniles who have white victims."***

If the alternative is nothing or just a slap on the wrist, then of course the death penalty might be necessary for adequate deterrence. However, the alternative is long-term imprisonment, a punishment even more feared by adolescents. This was illustrated vividly in the Missouri case involving Heath Wilkins, a murderer at sixteen. When the judge asked Wilkins whether he preferred life imprisonment or the death penalty, Wilkins was certain of his answer: "I prefer the death penalty. One I fear, and one I don't."

Criminological research clearly establishes that the death penalty is not as great a deterrent to violent juvenile crime as long-term imprisonment is. The only question left open in this regard is how long the imprisonment must be in order to provide satisfactory deterrence, a question answered in widely varying ways by different jurisdictions.

Fourth. Is it unreasonable to totally disregard the goals of reform and rehabilitation for juvenile offenders? In some cases, such as that of Dalton Prejean, who killed first at age fourteen and then again at seventeen, it may appear that reform and rehabilitation are unlikely to occur. Certainly, the defiant, swaggering attitudes of some juvenile gang members seem to portend nothing but terrible behavior for their entire lives.

But others note that behavior patterns change significantly as persons mature from adolescence to adulthood and into middle age. All of us have mellowed since our teenage years and are now embarrassed by some of our wilder activities during that stage of life. Given long-term imprisonment, juvenile murderers also may change their behavior, usually to ways more acceptable to society. Imposing the death penalty for juvenile crimes totally disregards these universally accepted truisms about maturation beyond adolescence. Long-term imprisonment holds out the possibility of such a destructive teenager's becoming a responsible adult at some time in the future.

Undeniable Racism

Fifth. The problem of racism is so pervasive in our society that we could not expect the death penalty systems to be immune. And in this literally life-and-death system, racism seems most unacceptable. That the juvenile death penalty system is racially skewed is undeniable. In Dalton Prejean's case, he is a black male who killed a white victim in Louisiana and was convicted and sentenced to death by an all-white jury. Louisiana has executed only eight offenders for juvenile crimes, the first in 1878 and the latest in 1948. In these previous juvenile executions, all eight offenders were black, all eight victims were white, and all eight juries were all white.

Racism and the Death Penalty

Some would downplay this issue by noting that black males are arrested for murders in greater numbers than their proportion in the general population would predict, leading to the conclusion that black males might understandably then be overrepresented among those sentenced to death and executed. However, this explanation does not reach the magnitude of the phenomenon in states such as Louisiana, where it seems clear that the juvenile death penalty is reserved solely for black juveniles who have white victims.

Others would note that racism is a pervasive problem throughout society and that the criminal justice system simply cannot expunge that problem. To require it to do so would be to close down the entire system. One response may be that if racism cannot be eradicated from criminal justice, then this may be a good reason to back away at least from the ultimate punishment and to replace it with something less final.

"We simply must do something now to stop convicted murderers from continuing their rampages."

Sixth. The element of cost may seem less important in matters of life and death such as these, but it is clear that criminal justice systems cannot afford to waste any of their funds. If the juvenile death penalty was head and shoulders above any of the other alternatives, it might be worth the increased cost to gain this additional effect. However, the death penalty seems to be less effective than life imprisonment. In fact, many states (most recently Kansas) have rejected the death penalty altogether because its cost is many times that of long-term imprisonment.

When a state allows the death penalty for juveniles, it can expect many capital trials and very few capital sentences. Capital trials are very complex and expensive, and the appellate process following a death penalty seems to go on forever—certainly in contrast to that usually pursued by prison inmates. For example, Dalton Prejean has turned thirty while pursuing his appellate process for a crime committed when he was seventeen. At the end of this enormously expensive procedure, the state may get an occasional execution. Studies of such systems have concluded that each of these executions costs the state several million dollars, much more than long-term imprisonment would. This leads to a conclusion that the death penalty for juveniles may be the high-cost alternative that delivers less-effective results.

Seventh. Consider the message juveniles receive from juvenile death sentences. The crimes they have committed are often the killing of a person in order to solve some problem the juvenile perceives as otherwise unsolvable. The girl with whom they wish to have sexual relations or the victim they wish to rob struggles and causes them major problems. Their solution to their problem is to kill the person who is causing the problem.

"Many believe that the death penalty for juveniles has been given a long trial period and has been found wanting."

Now they see government officials struggling with a problem of their own, a person whose behavior is unacceptable to them. How do government officials solve their problem? They kill [execute] the person who is causing the problem. Is it wrong to kill someone to solve a problem? It is most difficult to convince teenagers not to do something that government officials do with the apparent blessings of society.

Teenagers are careful observers of the actions of their adult role models. The father who lectures his son not to smoke with a cigarette hanging out of his mouth is likely to find that his actions speak louder than his words. If we as a society lecture our children that to kill a person is the worst crime they could commit, and then set about executing juvenile offenders to make our point, the message children receive may be exactly the opposite of the one we wanted to send.

Eighth. Concern over the death penalty for juveniles is often a common ground on which death penalty proponents and opponents can meet and agree. The acrimonious and interminable debate about the death penalty in general has resulted in deep divisions between the opposing camps. Such debates so often end in name-calling and angry shouting matches relying upon bumper-sticker slogans for rationale. The death penalty for juveniles is only a small part of the general death penalty issue, but it can bring the warring parties together at least on this point.

Levy Long Prison Sentences

A majority would agree that this branch of the death penalty laws should be trimmed back. If everyone can reason together on this small issue, avenues of dialogue and understanding may well be opened for more rational and constructive discussion of the death penalty for adults and for the appropriate application of criminal punishment in general.

Ninth. If we renounce the death penalty for juveniles, what can be done about violent juvenile crime? The fear and outrage such crimes provoke are shared by all reasonable persons, whether for or against the death penalty. We simply must do something now to stop convicted murderers from continuing their rampages.

The temporary solution is to impose long-term prison sentences on such violent juveniles. This will ensure that they are reasonably mature adults and have been subjected to whatever rehabilitative programs are available before they again go free. Probably a minimum of twenty years is the best place to start, but criminologists debate the best conditions and term of years. After such a minimum, parole should be sparingly—not automatically—granted.

Life imprisonment without chance of parole tends to satisfy our visceral demands for retribution. However, many note that this means deciding in 1990 to lock a boy up through the years 2025, 2050, and on, and absolutely removing any mechanism for ever changing our minds, regardless of what the world may be like in the twenty-first century. Is it ever a wise business, personal, or societal decision to make a choice that can never be altered or modified, no matter what the future brings?

Tenth. The long-term solution to violent juvenile crime, or all crime for that matter, probably will not come from harsh criminal punishment, whether imprisonment or death. Given the individual freedom in our society, the resultant ample opportunity for violent juvenile crime, and the low probability of being caught and punished, prevention through threatened punishment will always be insufficiently effective.

Our society must be willing to devote enormous resources to the search for causes and cures of violent juvenile crime, just as it has for the causes and cures of diseases such as cancer and AIDS. And we must not demand a complete cure in a short time, since no one knows how long it will take. Unfortunately, no one now has the cure for violent juvenile crime. However, many believe that the death penalty for juveniles has been given a long trial period and has been found wanting. Its societal costs are enormous, and it delays our search for a rational and acceptable means of reducing violent juvenile crime.

Bibliography

Books

Falcon Baker — *Saving Our Kids from Delinquency, Drugs, and Despair*. New York: HarperCollins, 1991.

Elissa P. Benedek and Dewey G. Cornell — *Juvenile Homicide*. Washington, DC: American Psychiatric Press, 1989.

Thomas J. Bernard — *The Cycle of Juvenile Justice*. New York: Oxford University Press, 1992.

Léon Bing — *Do or Die*. New York: HarperCollins, 1991.

Cristina Bodinger-de Uriarte and Anthony R. Sancho — *Hate Crime*. Los Alamitos, CA: Southwest Regional Laboratory, 1991.

John A. Calhoun — *Violence, Youth, and a Way Out*. Washington, DC: National Crime Prevention Council, 1989.

Richard C. Cervantes — *Substance Abuse and Gang Violence*. Newbury Park, CA: Sage Publications, 1992.

Deborah W. Denno — *Biology and Violence from Birth to Adulthood*. Portchester, NY: Cambridge University Press, 1990.

Charles Patrick Ewing — *Kids Who Kill*. Lexington, MA: Lexington Books, 1990.

R. Barri Flowers — *The Adolescent Criminal*. Jefferson, NC: McFarland & Company, 1990.

James Garbarino, Kathleen Kostelny, and Nancy Dubrow — *No Place to Be a Child*. Lexington, MA: Lexington Books, 1991.

Susan Geason and Paul Wilson — *Preventing Graffiti and Vandalism*. Monsey, NY: Criminal Justice Press, 1990.

Seymour Gelber — *Hard-Core Delinquents*. Tuscaloosa: The University of Alabama Press, 1988.

Arnold P. Goldstein — *Delinquent Gangs: A Psychological Perspective*. Champaign, IL: Research Press, 1991.

Arnold P. Goldstein — *Delinquents on Delinquency*. Champaign, IL: Research Press, 1990.

Boronia Halstead et al. — *Youth Crime Prevention: Proceedings of a Policy*. Monsey, NY: Criminal Justice Press, 1991.

C. Ronald Huff — *Gangs in America*. Newbury Park, CA: Sage Publications, 1990.

Mark D. Jacobs — *Screwing the System and Making It Work.* Chicago: University of Chicago Press, 1990.

Martin Sanchez Jankowski — *Islands in the Street: Gangs and Urban American Society.* Berkeley: University of California Press, 1991.

George W. Knox — *An Introduction to Gangs.* Laurel, MD: American Correctional Association, 1991.

Jerome G. Miller — *Last One over the Wall.* Columbus: Ohio State University Press, 1991.

Paul A. Mones — *When a Child Kills: Abused Children Who Kill Their Parents.* New York: Pocket Books, 1991.

Ivan Potas et al. — *Young People and Crime: Costs and Prevention.* Monsey, NY: Criminal Justice Press, 1990.

Deborah Prothrow-Stith — *Deadly Consequences.* New York: HarperCollins, 1991.

David M. Sandberg — *The Child Abuse-Delinquency Connection.* Lexington, MA: Lexington Books, 1989.

Darly Sander — *Focus on Teens in Trouble.* Santa Barbara, CA: ABC-CLIO, 1991.

Ira M. Schwartz — *(In)Justice for Juveniles.* Lexington, MA: Lexington Books, 1989.

Mercer L. Sullivan — *"Getting Paid": Youth Crime and Work in the Inner City.* Ithaca, NY: Cornell University Press, 1989.

Carl S. Taylor — *Dangerous Society.* East Lansing: Michigan State University Press, 1990.

Julia Vernon — *Preventing Juvenile Crime.* Monsey, NY: Criminal Justice Press, 1991.

Neil Alan Weiner, Margaret A. Zahn, and Rita J. Sagi — *Violence: Patterns, Causes, Public Policy.* San Diego, CA: Harcourt Brace Jovanovich, 1990.

Periodicals

George M. Anderson — "Punishing the Young: Juvenile Justice in the 1990's," *America*, February 29, 1992.

Brian Bird — "Reclaiming the Urban War Zones," *Christianity Today*, January 15, 1990.

William Broyles Jr. — "Letter from LA," *Esquire*, July 1992.

William F. Buckley Jr. — "Guns and Children," *National Review*, October 21, 1991.

Janice Castro — "In the Brutal World of L.A.'s Toughest Gangs," *Time*, March 16, 1992.

Brandon S. Centerwall — "Television and Violence," *The Journal of the American Medical Association*, June 10, 1992.

Sabra Chartrand — "Capital Is Capital of Gunfire Deaths," *The New York Times*, June 11, 1992.

Fortune — Entire issue on children in crisis, August 10, 1992.

David Gelman — "When Kids Molest Kids," *Newsweek*, March 30, 1992.

Katharine Greider	"Frances Sandoval: Against the Gangs," *In These Times*, June 20-July 3, 1990.
Kathleen M. Heide	"Why Kids Kill Parents," *Psychology Today*, September/October 1992.
Philip J. Hilts	"Gunshot Wounds Become Second-Leading Cause of Death for Teen-agers," *The New York Times*, June 10, 1992.
Jon D. Hull	"No Way Out," *Time*, August 17, 1992.
Thomas L. Jipping	"A Generation at Risk: What Can Be Done?" *The World & I*, April 1992. Available from 2800 New York Ave. NE, Washington, DC 20002.
Felicia R. Lee	"For Gold Earrings and Protection, More Girls Take Road to Violence," *The New York Times*, November 25, 1991.
Charles Leerhsen	"Going like Gangbusters," *Newsweek*, June 17, 1991.
Art Levine	"America's Youthful Bigots," *U.S. News & World Report*, May 7, 1990.
Alan McEvoy	"Combating Gang Activities in School," *The Education Digest*, October 1990.
Salvador A. Mendez	"Community Struggles to Prevent Youths from Joining Growing Number of Gangs," *Corrections Today*, July 1992.
Eugene H. Methvin	"When the Gangs Came to Tacoma," *Reader's Digest*, May 1992.
Lance Morrow	"Childhood's End," *Time*, March 9, 1992.
Seth Mydans	"F.B.I. Setting Sights on Street Gangs," *The New York Times*, May 24, 1992.
The New York Times	"Life at 'Jeff': Tough Students Wonder Where Childhood Went," March 7, 1992.
Rod Nordland	"Deadly Lessons," *Newsweek*, March 9, 1992.
Clarence Page	"Reading and Writing and Reality," *Liberal Opinion*, March 23, 1992. Available from Living History, Inc., 108 E. 5th St., Vinton, IA 52349.
Deborah Prothrow-Stith	"Dealing with Deadly Consequences," *Essence*, January 1992.
William Raspberry	"The Three R's Plus One," *The Washington Post National Weekly*, January 28-February 3, 1991.
Eloise Salholz	"How to Keep Kids Safe," *Newsweek*, March 9, 1992.
William E. Schmidt	"A Growing Urban Fear: Thieves Who Kill for 'Cool' Clothing," *The New York Times*, February 6, 1990.
Brent Staples	"The War Against Street Gangs," *The New York Times*, May 31, 1992.
Joseph B. Treaster	"Teen-Age Murderers: Plentiful Guns, Easy Power," *The New York Times*, May 24, 1992.
Gary Turbak	"Children of the Nightmare," *The American Legion*, February 1992.
Gordon Witkin	"Kids Who Kill," *Newsweek*, April 8, 1991.
The World & I	Special issue on youth violence, April 1990.

Organizations to Contact

The editors have compiled the following list of organizations that are concerned with the issues debated in this book. All of them have publications or information available for interested readers. For best results, allow as much time as possible for the organizations to respond. The descriptions below are derived from materials provided by the organizations. This list was compiled at the date of publication. Names, addresses, and phone numbers of organizations are subject to change.

American Civil Liberties Union (ACLU)
132 W. 43d St.
New York, NY 10036
(212) 944-9800

The ACLU champions the rights set forth in the Declaration of Independence and the U.S. Constitution. In addition to many other civil rights issues, the ACLU works for the legal rights of juveniles accused of crimes. The ACLU supports the right of juveniles to a jury trial excluding both public and press. It believes that juveniles should never be executed or jailed but, rather, placed in nonsecure facilities. ACLU publications include the monthly newsletter *First Principles* and the bimonthly newspaper *Civil Liberties*.

American Correctional Association (ACA)
8025 Laurel Lakes Ct.
Laurel, MD 20707-5075
(301) 206-5100

The ACA is comprised of correctional administrators, prison wardens, superintendents, and other corrections professionals who want to improve correctional standards. ACA studies the causes of crime and juvenile delinquency and reports regularly on juvenile justice issues in its bimonthly magazine *Corrections Today*.

Center for the Study of Youth Policy
University of Michigan School of Social Work
1015 E. Huron St.
Ann Arbor, MI 48104-1689
(313) 747-2556

The center studies issues concerning juvenile justice and youth corrections. The center itself does not take positions regarding these issues, but it publishes individuals' opinions on these issues in booklets, including *Programs for Serious and Violent Juvenile Offenders* and *Violent Juvenile Crime: What Do We Know About It and What Can We Do About It?* It also publishes the monograph *A Blueprint for Youth Corrections*.

Milton S. Eisenhower Foundation
1660 L St. NW, Suite 200
Washington, DC 20036
(202) 429-0440

The foundation is comprised of individuals dedicated to reducing crime in inner-city neighborhoods through community programs. The foundation believes that more federally funded programs like Head Start and Job Corps would improve education and job opportunities for youths, thus reducing juvenile crime and violence. Its publications include the report *Youth Investment and Community Reconstruction* and the monthly newsletter *Challenges from Within.*

Mothers Against Gangs
110 W. Madison St.
Chicago, IL 60602
(312) 853-2336

Mothers Against Gangs is an organization of parents and community members dedicated to reducing gang crime and violence. It lobbies for legislation to deter gang violence, advocates increased law enforcement and youth activity programs, and educates the public about the warning signs of gang activity. The organization publishes the *Mothers Against Gangs* quarterly newsletter.

National Association of Juvenile Correctional Agencies (NAJCA)
55 Albin Rd.
Bow, NH 03304-3703
(603) 271-5945

NAJCA promotes research and legislation to improve the juvenile justice system. It opposes the death penalty for juveniles and the placement of juvenile offenders in adult prisons. NAJCA publishes the quarterly newsletter *NAJCA News.*

National Center on Institutions and Alternatives (NCIA)
635 Slaters Lane, Suite G-100
Alexandria, VA 22314
(703) 684-0373

The NCIA works to reduce the number of people institutionalized in prisons and mental hospitals. It favors the least restrictive forms of detention for juvenile offenders and opposes sentencing juveniles as adults and executing juvenile murderers. NCIA publishes the monthly journal *Augustus: A Journal of Progressive Human Services*, the book *Juvenile Decarceration: The Politics of Correctional Reform*, and the booklet *Scared Straight: Second Look.*

National Coalition to Abolish the Death Penalty (NCADP)
1325 G St. NW, Lower Level B
Washington, DC 20005
(202) 347-2411

NCADP works to abolish the death penalty for both juveniles and adults. It believes the death penalty does not effectively deter crime. NCADP compiles statistics on the death penalty and on the number of juveniles on death row. Its publications include the bimonthly newsletter *Lifelines.*

National Council of Juvenile and Family Court Judges
PO Box 8970
University of Nevada
Reno, NV 89557
(702) 784-6012

The council is comprised of juvenile and family court judges and other juvenile justice professionals. It seeks to improve juvenile and family court standards and practices. Its publications include the monthly *Juvenile and Family Law Digest* and the quarterly *Juvenile and Family Court Journal.*

National Council on Crime and Delinquency (NCCD)
685 Market St., Suite 620
San Francisco, CA 94105
(415) 896-6223

NCCD is comprised of corrections specialists and others interested in the juvenile justice system and the prevention of crime and delinquency. It advocates community-based treatment programs rather than imprisonment for delinquent youths. It opposes placing minors in adult jails and executing those who committed capital offenses before age eighteen. It publishes the quarterlies *Crime and Delinquency* and the *Journal of Research in Crime and Delinquency* as well as policy papers, including the *Juvenile Justice Policy Statement* and *Unlocking Juvenile Corrections: Evaluating the Massachusetts Department of Youth Services.*

National Crime Prevention Council (NCPC)
1700 K St. NW, 2d Fl.
Washington, DC 20006
(202) 466-6272

NCPC provides training and technical assistance groups and individuals interested in crime prevention. The council advocates job training, recreation, and other programs as means to reduce youth crime and violence. NCPC publishes the book *Preventing Violence: Program Ideas and Examples*, the booklet *Violence, Youth, and a Way Out*, and the newsletter *Catalyst*, published ten times a year.

National Criminal Justice Association (NCJA)
444 N. Capitol St. NW, Suite 608
Washington, DC 20001
(202) 347-4900

NCJA is an association of state and local police chiefs, judges, attorneys, and other criminal justice officials. It seeks to improve the states' administration of their criminal and juvenile justice programs. NCJA publishes the *Juvenile Justice* newsletter three times a year.

National Institute Against Prejudice and Violence (NIAPV)
31 S. Greene St.
Baltimore, MD 21201
(301) 328-5170

NIAPV studies the problem of violence and intimidation motivated by racial, religious, ethnic, or sexual prejudice. It believes that youth hate crimes are a serious problem. The institute believes that parents, clergy, and youth counselors can reduce this problem by helping to dispel harmful stereotypes of ethnic, religious, and minority groups and by teaching young people how to resolve conflicts. NIAPV publishes the quarterly newsletter *Forum*.

National School Safety Center (NSSC)
4165 Thousand Oaks Blvd., Suite 290
Westlake Village, CA 91362
(805) 373-9977

NSSC is a research organization that studies school crime and violence, including youth hate crimes. The center believes that teacher training is an effective means of reducing these problems. Its publications include the book *Gangs in Schools: Breaking Up Is Hard to Do* and the *School Safety Update* newsletter, published nine times a year.

U.S. Office of Juvenile Justice and Delinquency Prevention (OJJDP)
633 Indiana Ave. NW
Washington, DC 20531
(202) 307-0751

As the primary federal agency charged with monitoring and improving the juvenile justice system, OJJDP develops and funds programs to advance juvenile justice. Among its goals are the prevention and control of illegal drug use and serious juvenile crime. Through its National Youth Gang Clearinghouse, OJJDP investigates and focuses public attention on the problem of youth gangs. The office publishes the *OJJDP Juvenile Justice Bulletin* periodically.

Youth Policy Institute (YPI)
1221 Massachusetts Ave. NW, Suite B
Washington, DC 20005
(202) 638-2144

YPI monitors federal policies concerning youth and family in order to provide information on these policies to organizations and individuals. The institute believes that much of youth violence results from violence on television and in movies. It also believes that schools and communities should try to solve the problem of youth violence. YPI publishes the monthly magazines *American Family* and *Youth Policy* and the triannual journal *Future Choices*.

Index